D0147117

DUE DATE	RETURN DATE	DUE DATE	RETURN DATE
AUG 9 1990			
AUG 2 9 1990			
	FEB 2 5 1991		
FEB 2 1 1991			
DEC 1 5 2004			

Deselected Library Material

DO NOT RETURN
TO LIBRARY

Not for Resale

First Use of

Nuclear

Weapons

First Use of

NUCLEAR WEAPONS

Under the Constitution, Who Decides?

Edited by
PETER RAVEN-HANSEN

Contributions in Legal Studies, Number 38

GREENWOOD PRESS
New York • Westport, Connecticut • London

Library of Congress Cataloging-in-Publication Data

First use of nuclear weapons.

(Contributions in legal studies, ISSN 0147-1074 ;
no. 38)
Based on a symposium held at Airlie House,
Virginia, in Nov., 1985, and sponsored by the
Federation of American Scientists (FAS) and the
Lawyers Alliance for Nuclear Arms Control (LANAC).
Bibliography: p.
Includes index.
1. War and emergency powers—United States—
Congresses. 2. No first use (Nuclear strategy)—
Congresses. 3. Legislative power—United States—
Congresses. 4. Executive power—United States—
Congresses. I. Raven-Hansen, Peter, 1946-
II. Federation of American Scientists. III. Lawyers
Alliance for Nuclear Arms Control. IV. Series.
KF5060.A75F57   1987   342.73'062   86-33655
                             347.30262
ISBN 0-313-25520-2 (lib. bdg. : alk. paper)

British Library Cataloguing in Publication Data is available.

Copyright © 1987 by Peter Raven-Hansen

All rights reserved. No portion of this book may be
reproduced, by any process or technique, without the
express written consent of the publisher.

Library of Congress Catalog Card Number: 86-33655
ISBN: 0-313-25520-2
ISSN: 0147-1074

First published in 1987

Greenwood Press, Inc.
88 Post Road West, Westport, Connecticut 06881

Printed in the United States of America

The paper used in this book complies with the
Permanent Paper Standard issued by the National
Information Standards Organization (Z39.48-1984).

10 9 8 7 6 5 4 3 2 1

100279¥

Contents

Preface

This collection of essays grew out of a November 1985 symposium of constitutional scholars and lawyers at Airlie House, Virginia, on "First Use of Nuclear Weapons: Under the Constitution, Who Decides?" sponsored by the Federation of American Scientists (FAS) and the Lawyers Alliance for Nuclear Arms Control (LANAC). FAS Director Jeremy J. Stone had the inspiration for the symposium and wrote the article that was its focus; without him there would be no book. I would like to thank him, Vanessa Lide and the rest of the FAS staff who handled the logistics for the symposium, and LANAC Executive Director Anthony P. Sager.

Thanks are also due the contributors whose essays appear here. Their presentations of their essays sparked a spirited debate, only a few highlights of which could be reproduced. They were subsequently patient and tolerant with my editing, easing a task that I approached with some dread.

Special thanks and an apology are also due the many other scholars and lawyers, too numerous to list here, who dedicated a brilliant fall weekend to debating the issues posed by these essays. Thanks, because their participation made the symposium a success. An apology, because page limitations prevented me from including more than a few of their contributions in this collection.

Finally, I would like to thank my research assistant, Annemargaret Connolly, and chief typist and form controller, Carol Matsuuchi, for their assistance in completing the book.

ERRATA

Notes 1-6 below correspond to the Introduction and follow the text on page xii.

Notes

1. In pertinent part, the bill provided:
   Whereas, there would not be time in all cases for the Congress itself to deliberate as a whole over the question of first use of nuclear weapons;
   Whereas, in such cases as there was adequate time, Congress could work its will through a suitable statute, rescinding the delegation of authority herein;
   Now therefore be it resolved that
   (1) In any given conflict or crisis, whatsoever, and notwithstanding any other authority, so long as no nuclear weapons have been used by others, the President shall not use nuclear weapons without consulting with, and securing the assent of a majority of, a committee composed of the
   Speaker of the House of Representatives and Minority Leader
   Majority and Minority Leader of the Senate
   Chairman and Ranking Member of:
   Senate Committee on Armed Services
   House Committee on Armed Services
   Senate Committee on Foreign Relations
   House Committee on International Relations
   Joint Committee on Atomic Energy
   (2) Nothing herein shall preclude the President from using nuclear weapons first if Congress adopts a declaration of war that explicitly suspends the authority granted in this act.
   28 *F.A.S. Public Interest Report* 4 (Nov. 1975).
2. S. Rep. No. 606, 92d Cong., 2d Sess. 26 (1972) (additional views of J. William Fulbright).
3. Amend. No. 1085, 118 Cong. Rec. 12448 (1972).
4. *Id.* at 12456.
5. 462 U.S. 919, 951 (1983).
6. Youngstown Sheet & Tube Co. v. Sawyer, 343 U.S. 579, 635-38 (1952) (Jackson, J., concurring).

Introduction

Scholarly examination of the constitutional allocation of war powers has historically followed our most controversial wars. The Vietnam War in particular
produced an enormous volume of legal literature that seemingly exhausted, but
hardly resolved, the debate between presidential command and congressional
control. However, as some have said of our foreign and military policy, most
of that literature addresses the last war, not the next one. And, if the next war
is nuclear, we obviously cannot wait until its conclusion for scholarly analysis
of nuclear war powers. The purpose of this book is therefore to take up where
the Vietnam era literature left off by addressing issues of nuclear war powers
under the Constitution.

Ironically, the participants in the great Vietnam era war powers debates missed
an opportunity to look beyond that war. In 1971, the Federation of American
Scientists (FAS), a group of scientists and engineers originally organized in 1945
as the Federation of Atomic Scientists and dedicated to ending the arms race,
drafted a bill that could have required the assent of a committee of congressional
leaders before any first use of nuclear weapons by the United States, absent a
declaration of war.[1] The following year, Senator J. William Fulbright said in a
statement accompanying a report of the Senate Foreign Relations Committee
about the proposed War Powers Act that he "concur[red] wholly with the Federation of American Scientists that Congress must retain control over the conventional or nuclear character of a war."[2] He subsequently offered a floor
amendment providing that except in a declared war or "in response to a nuclear
attack or to an irrevocable launch of nuclear weapons, the President may not
use nuclear weapons without the prior, explicit authorization of the Congress."[3]
The amendment was defeated by the Senate 68–10.[4]

Now, more than a decade later, the emergence for the first time of a broad public debate about our first use policy again presents an occasion for addressing nuclear war powers issues. To that end, FAS Director Jeremy J. Stone resurrects and defends the original FAS proposal in Part I of this collection. He also clarifies the nuclear scenarios that are at issue, distinguishing the paradigm case to which the proposal applies—first use in response to a conventional Warsaw Pact attack on our NATO allies—from second strikes, launches-on-warning, and pre-emptive forestalling attacks, which he concedes *arguendo* are within the President's unilateral constitutional authority.

Dr. Stone's essay casts in sharp relief three important war powers issues that are the focus of the remaining parts of the collection.

THE ALLOCATION OF NUCLEAR WAR POWERS UNDER THE CONSTITUTION

The first issue was suggested by Senator Fulbright's 1972 statement of agreement with the FAS proposal: whether the "conventional or nuclear character of a war" affects the allocation of war powers under the Constitution. Even in a conventional war declared by the Congress or thrust upon the United States by an enemy, "going nuclear" sharply breaks the continuum of conventional escalation and arguably initiates a new and dangerously more threatening war. Does the Constitution therefore require a new authorization from Congress for the first use of nuclear weapons? Does the "nuclear character" of first use take it out of the realm of command decisions constitutionally committed to the President as commander in chief and place it within the realm of basic war and peace policy decisions committed to Congress?

In Part II, Professor John Norton Moore concludes that it does not, buttressing his argument by placing it in strategic context. Robert F. Turner, President of the United States Institute for Peace, also argues from history and case law that the FAS proposal would unconstitutionally invade the President's command authority. Professor Michael J. Glennon, former Legal Counsel to the Senate Foreign Relations Committee, responds by showing that the NATO Treaty confers no authority on the President that he does not already possess. Professor Allan Ides cites the Framers' intentions and constitutional text to make the case for congressional authority to control first use. Finally, excerpts from a debate between the contributors serve to highlight some differences between them.

THE FORM OF CONGRESSIONAL PARTICIPATION

The second issue presented by the FAS proposal is whether Congress may participate in nuclear war power decisions through a leadership committee. Even during the Vietnam era war powers debates, scholars and politicians cited Congress's cumbersome size, military inexpertise, leaky deliberations, and, above all, sluggish pace, to support their case for presidential war power. First use of nuclear weapons puts that case most strongly because of the speed with which a decision would need to be made in most settings. But any counter-argument that rests on by-passing the usual legislative procedure of full bicameral approval and presentment to the President has been seriously undercut by the Supreme Court's 1983 decision in *Immigration and Naturalization Service v. Chadha* striking down the one-house legislative veto.[5] After *Chadha*, the question is no longer just whether Congress *may* constitutionally participate in war powers decisions, but whether it *can*, given the impracticality of timely deliberation and action by the full bicameral body. Is the proposed congressional leadership committee a constitutionally permissible answer?

In Part III, Professor Stephen L. Carter concludes that it is not, because no committee can constitutionally convey the intent of Congress. Professor William C. Banks suggests that the committee solution is not a congressional veto in form, in substance, or in contemplation of the separation of powers, and that it therefore does not suffer the defects of the veto struck down in *Chadha*. Charles Tiefer, author of the brief for the Senate in *Chadha* and presently Deputy General Counsel to the Clerk of the House, distinguishes *Chadha* as a domestic delegation case that is inapplicable to arrangements for shared foreign affairs and war powers.

PROBLEMS OF IMPLEMENTATION OF CONGRESSIONAL CONTROL

The third issue presented by the FAS proposal is implementation. Virtually all the essays in this collection inevitably touch in passing on this issue, but a few problems are singled out for extended discussion in Part IV. Would a congressional leadership committee have the information and expertise to approve or disapprove first use? If it did, would the President abide its decision?

Professor Edwin M. Smith argues that the answer to both questions is no, citing analyses of command and control problems and the literature of social psychology. William G. Miller, formerly Staff Director to the Senate Select Committee on Intelligence, gives an affirmative answer to the first question, based on the experience of that committee. Professor Arthur L. Berney concludes that if the answer to the second question is no, Congress can expect no help from the courts, which will find the FAS proposal nonjusticiable in its present form.

Part V concludes the collection with a critical summary by organizing the President's nuclear war power in gradations from its apex, in a declared total war, to its nadir, in opposition to a clear congressional limitation. It also evaluates the major rebuttal arguments to the challenge that the *Chadha* decision poses to the FAS proposal for congressional first use decision by a leadership committee.

This summary evidences the analytic power of Justice Jackson's theory of graduated power,[6] by highlighting a few unexpected areas of agreement among the diverse contributors, as well as the inevitable disagreements. Above all, it confirms that first use *does* change the war powers debate by presenting the extreme case of war power, which forces us to look beyond foggy historical precedents of limited presidential military initiatives and arguments against domestic legislative ''shortcuts,'' and to confront instead the core issues of democratic control of the exercise of war power in a nuclear age.

I

RETHINKING PRESIDENTIAL FIRST USE

1

Presidential First Use Is Unlawful

Jeremy J. Stone

Few Americans question the right of the President of the United States to order promptly, alone, the use of nuclear weapons in response to the use of nuclear weapons against the United States, its forces, or its allies. In many such cases, little time would be available for consultations. Most would therefore concede the absolute necessity of giving a single decision maker, the President, the authority to respond in kind.

But what about the case in which the President is contemplating *first* use of nuclear weapons? Is there a comparable urgency justifying a comparable delegation of authority to the President to take this fateful act alone? Or would many hours be available for group decision making—as suggested by 1973 testimony of then Deputy Secretary of State Kenneth Rush when he observed: "Judgments are possible within a certain range of probability. The assertion that our nuclear forces in Europe would be overrun, destroyed or used within two days is not within that range."[1]

Most Americans have never focused on this question (discussed in Part I of this chapter). Indeed, it is only recently that most Americans have recognized the extent to which the threat of first use of nuclear weapons has been a staple of United States' plans for defending Western Europe. American rhetoric has generally assumed that, since the United States would never be the aggressor, war would be forced upon the country. And accordingly, once war had begun, the President should have all authority to use all United States weapons.

There are, however, two alternative views. The first (disscussed in Part II of this chapter) is that, absent a declaration of war or a nuclear attack, no single

A prior version of this essay was published in *Foreign Policy* 56 (1984), from which this excerpt was drawn with permission of The Carnegie Endowment for International Peace.

decision maker should have the authority to order the firing of nuclear weapons alone, and that Congress *may* limit and control this power, as it can control any other war power. A second, more fundamentalist point of view (discussed in Part III of this chapter) is that Congress *must*, whether it wants to or not. Indeed, according to this view, it is unconstitutional, in the absence of a declaration of war, for the President to order first use of nuclear weapons without specific authority at the time from Congress or from its authorized representatives, such as a joint nuclear planning committee created for the purpose.

These are no doubt startling assertions to many and may seem to some easy to ridicule. Nevertheless, there is reason to think that over the decades constitutional practice will, and should, drift in this direction. And for supporters of the doctrine that the United States should never use nuclear weapons first, a proposal to at least give a congressional committee a veto over first use of nuclear weapons (discussed in Part IV of this chapter) has special advantages.

I. THE FIRST USE OF NUCLEAR WEAPONS POSES QUITE DIFFERENT QUESTIONS FROM OTHER USES

For a third of a century, believing that there was Soviet conventional superiority in Europe, United States Presidents have threatened to respond to Soviet conventional attacks with American first use of nuclear weapons. These Presidents threatened, in effect, to turn a conventional war, declared or undeclared, into a qualitatively different conflict—one fought with nuclear weapons. In such escalation of the struggle, they proposed to raise the immediate United States' stakes in the war from risks to American armed forces in Western Europe to immediate risks both to the citizenry and to the republic itself. After all, no conventional war would lead to the destruction of the nation. But within hours of the President's first use of nuclear weapons, nuclear retaliation could lead to the end of the United States.

If it is not absolutely necessary to delegate such authority to a single individual, then this arrangement would seem to violate common sense. Individuals are prone to failures of judgment in much less tense situations, and some kind of check and balance would obviously be preferable.

Insofar as the fate of the nation is concerned, this matter was considered by the Founding Fathers. They recognized that the President was not a king and that the United States was not to be his kingdom, to do with and risk as he wished. They recognized that he needed the power to repel attacks that required immediate action. But the President was to turn to Congress for authority to go beyond such measures. The Constitution authorized Congress "to declare war," after which, but not before, the nation would be at risk. As retired Supreme Court Justice Arthur J. Goldberg has testified, "The President . . . constitutionally has no war making powers except perhaps to repel, as I have said earlier, a surprise attack, an emergency, following which he must immediately go to Congress."[2]

Consistent with this distinction, few would question the right of a President to respond with nuclear weapons. Such a response would be repelling a nuclear attack with like weapons and, most would presume, would need to be ordered almost immediately. But the first use of nuclear weapons raises quite different questions. Since no conventional war is lost in minutes and since the tactical nuclear weapons based in Western Europe that are most at issue could not even be released in less than hours, the President would have time to discuss this fateful issue with officials other than subordinates—in particular with at least some members of Congress. Indeed, setbacks in a conventional war overseas would not cost the United States its existence, its freedom, or its ability to pursue the conflict over time and in other ways, as America did in two world wars. What then gives the President the right to initiate nuclear war, alone, without new authority from Congress, when nuclear war has not been forced upon the country by the nuclear weapons of others?

II. CONGRESS HAS THE AUTHORITY TO CONTROL PRESIDENTIAL FIRST USE

A. The Conventional View

The conventional view asserts that the commander in chief clause in the Constitution gives the President the authority to order the use of any and all weapons once "war" has begun, and it treats any and all major conflicts as war. This view treats the first use of nuclear weapons much as it treats the first use of tanks or conventional artillery—as tactical decisions within the purview of the country's highest military authority, the commander in chief. This view also tends to assume that the war would be forced upon the United States and hence that Congress need not declare war to authorize the commander in chief to make all the decisions in a state of war created by others. No doubt this view would also point to the "inherent" powers of the President as chief executive. And it would point to a history in which the President has often waged war without congressional authority. Indeed, even with United States Marines being killed in Lebanon, Congress had trouble getting President Ronald Reagan to recognize the existence of the War Powers Resolution of 1973, a law designed to control just such undeclared wars. Has not time, at least, worn away such congressional pretensions to control war, if they ever existed?

B. The Historical Experience

Certainly, these claims did exist once. During the Revolutionary War, the Continental Congress designated General George Washington its commander in chief but put him under the control not only of the Congress as a whole, but of a committee of the Continental Congress. His commission of June 19, 1775, stated:

And you are to regulate your conduct in every respect by the rules and discipline of war, (as herewith given you) and punctually to observe and follow such orders and directions from time to time as you shall receive from this or a future congress of these United Colonies, or a committee of congress, for that purpose appointed.[3]

In other words, commander in chief, as delegates understood the title, was subordinate to a strategy committee of the Continental Congress. And this position reflected more than the lack of an executive branch to which the Continental Congress could delegate guidance. It was consistent with the delegates' understanding of the term "commander in chief." Alexander Hamilton asserted in *The Federalist No. 69* that commander in chief was to mean, under the new Constitution, "nothing more than the supreme command and direction of the military and naval forces, as first General and Admiral."[4]

During the last 200 years, while there have been few major conflicts between Congress and the President over war strategy, members of Congress have shown a consciousness of their oversight rights. For example, they have investigated Abraham Lincoln's pursuit of the Civil War and Harry Truman's firing of General Douglas MacArthur during the Korean War. In the case of Vietnam, Congress actually passed legislation asserting that "on or after August 15, 1973, no funds heretofore or hereafter appropriated may be obligated or expended to finance the involvement of United States military forces in hostilities in or over or from off the shores of North Vietnam, South Vietnam, Laos, or Cambodia, unless specifically authorized hereafter by Congress."[5]

C. "Necessary and Proper" Implementation of the War Power

Is the first use of nuclear weapons something appropriate for a first general or admiral or for that matter a chief executive to decide? Or is this decision something so fundamental in its risks for the nation that it would seem to exceed their authority? And in any case, could Congress pass legislation controlling that use as it limited the use of funds for hostilities in Southeast Asia?

During and after the war powers debate, a number of scholars addressed the issue of whether Congress could, by affirmative legislation, control presidential actions in the field of war. Former national security adviser McGeorge Bundy observed that Congress has "every right to assert itself on broad questions of place, time, and the size of forces committed."[6] An eminent authority on the commander in chief clause, Columbia University Law Professor Louis Henkin, wrote: "In my view, he would be bound to follow congressional directives not only as to whether to continue the war, but whether to extend it to other countries and other belligerents, whether to fight a limited or unlimited war, today, perhaps, even whether to fight a 'conventional' or a nuclear war."[7] Professor John Norton Moore ventured that Congress could prevent a President at war in Vietnam from bombing Beijing or from employing biological weapons in a conventional war.[8]

Much of this authority stems from the right of Congress, as stated in Article I, Section 8 of the Constitution, "to make all laws which shall be necessary and proper for carrying into execution the foregoing powers, and all other powers vested by this Constitution in the Government of the United States, or in any Department or Officer thereof." Referring to this clause, George Washington University Professor W. T. Mallison, Jr., observed:

It is appropriate to emphasize that the judgment as to what is "necessary and proper" is that of the Congress, and not of the Supreme Court. The aggregate of the war powers of the Congress are, therefore, sufficiently comprehensive to enable the Congress to have a large role in the conduct of the war. Based upon its expressed war powers combined with the "necessary and proper" clause, the Congress has power to conduct the war insofar as the war may be conducted under statutory authority as contrasted with the President's authority as Commander in Chief. This was recognized in the famous case of *McCulloch v. Maryland*—4 Wheaton 316, 1819—where Chief Justice Marshall referred to the powers of the Congress to "declare and conduct a war" as among its enumerated powers.[9]

Accordingly, most legal scholars would seem to admit the argument that the first use of nuclear weapons was so much more momentous than a tactical decision that Congress had the right to control that decision—if it wished to do so—and that it could control this decision by legislation.

Congress could, for example, legislate that under no circumstances was the President authorized to use nuclear weapons of any kind in any conflict in which they had not already been used by others. By passing a law—over the President's veto if necessary—it could simply remove nuclear weapons from the arsenal available in undeclared conventional wars abroad. If necessary, Congress could use the power of the purse to assert that no funds could be spent to use nuclear weapons except in specified contingencies.

Some will argue that such constraints will be meaningless in war, especially in issues involving nuclear war. But a closer examination of the situation suggests otherwise. No President is going to use nuclear weapons first, if he believes that it will lead to the destruction of the nation. On the contrary, he will be hoping and expecting that escalation will not result. Accordingly, he will ponder being held accountable to the nation for the risks to be taken and for the extent these actions would be in violation of law. If legislation exists precluding the contemplated actions, the President will be to that extent discouraged, deterred, and dissauded from going forward. Indeed, in that event subordinates might not follow the President's orders; the secretary of defense, the Joint Chiefs of Staff, and all the others in the chain of command are sworn to uphold the Constitution and the law, not merely to obey the President.

III. FIRST USE WITHOUT CONGRESSIONAL APPROVAL IS UNCONSTITUTIONAL

A. First Use as a New War

Congress thus has the authority to pass the affirmative legislation necessary to control nuclear first use, although it has yet to exercise it. But perhaps Congress has no choice. A presidential order to use nuclear weapons first during conventional hostilities would be more than just a major tactical and strategic decision, which Congress has the authority to limit. Such an order would start a nuclear war that would be qualitatively different from the ongoing conventional fighting. Certainly this description would be true of a conflict in Europe. A war that might otherwise engulf United States allies and armies would threaten to destroy the United States as well. First use in effect moves the nation into the line of fire—into the war zone. A war that promised to take days and weeks to run its course now may be over in minutes and hours. A war that would leave most of the population in Europe alive now threatens to leave most of them dead.

This is, in short, an entirely new war in common-sense terms. What about legal terms? In legal terms the President who uses nuclear weapons first, without a declaration of war, would have gone from trying to "repel" an attack on our forces and allies abroad to initiating just that kind of much wider commitment that the Founding Fathers wanted to be made by Congress. And obviously, even they never contemplated the immediacy and the magnitude of the risks that this one person would be taking with the nation itself.

In the central case to which all this analysis is really directed—the case of NATO—the original understanding of the NATO treaty was clear: a declaration of war was required before the United States could become fully engaged. True, Article 5 of the NATO treaty declares that an "armed attack" against any of the parties is an armed attack against each of them.[10] But the chief architect of the treaty, Secretary of State Dean Acheson, explained in Senate ratification hearings on April 27, 1949:

This naturally does not mean that the United States would automatically be at war if one of the other signatory nations were the victim of an armed attack. Under our Constitution, the Congress alone has the power to declare war. The obligation of this government under article V would be to take promptly the action it deemed necessary to restore and maintain the security of the North Atlantic area. That decision would, of course, be taken in accordance with our constitutional procedures.[11]

Indeed, Article 11 of the treaty confirms that the treaty "shall be ratified and its provisions carried out by the Parties in accordance with their respective constitutional processes,"[12] which is what Acheson had explicated.

B. The Likelihood of By-Passing Congress If It Fails to Act

Nevertheless, although the line of argument supporting prompt involvement of Congress in declarations of war is a strong one, especially in cases like that of NATO where no attacks have been made on our territory, there is no assurance that a future President would, in fact, ask for such a declaration before the war had escalated to the nuclear level. On the contrary, although obligated to use all available time to consult with the 15 other countries in NATO—an organization that has historically taken its decisions unanimously—and although consulting thoroughly with subordinates, the President may not turn formally to Congress at all even in those cases where time clearly permits asking the full Congress for a declaration of war. Presidents have, after all, by-passed Congress before.

The Vietnam and Korean wars alone show the readiness of the executive branch to exploit lesser authority than declaration of war to involve the country in war. Attacks on our forces or misinterpretations of Article 5 might be used to maintain America's undeclared involvement beyond the period in which Congress could be consulted. The temptation to do so would be enhanced by the fear that a declaration of war, unmodified by any limit, would be excessive and destabilizing in a conflict that both sides would be trying to contain, even as they tried to conduct it.

Further, the War Powers Resolution, while not permitting the war power to be inferred from treaties, does permit the introduction of forces into hostilities in a "national emergency created by attack upon the United States, its territories or possessions, or its armed forces."[13] Thus attacks upon our armed forces in Western Europe, inevitable in any major attack upon NATO, could be used with the authority of this congressional statute to justify the continuation of hostilities. As Bundy put it:

I think a major attack from the East would bring on war without much further "constitutional process," and I think we understand it that way. . . . We have not fully answered the question of the role of the Congress in a case where there may be a major military action in contemplation which is not so much a response to an instantaneous threat as it is a decision as to how to deal with a gradually deepening crisis.[14]

Consequently, if the Soviet Union attacked NATO, Congress might not, in fact, get an opportunity to express itself. And as the conflict escalated, first use of nuclear weapons, always under consideration, might be ordered by the President. In such circumstances, the President would certainly argue that the purpose of the first use would be indeed to repel immediate attacks and not to "declare war." The President's lawyers would note that in 1787 the draft constitution was amended at the Constitutional Convention to give Congress only the right to "declare war" rather than to "make war" so as to leave "to the Executive the power to repel sudden attacks" that might not permit recourse to the Congress.[15]

In fact, however, the initial nuclear weapons used in Europe would represent primarily an announcement of readiness to wage general and indeed nuclear hostilities, not a military effort to contain or repulse the attack. The strict military utility of the initial nuclear weapons to repel the attack, as in the destruction of tanks or command posts, would be minor indeed in comparison to their political utility in dissuading the other side's political leadership from continuing their conventional attack by forcing them also to escalate to nuclear weapons or to cease and desist entirely. It would thus be an effort—a quite dangerous effort— to decide the conflict itself. As Schlesinger put it in May 1975, first use is relevant only when defeat appears imminent:

The first use of theater nuclear forces, even in very limited ways, carries grave risks of escalation and should be considered only when the consequences of conventional defeat would be even more serious. If the alternative is, for example, major loss of NATO territory or forces, NATO political leaders may choose to accept the risks of first use.[16]

Thus first use would usurp the Congress' right to determine whether the nation wishes to go beyond normal efforts to repel the attack to such extraordinary methods as would gamble its very existence. Such presidential misuse of the right to repel attack is analogous to an early President's argument that continued attacks on United States merchant vessels by, for example, the French, could not be repelled in any fashion short of direct attacks on France or its allies and that this observation was sufficient to justify such attacks without further authorization. The first use of nuclear weapons would be far more akin to the initiation of a new military venture than it would be an expansion of the existing one.[17]

And since the United States itself, in this European scenario, would not have been attacked directly, it seems quite unlikely that James Madison and those who supported him would consider this line of argument a fair use of their "repel" amendment. As the distinguished scholar Edward Corwin put it in *The Constitution*, "It was clearly the original understanding of the Constitution that under it all measures of hostility toward another government, not justifiable immediately as acts of self-defense, must have the sanction of Congress."[18] Thus the President does not seem to have the authority, without specific congressional permission in the event itself, to risk the entire nation by moving the conflict onto this new and risky plateau.

It is worth emphasizing that the earlier cases in which presidents fought undeclared wars did not risk attacks upon American territory in response—and certainly did not risk prompt and massive responses, much less the totally destructive response now possible. Moreover, in any case, unconstitutional military actions of the past do not justify unconstitutional actions in the future.

IV. CONSTITUTIONAL SOLUTION?

A. The FAS Committee Proposal

The view expressed here is completely consistent with that of those scholars who demand and expect a declaration of war before the nation is fully committed to war because this view admits that such a congressional declaration, if unmodified by references to nuclear weapons, is a carte blanche authorization for the President.[19]

But many observers do not demand, expect, or even want a declaration of war. What are they to do about the President's otherwise unfettered authority to use nuclear weapons first without congressional involvement? They well understand that the critical issue in the modern day is not the declaration of war *per se* but the first use of nuclear weapons. As Representative L. H. Fountain (D-North Carolina) once asked, "The use of such weapons would amount to a declaration of war, would it not"?[20] Is there a constitutional solution that involves Congress but does not require a full-scale declaration of war or, indeed, full-scale involvement of Congress?

Some may share my view that a decision to use nuclear weapons first made by the President alone or with subordinates is and ought to be unconstitutional, even if the only alternative is the involvement of the entire Congress without any rules to expedite its procedures or to act in secret. Anticipated losses of allied territory in a conventional war abroad do not justify departing from the constitutional requirement of involving Congress. And a constitution that prevents a country that is in no danger of conventional invasion from risking destruction unnecessarily and on the decision of one person has much to be said for it.

But for those who accept the reasoning but dislike consulting Congress as a whole, an intermediate position would be to create a special committee of Congress that could grant the authority for any first use of nuclear weapons. Such a nuclear planning committee, containing a dozen or so members and composed of the two senior members from each of the most relevant existing committees of Congress, could act expeditiously and even secretly in any crises precipitated by a conventional war. Congress should create such a committee and should give it, by statute, a veto over first use. The Supreme Court, if subsequently asked, should find the statute constitutional because the alternative would be to leave the nation torn between the perceived unconstitutionality of one-person control that produced the statute and the perceived impracticality of control by the full Congress that inspired the committee.

With this in mind, a bill drafted by the FAS in 1975 proposed as a solution these provisions: "In any given conflict or crisis whatsoever, and notwithstanding any other authority, so long as no nuclear weapons have been used by others, the President shall not use nuclear weapons without consulting with, and securing the assent of a majority of, a committee" composed of the speaker and minority leader of the House of Representatives, the majority and minority leaders of the Senate, and the chairman and ranking member of the Senate and House committees on Armed Services, the Senate Committee on Foreign Relations, the House Committee on International Relations, and the Joint Committee on Atomic Energy. The bill also provided that "nothing herein shall preclude the President from using nuclear weapons first if Congress adopts a declaration of war that explicitly suspends the authority granted in this act."[21]

Under this proposal, the secretary of defense or chairman of the Joint Chiefs of Staff, through whom the order to initiate the use of nuclear weapons would pass, would check with the secretary of state to verify that the committee vote had been affirmative. This certification procedure would be in effect a two-key system at the top of the chain of command between the President and the secretary of state. Another provision was added calling for annual reports from the President to the committee with the thought that a presidential failure to report would set a possible stage for a peacetime legal test of the constitutionality of the statute.

B. *Chadha* and the Committee Proposal

The Supreme Court, it is true, had ruled against one-house vetoes and, *a fortiori*, against committee vetoes in its decision in the case of *Immigration and Naturalization Service v. Chadha.*[22] In deploring a "convenient shortcut," the *Chadha* decision justified what it called "governmental processes that often seem clumsy, inefficient, even unworkable" on the grounds that the records of the Constitutional Convention and the debates in the states showed a determination that legislation be a "step-by-step, deliberate and deliberative process."[23] But the convention obviously had non-emergency peacetime action in mind.

Indeed, the use of the word "shortcut" reveals the Court's premise that Congress had the capacity in due course to change any government regulations through its traditional means. Such reasoning does not extend to the question at hand. The first use of nuclear weapons may not be so immediate an issue that one decision maker need be given the authority to decide it, but it is a time-urgent matter that does not permit the usual congressional procedures. Nor does this question involve a veto over regulations; instead, it is a committee method of effecting a constitutionally granted congressional authority over war.

The Supreme Court has argued similarly that wartime justified congressional delegations of authority to the executive branch that would not otherwise have been justified. It asserted in 1948 in *Lichter v. United States*,[24] for example, that "a constitutional power implies a power of delegation of authority under it sufficient to effect its purposes." And Corwin has asserted, "[l]ikewise in wartime the constitutional ban on the delegation by Congress of its powers to the President is in almost complete abeyance. What are termed the 'cognate powers' of the two departments may be merged by Congress substantially at will."[25] Does this delegation always have to be from Congress to the executive or could the merging of cognate powers take the form required by the creation of the proposed congressional committee?[26]

After all, a sustained refusal of the Court to sanction any congressional involvement in the first use of nuclear weapons short of a full-scale formal declaration of war could leave the nation with what some would consider no satisfactory defense. And, in particular, it could leave Congress with no effective method of implementing in a timely and flexible fashion a power conceded to belong to it. These issues are too serious for a proposal concerning them to be ruled unconstitutional simply because it has to be distinguished from everyday legislation. Accordingly, it seems clear that a Court that wished to do so could accommodate this position. Whether it would wish to do so could depend on public opinion and the position of the other two branches.

C. Practical Advantages

The proposal for a planning committee has a number of practical advantages as well as constitutional ones. A committee veto represents, in perspective, a natural evolution from the no first use posture that so many citizens are coming to desire. Rather than moving in one giant step from unilateral presidential authority for first use to a world in which our entire political system pledges never again to use nuclear weapons first under any authority, the committee approach spreads the responsibility for first use, making it less likely to occur by putting an additional lock on the trigger.[27]

This approach substitutes a less controversial issue of "no one first decision maker" for a relatively difficult political effort to secure a declaration of no first use under any circumstances. Moreover, where the no first use declaratory policy of one President can be reversed by a later President or ignored in a crisis, the legal and bureaucratic process created by a committee would be much harder to ignore. Those who want above all to suppress the possibility of our first use of nuclear weapons ought to think carefully about which road is more effective.

In spreading the responsibility for Western first use, rather than banning it, the approach of committee oversight also avoids rupturing our commitments to NATO. As before, the United States would have the right to use nuclear weapons and the obligation to respond in NATO in accordance with its constitutional responsibilities. America would simply have reconsidered what those processes are and would have adjusted its internal governmental processes accordingly. Washington would not have withdrawn its main weapon from the West's protective arsenal. And since all other NATO countries value highly their rights to be consulted on just such matters, they could hardly complain too heatedly if America's own government consultation were extended to a congressional committee.

Nor does it seem that this approach would undermine deterrence in any significant way. By comparison, our decision to protect against unauthorized use of nuclear weapons by installing "permissive action links," electronic locks on individual nuclear weapons, probably did far more to allay Soviet fears of an early first use of nuclear weapons than would this method of preventing unauthorized presidential first use. The threat of a timely and even of a surprise first use of nuclear weapons remains because the committee could function in secret. Moreover, an announcement that the committee had given its authorization to the President could represent, like a revolver being drawn from a holster, an optional sign of warning. Such a signal clearly would be preferable to the demonstration firing of a nuclear weapon sometimes discussed as a possible method of showing NATO determination if a conventional war were to reach a point of no return. Such a firing would combine all the dangers of a verbal announcement, as well as the danger of being interpreted by the other side as a precursor to a general firing, with the finality of having jumped the nuclear fire gap.

The congressional authorization procedure *would*, on the other hand, lower the *popular perception* of the likelihood of our first use of nuclear weapons. One benefit could be more support for the alliance among that younger Western European generation that fears America's trigger-happiness, thus offsetting to some degree whatever opposition can be expected from allied governments. Yet this proposal's fate should not turn on whether Western Europeans approve it. America's obligations to its own security, its own Constitution, and its own judgment on how best to assist in the defense of Western Europe should be the decisive factors.

There would be other political advantages. Presidents who do not wish to use nuclear weapons first could find political shelter in their inability to get support from a congressional committee. Recall that President John Kennedy is said to have told his brother Robert that he would be impeached if he did not win the Cuban missile crisis. At least under this system Presidents will find it easy to orchestrate a spreading of the responsibility for restraint.

Not least important, since the secretary of state would have the responsibility to certify to the secretary of defense that the congressional committee had opted for giving its authority, the specter of aberrant behavior on the part of a psychologically exhausted, politically committed, and deeply involved individual in a drawn-out crisis would be to that extent laid to rest. This possibility was a matter of some concern to lower-level officials immediately before President Richard Nixon's resignation, even though no military conflict existed.

Finally, this proposal can also be seen as a long-overdue measure drawing Congress into the decision making process on nuclear issues. Two decades ago, then Secretary of Defense Robert McNamara saw a similar need to draw NATO into an understanding of nuclear issues and to share responsibility with alliance members. From this notion came the idea of a nuclear planning group. The committee approach would represent, in a way, a long-overdue analogous development at home.

Obviously, conservative opponents of this approach will consider it an outrageous usurpation of presidential power. Perhaps less obvious is the inevitable hostility toward this idea from many on the Left. Arms control advocates who oppose first use of nuclear weapons have in the past considered congressional involvement to be an all-too-easy way to authorize and legitimate first use. They inaccurately assume that hawkish members of Congress are all too eager to risk the country's existence. And they often mistake the congressional veto approach herein advocated for a system in which Congress gets the right to encourage first use.

One cannot help but believe, however, that the Founding Fathers would look down with favor on some return to constitutional practice in, at least, this ultimate case of when and how America is taken into the ultimate war. During Jefferson's presidency, in the midst of a dispute with Spain about the Florida border, he advised Congress, "Considering that Congress alone is constitutionally invested with the power of changing our condition from peace to war, I have thought it my duty to await their authority for using force in any degree which could be avoided."[28] Nuclear force in a conventional war abroad would seem to be precisely force in a degree that "could be avoided" while congressional authority was awaited.

NOTES

1. *U.S. Forces in Europe; Hearing Before the Subcomm. on Arms Control, Internat'l Law and Organization*, 92d Cong., 1st Sess. 101 (July 27, 1971) (statement of Kenneth Rush, Deputy Secretary of State).

2. *War Powers Legislation: Hearing on S. 731 Before Senate Foreign Relations Comm.*, 93d Cong., 1st Sess. 773 (Oct. 6, 1973) (statement by Arthur Goldberg, retired U.S. Supreme Court Justice).

3. J. Marshall, II *Life of George Washington* 4 (1925).

4. *The Federalist No. 69*, at 465 (A. Hamilton) (Cooke ed. 1961).

5. P.L. 93–126 § 13, 87 Stat. 454 (1973) (Dept. of State Appropriations Act of 1973).

6. *War Powers Legislation: Hearings on S. 731 Before Senate Foreign Relations Comm.*, 92d Cong., 1st Sess. 422 (April 26, 1971) (statement of McGeorge Bundy, Pres. Ford Foundation).

7. L. Henkin, *Foreign Affairs and the Constitution* 108 (1972).

8. J. Moore, *Law and the Indochina War* 538–69 (1972).

9. *Congress, the President and the War Powers: Hearing Before House Foreign Affairs Comm.*, 91st Cong., 2d Sess. 32 (June 23, 1970) (statement of W. T. Mallison, Professor, George Washington University).

10. North Atlantic Treaty art. 5, Apr. 4, 1949, T.I.A.S. No. 1964, 34 U.N.T.S. 243 (hereinafter "NATO").

11. *North Atlantic Treaty: Hearings on Exec. L. Before the Senate Comm. on Foreign Relations*, 81st Cong., 1st Sess. 11 (1949).

12. NATO, *supra* note 10, art. 11.

13. War Powers Resolution, 50 U.S.C. § 1541(c) (1982).

14. *Congress, the President and the War Powers: Hearings Before the House Subcomm. on National Security and Scientific Developments*, 91st Cong., 2d Sess. 14 (June 28, 1970) (statement of McGeorge Bundy, President, Ford Foundation).

15. III M. Farrand, *The Records of the Federal Convention* 318–19 (1966); *See generally* W. T. Reveley II, *War Powers of the President and Congress* 82–86 (1981).

16. *See Report to Congress on Nuclear Force Posture* under P.L. 93–365 (May 1975).

17. *See* Reveley, *supra* note 15, at 356–57.

18. E. Corwin, *The Constitution* (1973).

19. Our declarations of war have sometimes involved special instructions and could presumably be adopted in the future with limitations. In 1812 when war was "declared to exist," the President was authorized not only to use "the whole land and naval force" against Great Britain but also to issue letters of reprisal. 2 Stat. 102 (1812). In 1898 war was "declared to exist" against Spain after Spain declared war on the United States. The President was not only "directed and empowered to use the entire land naval forces," but also authorized to call up the militia as necessary. 31 Cong. Rec. 4244–45 (1898).

20. *Congress, the President and the War Powers: Hearing Before the House Foreign Affairs Comm.*, 91st Cong., 2d Sess. 13 (1970) (statement by L. H. Fountain, Rep., North Carolina).

21. *See* Raven-Hansen, *supra* Introduction notes 1–4 and accompanying text.

22. 462 U.S. 919 (1983).

23. *Id.* at 959.

24. 334 U.S. 742 (1948).

25. Corwin, *supra* note 18.

26. There may be additional ways to permit Congress to fulfill its constitutional function. The rules of each house of Congress, for example, are normally not subject to judicial review. Perhaps during hostilities these rules can be manipulated to transmute action of this unique bicameral committee into the functional equivalent of congressional action in some kind of superexpedited procedure.

27. The committee would have no authority to propose, urge, or insist on the first use of nuclear weapons but only to accede to or oppose presidential recommendations.

28. I *Messages and Papers of the President 1789–1897*, at 389 (J. Richardson ed. 1897).

2

Which Nuclear Scenarios Are at Issue?

Jeremy J. Stone

From the point of view of constitutional law, the following nine cases can be distinguished:

1. *Second Strike*: The nation is attacked with nuclear weapons. Here the President would be accorded the right to respond without further authorization from Congress on the theory that he was simply repelling an attack with like weapons.

2. *Irrevocable Launch*: The President determines that nuclear weapons have been "irrevocably launched' against the United States. Here the issue is the constitutionality of "launch-on-warning." If one believes that a determination can be made with certainty that opposing nuclear weapons have indeed been irrevocably launched, one can argue that the President ought not to be obligated to wait for their impact before moving to repel the attack. If, on the other hand, one sees in such policies much more likelihood of inadvertent war than of effective countering of such an attack, one might have another view. For the purposes of my essay,[1] "irrevocable launch" against the United States could be accepted as a justification for nuclear first use without damage to the fundamental points being made.

3. *Pre-emptive Forestalling Attack*: The President believes that he has information that a nuclear attack is about to be made on the United States and, while nuclear weapons have not been irrevocably launched against us, he wishes to launch a pre-emptive "forestalling" attack. According to certain constitutional authorities, such as Professor Louis Henkin, such forestalling attacks are probably constitutional.[2] They are not very likely in cases involving the Soviet Union since no plausible forestalling attack against that nation is likely to have sufficient

certainty of success in reducing retaliatory damage to persuade a President to attempt it—no advance information being that certain in any case. The President is far more likely to alert United States forces and to advise the Soviet Union that the forces are alerted—thus to attempt a political forestalling of the attack rather than a military one.

Nevertheless, as above, including a forestalling attack against an enemy country among the President's prerogatives without further consultation with Congress does not interfere with the essential point being made in my essay.

4. *Second Strike Abroad*: United States forces abroad, for example in Europe or Korea, are attacked with nuclear weapons. The President could, presumably, use a similar authority to repel the nuclear attack on United States forces by employing nuclear responses on enemy forces. However, in the European theater, as opposed to the Korean one, such a bilateral use of nuclear weapons would have a high likelihood of escalation to general nuclear war between the superpowers. Accordingly, the President would be usurping Congress's right to determine whether it did, indeed, want to risk the nation in that way. One possible solution would be to have Congress legislate restraints on the firing of nuclear weapons at the Soviet Union itself unless and until the Soviet Union had launched nuclear weapons at the United States. This would limit the President to repelling the attack in the theater and would lower the likelihood of escalation to general nuclear war between the superpowers. Such a policy of no first strike at the other's homeland has been urged by a number of specialists, including Paul C. Warnke.

5. *Forestalling an Attack Abroad*: The President asserts the right to use nuclear weapons first in the European theater in order to forestall an allegedly impending nuclear attack against United States forces. This scenario raises the above questions and, in addition, the possibility that a President might use the loophole of a forestalling attack to achieve the functional equivalent of that first use in Europe. However, the nuclear first use that would occur in the two cases would seem quite different. A true forestalling attack in the European arena would presumably require attacking a large number of Soviet nuclear weapon sites in Eastern Europe and the Western Soviet Union. On the other hand, contemplated first uses in Europe that are truly at the Western initiative are more likely to involve "demonstration" nuclear firings of an isolated kind or "tactical" uses designed, in fact, to show readiness to breach the nuclear threshold. Under these circumstances, it is, again, possible to admit even forestalling nuclear attacks in a theater without giving up on the principles being advocated here. The wisdom, however, of conceding the right to the President of nuclear forestalling attacks in Europe on his own authority is highly questionable since it means risking the nation, in the resultant escalation, in the absence of even an alleged attack on the nation itself.

6. *Conventional War Abroad*: In an on-going conventional war, or otherwise, Congress enacts a declaration of war that is unlimited by any relevant constraining references to the use of nuclear weapons. In this event, the President presumably has the authority to use all weapons available at his discretion unless the Congress intervenes subsequently and countermands this authority.

7. *Conventional Attack at Home*: A conventional attack on United States territory is deemed to have thrust war upon the nation without any congressional declaration of war. Perhaps, in the pre-nuclear era, attacks upon our territory might have produced a state of war that needed no congressional recognition. Perhaps President Roosevelt was not really required to ask Congress for a declaration of war against Japan despite Pearl Harbor except as a recognition of a pre-existing state of war.

But in the nuclear age, if Hawaii were attacked again by a nuclear power, there are two quite different states of war that might be produced, depending upon whether nuclear weapons had or had not been employed. Thus in the nuclear age, a conventional attack by a nuclear power is not an unlimited attack and would presumably not establish a state of total war in and of itself. It would be a more limited act. And since this more limited act might not require, or make wise, an unmodified or unlimited declaration of war from Congress, it can hardly, in and of itself, be the basis of a presidential presumption of total or unlimited war. Accordingly, it is argued here that first use is not constitutional, in the absence of a declaration of war, even after a conventional attack on United States territory. And this certainly accords with the common-sense fact that no such conventional attack on our nation will win a conventional war against us within a time period that would preclude consulting Congress—much less destroy the nation, which nuclear war threatens to do.

8. *Conventional Attacks Abroad with Treaty*: A conventional attack on our allies is deemed, via a treaty like the NATO treaty, to be an armed attack against the United States that justified presidential first use. These treaties do not pre-empt the right of Congress to determine the extent and nature of our military involvement in the event itself. The treaties are not advance declarations of war. For one thing they are not approved by Congress, but only ratified by the Senate, whereas declarations of war must be passed by Congress itself. More generally, as in the case of the NATO treaty, Congress has been advised of quite the opposite. The view here is that declarations of war in advance, in any form, are at variance with the intentions of those who drafted the Constitution.

9. *Conventional Attack Abroad without Treaty*: A conventional attack occurs on our forces abroad and there is no treaty binding our response. Here, *a fortiori*, the President should not have the right to use nuclear weapons first because it goes beyond force immediately necessary to repel attacks.

It is finally, perhaps, possible to concoct cases in which the nuclear weapon is necessary to forestall or prevent defeat of local forces somewhere—and, indeed, to find a scenario in which the opposing forces are so little linked to the immediate use of nuclear weapons in response that no risk of nuclear escalation exists.

NOTES

1. *See* Stone, *supra* Chap. 1.
2. *See* L. Henkin, *Foreign Affairs and the Constitution* 107–8 (1972).

II

ALLOCATING NUCLEAR WAR POWERS UNDER THE CONSTITUTION

3

The Constitution, Nuclear Weapons, and Deterrence: An Analysis of the FAS Proposal

John Norton Moore

Together with the problem of enhancing stability at the central strategic level, there is no more important and vexing problem in global strategic stability than enhancing stability in the NATO-Warsaw Pact area. Protection of the democracies of NATO from coercion and war has understandably been a priority concern of every American President and Congress since World War II. An underlying reality in implementing the cooperative defense of NATO is that the Warsaw Pact nations have traditionally maintained a conventional superiority in the NATO-Warsaw Pact area. Until recently, that conventional imbalance has been offset by unquestioned United States superiority at the central strategic level and a United States battlefield nuclear superiority in the NATO-Warsaw Pact area. In recent years, however, the problem of European strategic stability has been made more difficult by a setting of rough United States-Soviet equivalence at the central strategic level and, with the substantial Soviet deployment of SS-20 and upgraded nuclear systems in Eastern Europe, a battlefield and European intermediate nuclear balance no better, if not worse, than rough equivalence. This changing reality has created a dilemma for NATO—as it seeks to enhance regional stability and reduce the risk of war. If NATO forswears any use of nuclear weapons to deter conventional attack then, at least at current conventional levels, it may undermine deterrence against a conventional attack it could not stop with conventional means. Indeed, such an attack could, *in extremis*, result in a fallback use of nuclear weapons despite any pre-existing NATO policy of no first use. On the other hand, if NATO relies on battlefield nuclear weapons or escalation to the central strategic level, it faces a risk of comparable response

The views expressed are those of the author and do not necessarily represent the views of any organizations with which the author is or has been affiliated.

or escalation. Faced with this dilemma, NATO has adopted a policy of "flexible response" indicating that NATO will respond to any attack with appropriate levels of force, not excluding battlefield or strategic nuclear forces. And NATO defense planners have been concerned to link the defense of NATO with the United States strategic deterrent.

Given the nature of the dilemma facing NATO as it seeks to reduce the risk of war, it is not surprising—indeed it is a healthy feature of our democracies—that scholars and politicians will examine other alternatives to the dilemma. One such, most recently prominently debated in the pages of *Foreign Affairs*,[1] is that NATO should, as a matter of alliance policy, adopt a position of nuclear no first use, thus delinking American strategic nuclear forces, as well as potential battlefield first use of nuclear weapons, in response even to an overwhelming and possibly conventionally unstoppable Warsaw Pact attack. This doctrine of nuclear no first use in response to a massive Warsaw Pact conventional, or even conventional combined with chemical-biological, attack has been consistently rejected by NATO because of the perceived risk of such a policy in undermining deterrence, and paradoxically of possibly even increasing the risk of ultimate nuclear use should deterrence and conventional defense fail, as well as other political and tactical concerns.

More recently, Dr. Jeremy Stone, as a supporter of the "no first use" approach, has suggested an alternate approach, either as an intermediate option on the way to "no first use" or in combination with "no first use."[2] Dr. Stone suggested that any decision by the President to first use nuclear weapons in response to even an overwhelming non-nuclear attack—possibly with certain limited exceptions[3] not then fully developed by Dr. Stone—may be unconstitutional absent prior congressional approval of the decision. Dr. Stone has also advanced the Federation of American Scientists (FAS) suggestion that one possible way to structure the process of congressional approval would be to create a congressional leadership committee and give it "by statute, a veto over first use."[4]

This conference is in large measure an occasion to consider the generic structural issue suggested by the Stone essay, as well as the specific FAS proposal. The generic issue, as well as the specific FAS proposal, are being raised in a context heavily involved with the NATO-Warsaw Pact dilemma but are in part a response to broader contexts and issues and thus have not been limited to any one issue in use of nuclear weapons against non-nuclear attack.

No issue is of greater importance than strengthening global stability and reducing the threat of coercion and war, particularly the threat of nuclear war. As such, it is imperative that new and imaginative proposals, advanced in the shared interest in strengthening stability, receive a careful and fair hearing. It is equally important that they be candidly and fully critiqued precisely in terms of their contribution, or lack thereof, to enhancing deterrence, reducing the risk of war—including nuclear war—and generally strengthening the United Nations Charter normative protections for self-determination and freedom from coercion. Discussion of issues of such critical dimension may easily become heated and polarized. The shared human stakes, however, suggest that there is no greater intellectual error either than failing to fully consider the views advanced by others—even if novel or unpopular—or failing to candidly critique such proposals on the merits. On an issue of such importance, any lesser intellectual engagement may well be immoral.

In the spirit, then, of welcoming the discussion triggered by the FAS proposal, but not drawing back from full on the merits critique even in a conference seemingly largely composed of friends of the proposal, I must in candor and moral duty report to this conference that I regard the proposal as, sadly, likely to at least marginally increase the risk of war, rather than decreasing it as intended by the author, and I believe its constitutional underpinnings are seriously flawed.

I. BACKGROUND CONTEXT

The legal realists, and everything we know from modern jurisprudence, have indelibly taught us that legal problems cannot be usefully divorced from context and policy. To seek to do so on an issue of such momentous importance would be to multiply the intellectual error by the enormous stake we have in the goals of war avoidance and the protection of democratic institutions against coercive threat.

To fully explore the broadest context of the problem, however, would require not a paper—or even a book—but many such books on the important interrelated dimensions of the issues. Not having the luxury of time to fully set out the context of the problem, it nevertheless seems useful to briefly examine the most important features of context.

First, we should remember that the United Nations Charter, the Helsinki Final Act,[5] and virtually every normative statement on initiation of coercion in modern international law, establish that it is illegal to aggressively use force in international relations, whether such an aggressive attack is conventional or nuclear. This may well be the most important principle in over 2,000 years of human thought about war prevention. Support for the United Nations Charter prohibition of aggression in international relations is among the most important principles historically supported by the democracies. Pursuant to this principle, the United States and NATO have no doctrine of aggressive attack against the Warsaw Pact or first strike against the Soviet Union with or without nuclear weapons. Nor does the United States or any other democratic nation lightly contemplate use of nuclear weapons. Nothing is better understood in the democracies, by the public and decision makers alike, than the awesome destructive potential of nuclear weapons and the constraints of living in a world of shared nuclear equivalence. Any discussion of the "first use" of nuclear weapons by the United States or NATO, then, assumes *both* a prior aggressive attack against the United States, NATO, or other allies in violation of Article 2(4) of the United Nations Charter, giving rise to a right of effective defense and even an obligation for effective collective defense as is embodied in the NATO Treaty, *and* a horrendous *in extremis* setting of probable defeat from a massive conventional or even combined conventional and chemical-biological attack where the stakes are extraordinarily high as, for example, in protecting the self-determination and national sovereignty of the democratic nations of Europe. The debate about first use of nuclear weapons is emphatically not a debate about a United States first strike on the Soviet Union, or a NATO attack against the Warsaw Pact, or even a response to a conventional attack not imminently threatening the most fundamental values. Thus by simply never attacking NATO, and thereby complying with their obligation under the United Nations Charter and the Helsinki Final Act, the Warsaw Pact need never fear any NATO option of nuclear "first use" against a prior massive attack.

Second, although experts differ as to the precise NATO-Warsaw Pact military balance, it is widely recognized that the Warsaw Pact has conventional superiority in the European theater and many experts believe that NATO might not prevail if the target of a sudden and sustained conventional attack. It is also of concern that the Warsaw Pact strategy and force structure has many features suggestive of a modern armored blitzkrieg *into* NATO territory rather than the more cautious NATO strategy oriented to defense of its territory. Looking briefly at comparative force levels, in its careful 1984 study of force comparisons between NATO and the Warsaw Pact, NATO itself provided some of the important comparisons as of 1983:[6]

	NATO	*Warsaw Pact*
manpower	4.5 million	6.0 million
main battle tanks	17,730	46,230
other armored fighter vehicles	39,580	94,800
artillery and large mortars	14,700	38,800
attack helicopters	900	1,175
total aircraft in Europe	2,990	7,430

Numerical force comparisons certainly do not tell the whole story, but they are equally certainly relevant. Because of the present conventional imbalance—and a skepticism by many that the imbalance can be reversed at acceptable political and economic costs—NATO has, in order to enhance deterrence against conventional attack, adopted a policy, as discussed above, of "flexible response"— not ruling out the use of nuclear weapons against an overwhelming conventional attack. While no one should underestimate the enormous destructive potential of nuclear attack—such an attack must simply never occur—the great destructive potential of modern conventional weapons—an order of magnitude greater than in World War II—should also not be underestimated. The cost in human life, civilian casualties and property damage from a full-scale Warsaw Pact conventional attack against NATO would itself be a human catastrophe of monumental proportions.

Third, any decision by an American President to use nuclear weapons in the

NATO area in response to a massive conventional attack would require some degree of NATO government coordination and cooperation. In order not to undermine deterrence, the precise modalities of such consultation and cooperation are not publicly known.

Fourth, NATO has, since 1973, pursued negotiations with the Warsaw Pact, within the talks on Mutual Reduction of Forces and Armaments and Associated Measures in Central Europe (known by NATO participants as Mutual and Balanced Force Reduction talks or MBFR), on substantial reductions in conventional force levels to balanced levels not offensively threatening NATO nations. It is generally believed that the Warsaw Pact nations, enjoying substantial conventional superiority, have not been seriously interested to date in reducing force levels to a balanced non-threatening posture. If such a balanced reduction could be achieved, of course, the dilemma requiring possible NATO first use of nuclear weapons would largely be ameliorated. The Warsaw Pact, then, would seem to have an additional readily available, non-threatening option, which would largely eliminate any threat of allied nuclear first use.

Fifth, whatever the underlying constitutionality of the War Powers Resolution, an issue on which constitutional scholars differ, that Resolution requires—in a non-controversial provision—the President to make a report in writing to Congress within 48 hours of the introduction of United States armed forces into hostilities. It seems inconceivable, with or without a War Powers Resolution, that the kind of major conventional attack against the United States or NATO that would pose a realistic possibility of nuclear response would not be the subject of immediate congressional debate and consideration. In such a setting, Congress clearly has the power to authorize hostilities—and to exercise whatever constitutional power it possesses to constrain possible United States responses. No new mechanism is required for Congress to have this authority. The War Powers Resolution also confirms, as is the view of the overwhelming majority of constitutional scholars, that the President has the power to repel attacks against the United States "or its armed forces" and that authorization of any hostilities that may be constitutionally required can be accomplished legally by joint resolution as well as legislation formally denominated a "declaration of war." As a matter of international practice, there seem to have been no formal declarations of war anywhere in the world since the late 1940's. It should also be pointed out that the War Powers Resolution, itself advanced as a congressional check to promote stability, has engendered a lasting—even an intensifying—debate as to its constitutionality and effect on deterrence. For example, as superb a constitutional scholar as Eugene Rostow, the former Dean of the Yale Law School and former Director of the Arms Control and Disarmament Agency, has repeatedly called for its repeal as unconstitutional and as undermining deterrence.[7] And certainly the most careful study to date of practice under the Resolution, that of Robert F. Turner, has seriously called into question its constitutionality, its efficacy and its impact on deterrence.[8] Any proposal for a new "congressional check" dealing with the core *presidential* power as commander in chief should consider that a similarly inspired measure dealing only with the core *congressional* power to authorize major hostilities has itself strongly polarized the legal and strategic community.

These factors provide a brief but necessary context to examine the constitutional and policy issues in the FAS proposal.

II. THE CONSTITUTIONAL ISSUES

The division of powers between Congress and the President in the use of armed force has not been an area of the law characterized by great certainty.[9] Within that general context, however, a few issues stand out as relatively clear. Most importantly for analysis of the FAS proposal, it is generally accepted that the President has authority to conduct hostilities during constitutionally authorized hostilities: that is, to make decisions concerning the employment of defense assets placed at his disposal by Congress. And as previously noted, an attack on American forces, as would certainly accompany a major Warsaw Pact attack against NATO, would provide constitutional authority for the President to repel the attack without any requirement of prior congressional authorization.

The President's power to conduct hostilities stems, in part, from the specific constitutional grant of authority to him to serve as "commander in chief." From the background of the Constitutional Convention, we know that this power was a reaction against the effort of the Continental Congress to conduct the Revolutionary War by committee. The Stone essay cites the commission of George Washington placing him as commander in chief under the control of the Continental Congress. But surprisingly it does not inform the reader that it was in reaction to this practice that the Framers of the Constitution specifically spelled out that the President would be commander in chief, something they did not need to do given the general delegation of executive power to the President unless they wanted to be absolutely clear on the point. There is no historical evidence to suggest that the Framers intended, as Stone implies, to continue the Continental Congress practice that the conduct of hostilities would be subject to the "order and direction" of the Congress. There is strong evidence to the contrary, such as the remark of Mr. King in the Convention debate which makes it evident that one reason for the Framers changing "make war" to "declare war" in the congressional grant of authority was to make it clear that the conduct of hostilities was an executive, not a congressional function.[10] Similarly, Mr. Miller, in the North Carolina convention, clearly indicated that the constitutional rule was to the contrary when he "considered it as a defect in the Constitution, that it was not expressly provided that Congress should have the direction of the motions of the army."[11]

The broad authority of the President as commander in chief is illustrated by Dr. Clarence Berdahl in his classic study of the *War Powers of the Executive in the United States*. Dr. Berdahl writes:

Altho there has been some contention that Congress, by virtue of its power to declare war and to provide for the support of the armed forces, is a superior body, and that the President, as commander in chief, is "but the Executive arm"—in every detail and particular, subject to the commands of the lawmaking power, practically all authorities agree that the President, as commander in chief, occupies an entirely independent position, having powers that are exclusively his, subject to no restriction or control by either the legislative or judicial departments.[12]

As this summary suggests, the real constitutional issue is not the power of the President to conduct hostilities absent specific statutory authority, but in what areas, if any, Congress can restrict that power.[13] I regard it as a paradigm principle of American constitutional law that the President may conduct hostilities against an attacking nation, including *in extremis* making decisions to employ nuclear weapons in settings where, as here, Congress has not enacted any prohibition on such use. Thus, a premise of the Stone essay, embodied in its title, that "Presidential First Use is Unlawful," seems to me, in a setting in which Congress has even rejected a no first use approach, as simply hyperbole by Dr. Stone.[14]

As indicated, the more interesting—and real—constitutional issue is the power of Congress to place policy limits on the exercise by the President of his power as commander in chief to conduct hostilities. Congress certainly cannot intervene to make day-to-day tactical command decisions but it is arguable that it may under its power to make "rules for the government" of the army, or its other congressional powers, place certain policy restrictions on command decisions, such as those limiting conduct of hostilities by area or with nuclear weapons. Even this proposition, however, is unclear and certainly many command decisions are constitutionally exclusive in the President. Thus, Dr. Berdahl points out that a distinguished ex-Justice of the Supreme Court, Charles E. Hughes, among others, viewed congressional efforts at area restrictions on use of forces as impermissible. Hughes wrote: "There is no limitation upon the authority of Congress to create an army and it is for the President as commander-in-chief to direct the campaigns of that army wherever he may think they should be carried on."[15] The pervasive ambiguity on this issue is illustrated by the classic language in the 1893 Court of Claims case of *Swaim v. United States*:

The President cannot, under the disguise of military orders, evade the legislative regulations by which he in common with the Army must be governed; and Congress cannot in the disguise of "rules for the government" of the Army impair the authority of the President as commander in chief.[16]

The case of *Myers v. United States*[17] makes it clear in an area exclusively entrusted to the President under the Constitution, whatever the precise parameters of such areas in relation to the Presidential power to conduct hostilities, Congress is powerless to encroach.

Even if we assume that Congress can constitutionally establish a nuclear no first use policy binding on the President in the exercise of his responsibility to conduct constitutionally authorized hostilities, the core FAS proposal to establish a committee of Congress to make specific real-time decisions to authorize first use of nuclear weapons would seem almost certainly unconstitutional for two—and possibly three—reasons. These are:

—decisions by a committee of Congress, as opposed to Congress as a whole, would be unconstitutional encroachments on both the bicameral and presentment provisions of the Constitution, as recently expounded by the Supreme Court in the case of *Immigration and Naturalization Service v. Chadha*.[18] Clearly a statute removing the existing power of the President to make such a use until Congress authorizes such use can in no sense constitute a "delegation of authority." A decision by the proposed Committee would, on its face, be a "legislative act" requiring compliance with the bicameral and presentment clauses. Indeed, to argue somehow that this momentous decision is less than a "legislative act" squarely within *Chadha* is to demean the importance of the decision and argue against the whole thrust of the argument for such a statute;
—it is one thing for Congress to enact a general no first use policy binding on the President or to enact general rules for employment of nuclear weapons. It is altogether another thing to place a committee of Congress, or even the Congress as a whole, in the real-time operational chain of command concerning a decision to use nuclear, or any other, weapon during constitutionally authorized hostilities. I believe the courts are virtually certain to regard any such effort as an encroachment on the commander in chief power; and
—the specific Stone suggestion to place the Secretaries of State and Defense in the chain of command to control Presidential action, although hardly necessary to his thesis, would also seem highly doubtful constitutionally.[19]

III. THE POLICY ISSUES

Constitutional constraints can, if warranted, always be changed by constitutional amendment. And, short of this ultimate legal issue of constitutional revision, there is a dynamic interrelation between legal appraisal and policy proposals concerning structural changes in the mechanism for conduct of foreign policy. Accordingly, any effort to artificially prohibit consideration of policy considerations in responsible performance of all intellectual tasks in legal appraisal—particularly in an area of such enormous human concern as war prevention—would seem grotesque. I would briefly suggest the following as policy reasons that seem to me persuasive, even if the law were not negative, in decisively rejecting the FAS proposal:

First, I believe the FAS proposal would at least marginally increase the risk of war and possible use of nuclear weapons—despite Dr. Stone's clear intention to reduce the risk of war and nuclear use. For all its obvious problems, I believe the doctrine of flexible response in NATO is—at current comparative force levels—a significant contribution to deterrence. To modify that doctrine, even by the FAS procedural proposal, would, I believe, somewhat—and perhaps substantially—reduce deterrence.

Deterrence would be affected by the probable (and at least possible) added time required to fully involve a congressional committee and to await a decision from such a body. What, for example, is the possibility that key congressional committee members might be out of the country or otherwise unavailable during a crisis or that they simply could not agree in time? Deterrence would be affected by the enhanced likelihood of a negative decision if a veto were provided *any* additional decision maker. Indeed, it might be subject to reduction if a potential attacking power simply believed that a majority of any special committee favored no first use. And finally, since any no first use decision is only likely to arise in a setting where there has been a massive illegal attack and conventional forces are unable to hold, the perception in NATO-Europe may well be that the purpose of such a congressional check is to permit a decoupling of the security of NATO and American strategic forces. This perception seems to me highly likely to result from such a policy whatever its motivation. And this perception alone could reduce deterrence, as well as the NATO political bond with the United States.

The proposal might also serve to reduce deterrence by convincing a potential adversary that nuclear weapons might not be authorized in response but that if they were authorized then a preemptive nuclear strike might still be launched before retaliation because of the likely notice attendant on committee authorization. It is possible that committee authorizaton—or even erroneously perceived committee authorization—if committee decisions were secret, would even trigger a nuclear attack out of fear of such a first use.

And if committee real-time nuclear use decisions are to be different than simply a no first use or other congressionally mandated general policy, then the committee would have specific information concerning a decision to use nuclear weapons. Such an added intelligence target would be likely to trigger an enormous intelligence effort directed at the committee—and possible reduction in deterrence based even on leaks of erroneous information. To decrease the size of the committee and reduce this risk reduces any policy "check" offered by the committee but to have a larger more useful "check" increases this risk—probably geometrically rather than arithmetically under normal principles concerning access to intelligence information. And if the FAS proposal were clarified to involve the full Congress, I would regard these timing and secrecy issues as very substantially undermining deterrence and thus unworkable in the real world. These problems of Congress as a whole making real-time command decisions concerning the conduct of hostilities were, after all, precisely the characteristics that wisely led the Framers to reject a role for Congress in the operational chain of command.[20]

Second, quite apart from its effect on deterrence, the FAS proposal would seem to amplify a criticism made with respect to the War Powers Resolution that it would undermine the ability of the United States to respond effectively in defense emergencies by creating a potential legal confrontation between Congress and the President when the Nation could least afford it. As is Congress, the President is sworn to uphold the Constitution of the United States. If, in a critical NATO defense emergency, the President believed that nuclear weapons were required to stop an attack, and if the congressional committee disagreed, the President might be tempted to use nuclear weapons if he believed—as he would have good reason to believe—that the Act, establishing such a committee decision in the operational chain of command, were unconstitutional. And in such a setting, if he did use such weapons, the resulting disagreement about his legal authority could severely inhibit the effect of such use and invite miscalculation and escalation. A setting requiring a nuclear response against a massive Warsaw Pact attack against NATO would be a time of unimaginable strain. Is it wise to fuse a possible simultaneous constitutional dispute about the respective powers of Congress and the President in such a setting?

For these and other reasons concerning negative effects on deterrence and crisis stability, as well as the network of real world checks on any presidential first use decision, existing mechanisms for executive and congressional branch coordination, and concerns that issues of such magnitude not be decided by a small committee of Congress not elected by the people of the Nation as a whole (that is not collectively representing the Nation as a whole as does Congress or the President), I believe the FAS proposal should be rejected on policy as well as constitutional grounds.

IV. ALTERNATIVES FOR ENHANCING STRATEGIC STABILITY AND REDUCING THE RISK OF NUCLEAR USE

In my judgment one of the most serious drawbacks of the no first use proposal—and the FAS procedural variant—is that they offer only a cosmetic solution to the real NATO dilemma. By making an advance pledge not to use nuclear weapons they seem to avoid the horn of the dilemma associated with the real risks in any use of nuclear weapons and in any coupling of NATO security with the United States strategic nuclear arsenal. In the process, however, they reduce deterrence against conventional attack and offer no solution—except unacceptable loss of the democracies of Europe—in the setting where the issue really arises, that is, in an overwhelming conventional or chemical-biological attack against NATO-Europe in which NATO forces are unable to hold. Even more dangerously, if we increase the risk of conventional war, we may be increasing the risk of nuclear war regardless of prior pledges. That is, the avoidance of war itself—particularly war in so sensitive an area as Central Europe— may be more critical in avoiding use of nuclear weapons than pledges concerning no first use of nuclear weapons. The Iraqi *in extremis* use of lethal chemical weapons despite the existing conventional and customary international law ban on first use of such weapons illustrates the point. Thus under these no first use related proposals, the real dilemma for NATO remains as acute, if not more so, after the proposed solution as before.

As such, I believe that our attention would be better directed to solutions which genuinely lessen or avoid the dilemma. These include, among others:

—an effort to raise the nuclear threshold by dramatically strengthening NATO conventional forces to provide high confidence of defeating a Warsaw Pact conventional attack (and simultaneously to modernize the United States chemical deterrent against Warsaw Pact chemical or toxin attack). Paradoxically, this is also a presumption of some no first use proponents such as the *Foreign Affairs* "gang of four." If realistically achievable, however, the dilemma largely gives way without a formal no first use pledge. The problem, of course, is that, given the enormous Warsaw Pact force levels, it seems extremely difficult for NATO to maintain the level of forces required for such a high confidence conventional deterrent without major increases in NATO military budgets already strained to the breaking point. Nevertheless, I would agree with those who believe every effort should be made to strengthen the NATO conventional (and chemical) deterrent;

—an effort to strengthen the United Nations Charter and Helsinki pledges on non-use of aggressive force as the critical tripwire rather than first use of nuclear weapons as a tripwire. One unfortunate by-product of these no first use proposals is they focus attention on first nuclear use rather than aggressive attack as the crucial normative standard for international behavior. Modern conventional war can be devastating and it may be that avoiding war of any kind is the most critical threshold in avoiding use of nuclear weapons. If so, any proposal which lessens deterrence could paradoxically increase the risk of use of nuclear weapons even while pledging no first use of such weapons;

—an effort to strengthen "confidence building measures" through bilateral and multilateral negotiations. In particular, it would be useful to pursue—perhaps through the framework of the Conference on Security and Cooperation in Europe (CSCE)—a reduction in the forward deployment and prepositioning of weapons and equipment which serve no purpose but to support an offensive ground attack into the territory of the other side. This would include Soviet and Warsaw Pact forward prepositioning of river crossing and pipeline laying equipment;[21] and

—an effort to encourage balanced force reductions in the NATO-Warsaw Pact area, and in other dangerous areas of confrontation, leading to enhanced stability and a "no need to use nuclear weapons" policy as a result of high levels of confidence in regional strategic balance. It might even be an interesting proposal in MBFR and elsewhere to suggest a willingness to accept a mutual no first use policy in any region with a military balance negotiated to provide high confidence levels in the conventional balance. The Latin American nuclear free-zone is *de facto* such an area. Such a policy might also place the onus for potential first use policies squarely where they belong—on the regimes maintaining a regional imbalance and a threatening posture in conventional forces, despite repeated efforts at negotiating a balance.[22]

V. CONCLUSION

The proposal by Dr. Jeremy Stone is an imaginative proposal that unequivocally deserves a fair, on the merits, appraisal of both its legal and policy dimensions. Despite its laudable intentions to reduce the risk of nuclear use, however, it should just as unequivocally be rejected. It is, on multiple grounds, unconstitutional even if the existing ambiguity in congressional power to regulate the presidential power as commander in chief to conduct constitutionally authorized hostilities were to be resolved in favor of a congressional power to establish a general no first use policy—a conclusion which is far from established. And, even more decisively, its real world effect would be to reduce deterrence and crisis stability. There are more promising policies that deserve our attention in reducing the risk of nuclear use. All such alterntive policies have in common an effort to deal directly with the unhappy real dilemma faced by NATO in light of the massive Warsaw Pact conventional forces and rough equivalence between United States and Soviet forces at the central strategic level. In contrast, the no first use proposals, in both their substantive and procedural variants, seem largely cosmetic and suggest the exchange during the Constitutional Convention when it was proposed that the armed forces of the United States be constitutionally limited to 3,000 men. General Washington was heard to whisper that perhaps the Constitution should also deny any foreign power the right to invade the United States with more than 3,000 troops.

NOTES

1. *See* Bundy, Kennan, McNamara, Smith, *Nuclear Weapons and the Atlantic Alliance*, 60 Foreign Affairs 753 (Spring 1982) (proposing for NATO a "no first use policy" for nuclear weapons); and Kaiser, Lebe, Mertes, and Schulze, *Nuclear Weapons and the Preservation of Peace*, 60 Foreign Affairs 1157 (Summer 1982) (opposing the Bundy *et al.* proposal).

2. *See* Stone, *supra* Ch. 1.

3. *See supra* Ch. 2.

4. Stone, *supra* Ch. 1, text preceding note 21.

5. *See* Principle II, "Refraining from the Threat or Use of Force," and associated principles, in the Helsinki Final Act *reprinted in* 14 *I.L.M.* 1292 (1975) (The Helsinki Final Act is technically regarded as creating only a *political* obligation.) Article 2(4) is the principal applicable provision of the U.N. Charter.

6. *See, e.g.*, NATO Information Service, *NATO and The Warsaw Pact: Force Comparisons* 8 and 11 (1984) (hereinafter *NATO and the Warsaw Pact*).

7. *See, e.g.*, Restow, *The "Lessons" of Vietnam and Presidential Powers*, 12 Strategic Review 30 (1984).

8. *See* R. Turner, *The War Powers Resolution: Its Implementation in Theory and Practice* (1983).

9. *See generally*, L. Henkin, *Foreign Affairs and the Constitution* (1972); A. Sofaer, *War, Foreign Affairs, and Constitutional Powers: The Origins* (1976).

10. *See* II M. Farrand, *The Records of the Federal Convention of 1787* 319 (rev. ed. 1937); *The Constitution of the United States of America: Analysis and Interpretations* 326, S. Doc. No. 82, 92d Cong., 1st Sess. (1973).

11. C. Berdahl, *War Powers of the Executive in the United States* 116 (1920).

12. *Id.* at 116–17. This is illustrative of the views of most writers on the issue. Whatever the parameters of congressional power, if any, to place constraints, such as area constraints, on presidential use of American forces, there is no doubt that in the absence of such constraints the President has sole authority to command American forces, including

use of nuclear forces if absolutely necessary in defense against a massive aggressive attack.

13. *See, e.g., Congress, The President, and the War Powers: Hearings before the Subcommittee on National Security Policy and Scientific Developments of the House Committee on Foreign Affairs*, 91st Cong., 2d Sess. 129–31 (1970) (statement of John Norton Moore, Professor of Law, the University of Virginia).

14. Stone, *supra* at Ch. 1. This seems a particularly strange title in view of Dr. Stone's concession that "the conventional view asserts that the commander in chief clause of the Constitution gives the President the authority to order the use of any and all weapons" (*id.* at Part II(A)) and the Senate rejection 68–10 of a no first use proposal (*supra* Introduction, text accompanying note 4).

15. *See* Berdahl, *supra* note 11 at 121 (quoting Hughes).

16. Swaim v. United States, 128 Ct. Cl. 173, 221 (1893), *aff'd*, 165 U.S. 553 (1897).

17. 272 U.S. 52 (1926).

18. 462 U.S. 919 (1983). *See generally infra* Part III of this collection.

19. Professor John Kester argues that Congress is powerless to adjust the chain of command, much less place the Secretaries of State and Defense in the operational chain of command as checks on presidential decision. *See* Kester, *Thoughtless JCS Change Is Worse Than None*, Armed Forces J. Int'l 115 (Nov. 1984). One need not accept the Kester position to recognize that any congressional claim of power to place chain of command subordinates *over* the President would be an extraordinary claim in terms of the language and the underlying policy of the commander in chief power.

20. For a reminder of some of the attributes of presidential power in foreign policy and some examples of past congressional abuses, see J. Moore, "The Effects and Limits of Congressional Micro-Management of Foreign Policy," in Amer. Bar Ass'n, *Congress, the President, and Foreign Policy* 141 (1984).

21. Soviet and Warsaw Pact forces have currently prepositioned in Eastern Europe substantial stocks of bridging and tactical pipeline materials, including 12,000 kilometers of pipeline. *See* Dept. of State, *Soviet Military Power* 80 (1984).

22. NATO also faces a determined Warsaw Pact nuclear buildup in the NATO-Warsaw Pact area requiring what most NATO defense planners regard as either an effective NATO nuclear force structure in response or preferably a substantial reduction in levels of intermediate nuclear weapons. The United States zero-option and 420 aggregate world-wide warhead limit proposals for intermediate range missiles were efforts, in an ongoing, difficult, and controversial arms control process, to deal with this problem. According to NATO figures, at the end of 1983 NATO and the Warsaw Pact deployed the following longer range INF missile systems:

NATO	*Warsaw Pact*
32 Ground launched cruise missiles (GLCMS) (single warhead)	378 SS–20 (three warhead reloadable)
9 Pershing II missiles (single warhead)	200 SS–4 missiles (single warhead)

See NATO and the Warsaw Pact, supra note 6, at 34. Today these deployments total over 80 GLCMS and Pershing IIs for NATO and well over 400 SS–20 (plus the SS–4) for the Warsaw Pact.

4

Congressional Limits on the Commander in Chief: The FAS Proposal

Robert F. Turner

One of the most alarming legislative proposals in recent years in my view is the proposal by the Federation of American Scientists (FAS) to empower a committee of congressional leaders with a veto over a presidential decision to use nuclear weapons in response to a foreign attack—unless the aggressor state used such weapons first.[1] I don't question the sincerity of the people who propose this legislation, and I certainly share their view that a nuclear war would be horrendous. But after looking it over I can't find a single element in the proposed bill that is useful. Such a law would in my view be flagrantly unconstitutional on at least two grounds, and rather than promote peace the bill would weaken our deterrent and make both conventional and nuclear war more likely.

I. FOREIGN AFFAIRS IS PRIMARILY AN EXECUTIVE FUNCTION

In trying to determine the intentions of the Founding Fathers in this area, it is important to keep in mind that Locke,[2] Montesquieu, and other theoretical writers who influenced the constitutional Framers viewed the control of foreign affairs to be an "executive" function.

The late Professor Quincy Wright—who among his many other accomplishments served as President of the American Political Science Association, the International Political Science Association, and the American Society of International Law—wrote in his classic study, *The Control of American Foreign Relations*, that "when the constitutional convention gave 'executive power' to the President, the foreign relations power was the essential element of the

All views expressed and responsibility for accuracy of facts are the author's.

grant. . . . "[3] The preeminent position of the President in foreign affairs was recognized by early political figures in both the executive and the legislative branches. For example, in 1790 Thomas Jefferson wrote:

The transaction of business with foreign nations is executive altogether; it belongs, then, to the head of that department, except as to such portions of it as are specially submitted to the Senate. Exceptions are to be construed strictly. . . . [4]

Similarly, three years later, in his first *Pacificus* letter Alexander Hamilton wrote:

It deserves to be remarked, that as the participation of the Senate in the making of treaties, and the power of the legislature to declare war, are exceptions out of the general "executive power" vested in the President, they are to be construed strictly, and ought to be extended no further than is essential to their execution.[5]

Congress, too, recognized the preeminent status of the President in the realm of foreign affairs. Three examples illustrate the point. The First Congress, in 1789, established a Department of Foreign Affairs (later to become the Department of State) under the President's exclusive control. Whereas the Secretary of the Treasury was required to "make reports" and "give information" to either house of Congress on demand, the Secretary of Foreign Affairs was simply charged with conducting the business of the Department "in such manner as the President . . . shall from time to time order or instruct."[6] Similarly, the following year—1790—when Congress first appropriated funds for foreign affairs purposes, the President was given complete discretion not only as to how the funds were to be expended, but even as to whether a particular expenditure should be made known to Congress. If the President deemed a particular expenditure "advisable not to specify" in his annual report, he was required only to notify Congress of the total sum expended from this contingent account.[7] A few years later, when the Senate in 1816 created its first Committee on Foreign Relations, that committee concluded in one of its first reports that "[t]he President is the constitutional representative of the United States with regard to foreign nations. He manages our concerns with foreign nations. . . . *For his conduct he is responsible to the Constitution.*"[8]

Under our Constitution the President is granted certain independent powers that are beyond the control of Congress. This was acknowledged in the landmark 1803 Supreme Court decision of *Marbury v. Madison,*[9] in which Chief Justice John Marshall recognized that "by the Constitution . . . the President is invested with certain important political powers, in the exercise of which he is to use his own discretion, and is accountable only to his country in his political character and to his own conscience." Marshall explained that these powers "respect the nation, not individual rights, and being intrusted to the executive, the decision of the executive is conclusive. . . . *[T]here exists, and can exist, no power to control that discretion.*"[10]

Time and again the Supreme Court has recognized the special role of the President in international affairs. For example, in *Kennett v. Chambers*,[11] the Court referred to the executive branch as "that department of our government exclusively which is charged with our foreign relations." In *United States v. Curtiss-Wright Export Corp.*,[12] one of the most famous of modern foreign affairs cases, the Supreme Court said in 1936:

Not only . . . is the federal power over the external affairs in origin and essential character different from that over internal affairs, but participation in the exercise of the power is significantly limited. In this vast external realm, with its important, complicated, delicate and manifold problems, the President alone has the power to speak or listen as a representative of the nation. He makes treaties with the advice and consent of the Senate; but he alone negotiates. Into the field of negotiation the Senate cannot intrude; and Congress itself is powerless to invade it.

II. THE "SUPREME COMMAND" IS VESTED EXCLUSIVELY IN THE COMMANDER IN CHIEF

The Constitution gives to the Congress the powers "to declare war," and "to raise and support armies," while vesting in the President the nation's "executive power," and making the President "commander in chief of the army and navy of the United States. . . . ' '[13] It is clear from the convention debates that Congress at first was to be empowered "to *make* war," but this was overwhelmingly rejected at the motion of James Madison, in order to leave the President as commander in chief free to respond to "sudden attacks," and to avoid any implication that Congress had any role in the actual command of the armed forces.[14]

Unless, therefore, war is forced upon us by the military actions of a hostile state (in which case a "declaration of war" would be unnecessary), the President violates his oath to "protect and defend the Constitution" if he intentionally initiates a "war"[15] against a foreign State without affirmative congressional approval. The remedy for such a breach of duty is provided by article II, section 4 of the Constitution: the President may be impeached.

Under its power "to raise and support armies," Congress can directly influence the President's role as commander in chief. But the supreme command—and all decisions which accompany it, such as where to deploy forces in peacetime to deter war, and what forces and weapons to employ, and in what manner in order to defeat an enemy in the event hostilities break out—are confided exclusively by the Constitution in the President. Congress cannot, without violating the Constitution, either directly or indirectly seek to assume the commander in chief function by directing the President where to employ whatever army it creates, or specifying what weapons from the existing arsenal to use in the event of hostilities. As Chief Justice Chase wrote in *Ex parte Milligan*[16] in 1866:

Congress has the power not only to raise and support and govern armies, but to declare war. It has, therefore, the power to provide by law for carrying on war. This power necessarily extends to all legislation essential to the prosecution of war with vigor and success, *except such as interferes with the command of the forces and the conduct of campaigns. That power and duty belong to the President as Commander-in-Chief.* . . . [N]either can the President, in war more than in peace, intrude upon the proper authority of Congress, nor Congress upon the proper authority of the President. Both are servants of the People, whose will is expressed in the fundamental law.

Similarly, the U.S. Court of Claims observed in *Swaim v. United States*[17] in 1897:

Congress may increase the Army, or reduce the Army, or abolish it altogether, but so long as we have a military force Congress cannot take away from the President the Supreme Command. . . . Congress cannot in the disguise of "Rules for the Government" of the Army impair the authority of the President as Commander in Chief.

This interpretation is consistent with the contemporaneous explanation of the Constitution contained in the *Federalist Papers.* For example, in *The Federalist No. 72,*[18] Alexander Hamilton wrote:

The Administration of government . . . falls peculiarly within the province of the executive department. *The actual conduct of foreign negotiations, . . . the arrangement of the army and navy, the direction of the operations of war,* these and other matters of a like nature constitute what seems to be most properly understood by the administration of government.

In *The Federalist No. 74*[19] he addressed this theme once again, arguing:

Of all the cares or concerns of government, *the direction of war most peculiarly demands those qualities which distinguish the exercise of power by a single hand. The direction of war* implies the direction of the common strength; and the power of directing and employing the common strength, *forms [a] usual and essential part of the definition of the executive authority.*

In his book *War Power Under the Constitution of the United States,*[20] William Whiting wrote more than one hundred years ago:

Congress may effectually control the military power, by refusing to vote supplies or to raise troops and by impeachment of the President; but for the military movement, and measures essential to overcome the enemy—for the general conduct of the war—the President is responsible to and controlled by no other department of Government.

In 1886, Professor John Norton Pomeroy wrote in his *Introduction to the Constitutional Law of the United States:*[21]

Congress raises and supplies armies and navies, and makes rules for their government, and there its power and duty end; the additional power of the President as supreme commander is independent and absolute. . . . He commands the army and navy; Congress does not. He may make all dispositions of troops and officers, stationing them now at this post, now at that; he may send out naval vessels to such parts of the world as he pleases; he may distribute the arms, ammunition, and supplies in such quantities and at such arsenals and depositories as he deems best.

While a Professor at Yale Law School in 1916, prior to becoming Chief Justice of the United States, William Howard Taft wrote in the *Yale Law Review*:[22]

Now what can we lay down as undoubted limitations upon the power of Congress in legislating as to the duties of the Executive? In the first place, it is clear that Congress may not usurp the functions of the Executive . . . by forbidding or directing the movement of the army and navy. . . . When we come to the power of the President as Commander-in-Chief it seems perfectly clear that Congress could not order battle to be fought on a certain plan, and could not direct parts of the army to be moved from one part of the country to another.

Similarly, writing in *The Control of American Foreign Relations*,[23] Professor Quincy Wright argued in 1922:

By reduction of the Army and Navy or refusal of supplies, Congress might seriously impair the *de facto* power of the President to perform these duties, but it can not limit his legal power as Commander-in-Chief to employ the means at his disposal for these purposes.

These excerpts from the writings of prominent scholars are consistent with the actual practice of this country until very recently, and indeed have been frequently reflected in the statements of prominent members of the legislative branch. In 1798, for example, a bill was considered in Congress which, among other things, would have "authorized" the President to use the navy in peacetime to convoy merchant ships. Speaker of the House John Dayton—who nine years earlier had been the youngest man to sign the Constitution—objected to this provision, arguing that it was unnecessary and might prove to be a "dangerous precedent."[24] He said that the President "already possessed" the power to deploy the Navy to convoy ships in peacetime, and that the authority was "derived . . . from a higher source" than the Congress—from the people and the Constitution. Worried that enactment of unnecessary "authority" might imply to future generations that the President could not act without such a statute, Dayton moved that the language be deleted—which was immediately done by voice vote.[25]

To take a more recent example, in 1922, shortly after the end of World War I, an interesting exchange occurred on the Senate floor between Senator James Reed of Missouri and Senator William Borah of Idaho. This colloquy is all the more important because of Senator Borah's reputation as a constitutional lawyer and because he served as Chairman of the Senate Foreign Relations Committee during six of his thirty years in the Senate.

MR. REED: Does the Senator think and has he not thought for a long time that the American troops in Germany ought to be brought home?

MR. BORAH: I do.

MR. REED: So do it. . . . Would it not be easier to bring the troops home than it would be to have the proposed [disarmament] conference?

MR BORAH: You can not bring them home, nor can I.

MR. REED: We could make the President do it.

MR. BORAH: We could not make the President do it. He is Commander in Chief of the Army and Navy of the United States, and if in the discharge of his duty he wants to assign them there, I do not know of any power that we can exert to compel him to bring them home. We may refuse to create an Army, but when it is created he is the commander.

MR. REED: I wish to change my statement. We can not make him bring them home . . . , but I think if there were a resolution passed asking the President to bring the troops home, where they belong, the President would recognize that request from Congress.[26]

On the eve of United States involvement in World War II, a similar debate occurred in the Senate over a proposal by first-term Senator Henry Cabot Lodge to prohibit the President from deploying draftees to Europe. While sharing Lodge's view that draftees should not be deployed outside the Western Hemisphere, Senator Henry Ashurst—then in his twenty-eighth year as a Senator from Arizona, and the former vice chairman of the United States Constitution Sesquicentennial Commission—explained that the Congress lacked the power to control the deployment by the President of U.S. armed forces. He argued that "under the Constitution," the President "may send the Navy or the Army anywhere he chooses. . . . "[27] Senator Lodge recognized that there was "much force" in what the Arizona Senator had said, and was followed by his fellow Republican, Senator Alexander Wiley of Wisconsin, who concluded: "There is no legislative way to curtail the constitutional powers of the Executive."[28]

Even during the Korean conflict—when in my view the President stretched (and may have exceeded) the proper limits of his authority—few members of Congress raised constitutional objections to the President's failure to involve Congress in the decision to commit hundreds of thousands of American soldiers to hostilities. Indeed, the few legislators who did raise such concerns were promptly chastised by such prominent scholars as Arthur Schlesinger and Henry Steel Commager. When Senator Robert Taft proposed legislation to require the President to obtain congressional approval in the future prior to committing United States forces abroad, for example, historian Commager wrote in the *New York Times Magazine* that: "Whatever may be said of the expediency of the Taft . . . program, this at least can be said of the principles involved—that they have no support in law or in history."[29]

III. A FORMAL DECLARATION OF WAR IS UNNECESSARY FOR A DEFENSIVE WAR AND PROBABLY OBSOLETE

Vietnam, of course, changed everything. According to the conventional wisdom, Presidents Johnson and Nixon unilaterally dragged the Congress and the nation kicking and screaming into that horrible tragedy. I think Congress is learning the wrong lessons from Vietnam. Whatever else it was, Vietnam was not a consequence of presidential usurpation of the power of Congress to "declare war." Nor did Congress resist the initial commitment. In my view, the contention that Vietnam was a "presidential war" is a bit of politically expedient historical revisionism that fails to withstand a review of the facts.

It might be useful at this point to draw a distinction between the role of a "declaration of war" in international law, and the requirement of the Constitution that such instruments issued by the United States have the formal authorization of a majority of both houses of Congress. As an international lawyer, I would contend that a formal "declaration of war" is essentially an outmoded instrument of the past, with little utility in the post-Charter era. Grotius tells us that even in early Greek and Roman times, such declarations were never considered to be necessary for "defensive" uses of force. Virtually all offensive uses of force—at least by individual states—are today outlawed by the United Nations Charter. I would note in this respect that state practice has been consistent with my analysis, since there has not been a single "declaration of war" anywhere in the world—despite hundreds of significant conflicts—since the late 1940s. Indeed, there is a school of thought that contends a "declaration of war" would constitute *prima facie* evidence of international aggression.

This is important to keep in mind in assessing our constitutional procedures for committing armed forces into hostilities, because in article I, section 8, the Founding Fathers were essentially trying to guard against executive adventurism of a sort no longer permitted by our treaty obligations. Although the matter was not without proponents on both sides, the better view in my assessment is that the Founding Fathers did not expect that formal congressional authorization would be necessary to fight a defensive war. As Alexander Hamilton explained during the 1801 debate over whether congressional sanction was necessary for President Jefferson to act offensively in response to a declaration of war against America by the Bey of Tripoli:

It is the peculiar and exclusive province of Congress, *when the nation is at peace* to change that state into a state of war, whether from calculations of policy, or from provocations, or injuries received: in other words, it belongs to Congress only, *to go to War*. But when a foreign nation declares, or openly and avowedly makes war upon the United States, they are then by the very fact *already at war*, and any declaration on the part of Congress is nugatory; it is at least unnecessary.[30]

Discussing this debate, a massive study of the Constitution prepared by the Congressional Research Service of the Library of Congress concluded in 1972:

Congress thereafter enacted a statute authorizing the President to instruct the commanders of armed vessels of the United States to seize all vessels and goods of the Bey of Tripoli "and also to cause to be done all such other acts of precaution or hostility *as the state of war will justify* . . . [.]" But no formal declaration of war was passed, *Congress apparently accepting Hamilton's view.*[31]

This reasoning was also accepted by the Supreme Court in *The Prize Cases*,[32] when President Lincoln's right to respond offensively to an armed attack against the United States without seeking formal legislative approval was upheld. Speaking for the Court, Justice Grier explained:

If a war be made by invasion of a foreign nation, the President is not only authorized but bound to resist force by force. He does not initiate the war, but is bound to accept the challenge without waiting for any special legislative authority. And whether the hostile party be a foreign invader, or States organized in rebellion, it is none the less a war, although the declaration of it be "unilateral." . . . The President was bound to meet it in the shape it presented itself, without waiting for Congress to baptize it with a name; and no name given to it by him or them could change the fact.[33]

On a related point, it is important to keep in mind that as a matter of United States constitutional law the power of Congress "to declare war" need not be exercised by a formal and unconditional "declaration of war." From the earliest days of our country the Supreme Court has recognized that Congress may authorize the President to initiate armed hostilities against another State by joint resolution without formally "declaring war." The use of such joint resolutions—which, I would note, are also the legislative vehicles for formally declaring war—dates back to the administrations of John Adams and Thomas Jefferson, and its constitutionality was upheld by the Supreme Court in 1800 in the case of *Bas v. Tingy*,[34] and again in 1801—this time by Chief Justice John Marshall—in the case of *Talbot v. Seeman*.[35]

Unlike the Korean conflict, the war in Vietnam was formally authorized by Congress in 1964 by the so-called "Gulf of Tonkin Resolution,"[36] which passed the House unanimously and received only two opposing votes in the Senate. The text of this statute was unambiguous. It declared as a matter of law that the United States was prepared "*as the President determines*, to take all necessary steps, *including the use of armed force*" to assist the non-communist states of Indochina to defend their freedom.[37]

During the Senate debate on this resolution, the following exchange occurred between the ranking Republican and the Chairman of the Senate Committee on Foreign Relations (who were managing the joint resolution on the Senate floor):

DR. [JOHN SHERMAN] COOPER: Then, looking ahead, if the President decided that it was necessary to use such force as could lead into war, we will give that authority by this resolution?

MR. [J. WILLIAM] FULBRIGHT: That is the way I would interpret it. If a situation later developed in which we thought the approval should be withdrawn, it could be withdrawn by concurrent resolution.[38]

Senator Fulbright once characterized the late Senator Sam Ervin as the "most distinguished" jurist in the Senate—a view widely held by others as well. Looking back on the Tonkin Gulf Resolution in 1970, Senator Ervin said:

I maintain that *the Gulf of Tonkin Resolution . . . constitutes a declaration of war in a constitutional sense.* . . . I am certain that when Congress passed the Gulf of Tonkin Joint Resolution, it was aware of what authority it was granting to the President. . . . I contend that *the Gulf of Tonkin Joint Resolution is clearly a declaration of war.*[39]

The following year, despite its chairman's open opposition to the war, the Senate Foreign Relations Committee stated in a report:

The committee does not believe that formal declarations of war are the only available means by which Congress can authorize the President to initiate limited or general hostilities. *Joint resolutions such as* those pertaining to Formosa, the Middle East, and *the Gulf of Tonkin are a proper method of granting authority.*[40]

IV. THE STONE PROPOSAL IS UNCONSTITUTIONAL AND UNWISE

A. Its Historical Assumptions Are Wrong

Dr. Stone is not a lawyer, and I shouldn't be too critical of his attempts at constitutional analysis. However he is an intelligent man, and when he quotes one historian and two law professors in support of this position, and then writes: "Accordingly, most legal scholars would seem to admit . . . that Congress had the right to control" the decision to first use nuclear weapons—he fails to pass even the "straight face" test.

Dr. Stone notes that under the Continental Congress when George Washington was made "commander in chief" he was placed under the control of a congressional committee. From this he argues: "In other words, commander in chief, as delegates understood the title, was subordinate to a strategy committee of the Continental Congress." Let us be courteous and note that Stone is also not an historian. The *Federalist Papers* and other histories of the Constitution establish beyond doubt that a major reason for placing the control of foreign affairs and the direction of whatever military force Congress provided in the hands of an independent President was precisely because the earlier system had been such a disaster. As already noted, John Jay referred precisely to this early failure in *The Federalist No. 64* when he wrote: "So often and so essentially have we heretofore suffered from the want of secrecy and dispatch, that the Constitution would have been inexcusably defective if no attention had been paid to those objects."[41]

After discussing a number of alternative plans, the Founding Fathers agreed

upon a system of three separate, co-equal and independent branches of government, and rejected the idea that the President would be simply a subordinate
agent of the legislature. War related powers were given to both the Congress
and the President. Congress was given control of the size of the army, and also
a specific veto on any executive proposal to launch a "war" against another
state, as a guard against presidential adventurism. As Jefferson phrased it in a
1789 letter to James Madison: "We have already given . . . one effectual check
to the dog of war, by transferring the power of declaring war from the executive
to the legislative body, from those who are to spend, to those who are to pay."[42]

But I am aware of no evidence that the Founding Fathers intended to place
impediments in the path of the executive in the event war was forced upon the
country by foreign attack. Indeed, in *The Federalist No. 70* Hamilton explained
that "[e]nergy in the executive" was "essential to the protection of the community against foreign attacks."[43] He added:

> That unity is conducive to energy will not be disputed. Decision, activity, secrecy,
> and dispatch will generally characterise the proceedings of one man, in a much more
> eminent degree, than the proceedings of any greater number; and in proportion as the
> number is increased, these qualities will be diminished.
>
> This unity may be destroyed in two ways; either by vesting the power in two or more
> magistrates of equal dignity and authority; or by vesting it ostensibly in one man, subject
> in whole or in part to the controul and co-operation of others, in the capacity of counsellors
> to him. . . . [44]

Thus the strategic and tactical decisions on how best to subdue an enemy in
wartime are granted by the Constitution expressly to the President. Just as Congress would exceed its authority by enacting legislation directing the President
during hostilities to deploy a particular unit from one hill to another, it would
also exceed its proper authority by seeking to direct the President (at least in a
defensive setting) to use or not to use a particular weapon in the existing arsenal
against an armed enemy. As Professor Wright explained, Congress may not
"limit [the President's] legal power as commander in chief to employ *the means
at his disposal*" to subdue the enemy.[45]

B. Its "Leadership Committee" Cannot Constitutionally Act For Congress

Another fundamental problem with the FAS proposal is that it would place
the veto over the President's decision to employ weapons placed at his disposal
by Congress in an extra-constitutional small group of congressional leaders.
Even if the full Congress had the power to restrict the President's choice of
weapons—which might be arguable in a situation of United States-initiated hostilities—such authority is clearly beyond the authority of an ad hoc leadership
group. Article I, section 7, of the Constitution expressly requires that "[e]very

order, resolution or vote to which the concurrence of the Senate and House of Representatives may be necessary . . . shall be presented to the President of the United States'' for signature or veto. While there are exceptions to this rule expressly set forth in the Constitution (e.g., adjournment and amending the Constitution), there is no provision for the Congress to empower its leadership to act legislatively.[46] Any doubts about this issue should have been put to rest with the 1983 Supreme Court decision of *Immigration and Naturalization Service v. Chadha*,[47] which struck down a ''legislative veto'' exercised by a majority vote of one house of Congress in a subject area (naturalization) expressly delegated to the Congress by article I, section 8, of the Constitution. How one can argue in the wake of *Chadha* that Congress can constitutionally empower a few of its members to veto a decision by the commander in chief to use certain military resources provided to him by Congress is difficult to understand. If Congress had this power, it is difficult to distinguish it from the right to designate a single member of Congress to micromanage the President's deployment of troops or his use of other weapons systems as well, totally destroying in the process the principle of separation of powers.

C. Its ''Leadership Committee'' Cannot Practically Act at All

Given the propensity of legislative leaders for foreign travel, the proposed legislation is almost comical. It makes no provision, for example, for a massive Soviet attack against Western Europe and the United States during a congressional recess or period of adjournment. Under the FAS proposal, unless the President could track down a majority of the leaders of Congress, his hands would be tied—even if the Soviets were murdering tens of millions of Americans with a ''Yellow Rain'' and nerve gas attack. And if you doubt that it might be difficult to even locate a majority of congressional leaders during a recess—much less bring them together for the kind of detailed classified briefing and discussion that would be necessary for them to make an informed decision—I urge you to reflect upon the difficulties President Ford had during the Easter Recess of 1975 when he tried to ''consult'' with congressional leaders about the humanitarian evacuation of DaNang, Vietnam. As recounted in his autobiography, President Ford explained:

Not a single leader of either party remained in the capital. Three of them were in Greece, two in the People's Republic of China, two in Mexico, one in Europe, and another in the Middle East. The rest were in twelve widely scattered locations in the United States. Obviously, the ''consultation'' called for by the [War Powers Resolution] was impossible.[48]

Of course, that was essentially in peacetime, and Ford was eventually able to get a message to the Senate Majority Leader by sending a cable through the United States Embassy in Peking. If an attack were to take place while a congressional leadership delegation was visiting Moscow, the FAS proposal would presumably leave the President's hands permanently tied (unless of course Congress was able to meet and repeal the law).

I haven't even addressed the security problems that would accompany such a statutory scheme. In the event of a war, it would be extremely difficult for the President to convene the special congressional leadership committee without the event coming to the attention of the press. Given its willingness to publish other sensitive national security secrets, there is little reason to believe the *Washington Post* would not speculate that the President might be seeking permission to launch a massive nuclear strike on an adversary. Even if the meeting were in fact only to brief the congressional leaders on the progress of the conflict—or perhaps to seek their advice on a peace proposal—such speculation might well be present. And even without the help of the press, our adversaries have sophisticated intelligence services that would almost certainly go to great efforts to monitor the comings and goings of congressional leaders in time of crisis. Given a report that the President was meeting with the individuals empowered to authorize an American nuclear first strike, might not an adversary decide to strike the United States first? Perhaps it is not surprising that, when a milder version of the FAS plan was put to a vote on the Senate floor in 1972—with the sponsorship of the Chairman of the Foreign Relations Committee—it was defeated by a vote of 68 to 10.[49]

NOTES

1. *See* Stone, *supra* Ch. 1.
2. Locke, of course, defined "the Power of War and Peace, Leagues and Alliances, and all the Transactions, with all Persons and Communities without the Commonwealth," as the "Federative" power, but argued that "[t]hese two Powers, Executive and Federative, though they be really distinct in themselves, . . . yet they are always almost united" and "are hardly to be separated. . . . For both of them requiring the force of the Society for their exercise, it is almost impracticable to place the Force of the Commonwealth in distinct, and not subordinate hands. . . . " J. Locke, *Second Treatise of Government* §§ 146–48.
3. Q. Wright, *The Control of American Foreign Relations* 147 (1922).
4. III *The Writing of Thomas Jefferson* 15 (A. Lipscomb and A. Bergh, eds., 1904).
5. *Reprinted in* I. W. Goldsmith, *The Growth of Presidential Power* 398 (1974).
6. R. Turner, *The War Powers Resolution: Its Implementation in Theory and Practice* 85–86 (1983).
7. 1 Stat. 129 (1790).
8. *Quoted in* United States v. Curtiss-Wright Export Corp., 229 U.S. 304, 319 (1936) (emphasis added).
9. 5 U.S. (I Cr.) 137 (1803).
10. *Id.* at 165 (emphasis added).
11. 55 U.S. (14 How.) 38 (1852).
12. 299 U.S. 304 (1936).
13. U.S. Const. art. I, § 8, cls. 10 & 11, and art. II, § 2.

14. II M. Farrand, *The Records of the Federal Convention of 1787* 319 (1966).

15. There are uses of armed force that fall below the threshold of "war" and can be implemented by the commander in chief under his own authority, such as to rescue endangered Americans abroad.

16. 71 U.S. (4 Wall.) 139 (1866) (emphasis added). *See also* Turner, *supra* note 6, 43–44 n. 101.

17. 28 Ct. Cl. 173, *aff'd*, 165 U.S. 553 (1897).

18. *The Federalist No. 72*, at 486–87 (J. Cooke ed. 1961) (A. Hamilton) (emphasis added).

19. *The Federalist No. 74*, at 500 (J. Cooke ed. 1961) (A. Hamilton) (emphasis added).

20. W. Whiting, *War Power Under the Constitution of the United States* 82 n.* (1871).

21. J. Pomeroy, *An Introduction to Constitutional Law of the United States* 635–38 (1870).

22. W. Taft, *Branches of the Government—The Boundaries Between the Executive, the Legislative and the Judicial*, 25 Yale L. J. 599, 606, 610 (1916). That same year, Taft wrote: "The President is made Commander-in-Chief of the army and navy by the Constitution evidently for the purpose of enabling him to defend the country against invasion, to suppress insurrection and to take care that the laws be faithfully executed. If Congress were to attempt to prevent his use of the army for any of these purposes, the action would be void. . . . " W. Taft, *Our Chief Magistrate and His Powers* 129 (1916).

23. Wright, *supra* note 3, at 307. Similarly, in 1920 Professor Wright wrote in the *Columbia Law Review:* "Authority supported by practice shows that the President has independent power under the Constitution to employ the military or naval forces of the United States at home or abroad except as restricted by International Law, in time of peace to enforce the laws and treaties, to protect officers of the United States, . . . to protect the privileges and immunities of American citizens, to prevent foreign aggression and to protect inchoate interests of the United States abroad. . . . It is true that the Congress can authorize the use of armed forces either by declaration of war or by joint resolution in time of peace . . . but Congress cannot impair the concurrent power of the President to authorize the use of forces as given by the Constitution." Q. Wright, *Validity of the Proposed Reservation to the Peace Treaty*, 20 Colum. L. Rev. 135–36 (1920).

24. 7 Annals of Cong. 359 (1797).

25. *Id.* at 362–64.

26. 62 Cong. Rec. (1922).

27. 86 Cong. Rec. 10,895 (1940).

28. *Id.* at 10,896.

29. H. Commager, *Presidential Power: The Issue Analyzed*, N.Y. Times Magazine, Jan. 14, 1951, at 23–24. *See also* Turner, *supra* note 6, at 39 n. 58.

30. 7 *Works of Alexander Hamilton* 746–47 (J. Hamilton ed. 1851) (emphasis in original).

31. U.S. Library of Congress Cong. Res. Serv., *The Constitution of the United States of America: Analysis and Interpretation* 327 (1973). *See also* Turner, *supra* note 6, at 24 and n. 81.

32. 67 U.S. (2 Black) 635 (1863).

33. *Id.* at 668.

34. 4 U.S. (4 Dall.) 37, 40 (1800).

35. 5 U.S. (1 Cr.) 1, 27 (1801).

36. 78 Stat. 384 (1964).

37. *Id. See also* Turner, *supra* note 6, at 4–5.

38. 110 Cong. Rec. 18,409–18 (1964).

39. 116 Cong. Rec. 15,926 (1970).

40. *Quoted in* L. Henkin, *Foreign Affairs and the Constitution* 333 n. 61 (1972).

41. *The Federalist No. 64*, at 435 (J. Cooke ed. 1961) (J. Jay).

42. 7 *The Writings of Thomas Jefferson* 461 (A. Lipscomb and A. Bergh, eds. 1903).

43. *The Federalist No. 70*, at 471 (J. Cooke ed. 1961) (A. Hamilton).

44. *Id.* at 472–73.

45. Wright, *supra* note 3, at 149–50.

46. Even if one views the initial statute as a legislative prohibition, and the approval of the leadership committee as a modification of the prohibition, the proposal does not withstand challenge. The same legislative authority is required to repeal or modify a statute that is necessary to enact it in the first place.

47. 462 U.S. 919 (1983).

48. G. Ford, *A Time to Heal* 245 (1980).

49. 118 Cong. Rec. 12,448–56 (1972).

5

The NATO Treaty: The Commitment Myth

Michael J. Glennon

A selective reading of the NATO Treaty[1] would cut off any debate of the constitutionality of presidentially ordered first use of nuclear weapons to repel a Warsaw Pact attack on our NATO allies. Because the NATO parties "agree that an armed attack against one or more of them in Europe . . . shall be considered an attack against them all," and that each of them will assist the parties attacked by using armed force if necessary to restore the security of the North Atlantic area,[2] this bare language of the Treaty suggests that the President may consider an attack on our NATO allies as an attack on us and respond accordingly at his own initiative. Indeed, the General Counsel of the Defense Department has characterized the Federation of American Scientists (FAS) proposal for congressional committee approval of first use decisions as inconsistent with our NATO obligations,[3] and members of Congress have recently construed similar treaties to authorize presidential war making in fulfillment of alleged treaty obligations.[4] But debate would be cut off prematurely. This reading of the NATO Treaty[5] is seriously mistaken.

In mutual security treaties to which the United States is a party, the notion of commitment is a myth. A 1979 report of the Senate Foreign Relations Committee is correct:

No mutual security treaty to which the United States currently is a party authorizes the President to introduce the armed forces into hostilities or requires the United States to do so, automatically, if another party to any such treaty is attacked. Each of the treaties

Copyright © 1986, Columbia Journal of Transnational Law Association, Inc. A more extensive version of this article appears at 24 *Columbia Journal of Transnational Law* 201 (April, 1986). Reprinted with permission.

provides that it will be carried out by the United States in accordance with its "constitutional processes" or contains other language to make clear that the United States'
commitment is a qualified one—that the distribution of power within the United States
Government is precisely what it would have been in the absence of the treaty, and that
the United States reserves the right to determine for itself what military action, if any,
is appropriate.[6]

This article elaborates that conclusion by exploring two key issues raised by the
NATO Treaty.

First, can such a treaty constitutionally grant the President war making power
in excess of what he would otherwise possess? Part I of the article reviews the
Framers' intent, subsequent custom, and recent case law concerning the delegation doctrine in concluding that a treaty that did so probably would be unconstitutional.

Second, does the NATO Treaty in fact confer any such authority upon the
President? The answer depends upon the scope of the commitment undertaken:
if the United States is viewed as having bound itself automatically to intervene
militarily in the event one of its treaty partners is attacked, it is reasonable to
infer that the treaty in question confers such authority upon the President, for
under such circumstances any congressional role would be meaningless. Most
frequently the specific presidential authority at issue is the authority to introduce
the armed forces into hostilities, but the question also arises in connection with
other exercises of presidential war making power, such as the use of tactical
nuclear weapons. Part II of the article concludes that the NATO Treaty does not
in fact confer additional war making power upon the President.

I. CONSTITUTIONALITY

The text of the Constitution empowers the President "by and with the advice
and consent of the Senate, to make treaties, provided two-thirds of the Senators
present concur...."[7] Yet it also grants to Congress the power "[t]o declare
war,"[8] "[t]o raise and support armies...,"[9] "[t]o provide and maintain a
navy,"[10] and "[t]o make rules for the government and regulation of the land
and naval forces...."[11] These war making powers of Congress have been held
to subsume the lesser authority to determine the means to be employed by the
President,[12] including, presumably, the use or non-use of nuclear weapons. Can
they be exercised by the President and the Senate in making a treaty? Or are
such powers reserved to Congress, to be exercised either through the enactment
of implementing legislation to such a treaty or through a congressional-executive
agreement?

In oft-cited language the Supreme Court seemed to uphold a treaty power of
the broadest scope, extending to "any matter which is properly the subject of
negotiation with a foreign country."[13] Frequently overlooked, however, is the
Court's observation that the treaty power does *not* extend to "authorize what
the Constitution forbids, or a change in the character of the government...."[14]

A. Intent of the Framers

"A treaty may not declare war," the Senate Foreign Relations Committee said in its report on the Panama Canal Treaties, "because the unique legislative history of the declaration-of-war clause . . . clearly indicates that that power was intended to reside jointly in the House of Representatives and the Senate."[15] The events to which the Committee referred are recorded in Madison's notes of the Philadelphia convention. Alexander Hamilton submitted a plan which would have empowered the executive "to make war or peace, with the advice of the Senate."[16] After the Committee of Detail recommended instead that the war power be given to Congress, Hamilton's ally, Charles Pinckney, again proposed that the power should reside in the Senate:

Mr. Pinckney opposed the vesting of this power in the Legislature. Its proceedings were too slow. It wd. meet but once a year. The Hs. of Reps. would be too numerous for such deliberations. The Senate would be the best depository, being more acquainted with foreign affairs, and most capable of proper resolutions. If the States are equally represented in Senate, so as to give no advantage to large States, the power will notwithstanding be safe, as the small have their all at stake in such cases as well as the large States. It would be singular for one authority to make war, another peace.[17]

Sentiment opposing the Hamilton-Pinckney position was overwhelming. Oliver Ellsworth and George Mason argued that the concurrence of both houses of Congress should be required to declare war because the approval of only the Senate was required for peace treaties, and it should be easier to get out of war than into it. Mason further argued that the Senate was "not constructed as to be entitled to" the war power. Pierce Butler added that Pinckney's concerns about the institutional shortcomings of the House applied equally to the Senate.[18] Apparently Pinckney's proposal died for lack of a second. Speaking nine years later as a member of the House of Representatives, Madison pithily summarized his own objection to the view embodied in Hamilton's defeated proposal: "Congress, in case the President and Senate should enter into an alliance for war, would be nothing more than the mere heralds for proclaiming it."[19]

B. Custom

Under certain circumstances the existence of a custom is relevant in determining the allocation of constitutional power. The case law suggests that several criteria must be met.[20] Whether a constitutionally relevant custom exists depends upon how these criteria apply to the "act" in question—here, a mutual security treaty that automatically commits the United States to introduce its armed forces into hostilities upon the happening of a specified event (probably an armed attack by a third country). How frequently has this act been repeated?

The United States has never been a party to such a treaty.[21] Yet presidents on occasion have argued that a treaty conferred on them the discretionary authority to introduce the armed forces into hostilities to enforce the terms of that treaty: not that such introduction was required, but that it was permitted.[22] Although not always articulated this way, their claim might have been that the Constitution required that they "take care that the laws be faithfully executed,"[23] and that treaties constitute law for purposes of the Faithful Execution clause.

As a constitutional matter, it is doubtful that the Faithful Execution clause can serve as support for presidential introduction of the armed forces into hostilities to carry out treaties. Although a variety of interpretations are possible,[24] the Framers apparently intended to limit presidential enforcement power to laws resulting from legislative action.[25]

Moreover, assuming *arquendo* the existence of a custom of reliance upon the clause for such purposes, such a construction has hardly gone unchallenged in Congress. Following President Wilson's reliance upon the clause in 1917 when ordering the arming of United States commercial shipping,[26] for example, the Chairman of the Senate Foreign Relations Committee argued that Wilson's construction would rob the congressional war making power of all meaning:

I cannot consent that this clause confers, or was ever intended to confer, power upon the President to determine an issue between this Nation and some other sovereignty—an issue involving questions of international law—and to proceed to employ the Army and Navy to enforce his decision. A contrary view would clearly place the war making power in the hands of the President.[27]

Similar objections were voiced in Congress following executive reliance upon the SEATO treaty during the Vietnam War.[28] Because a custom is without constitutional relevance unless it is, at least, acquiesced in by the other branch, and because acquiescence requires an absence of objection,[29] it is doubtful that any custom of executive reliance upon the Faithful Execution clause to justify treaty enforcement has achieved constitutional legitimacy.

Finally, the terms of the NATO Treaty themselves belie any intent to provide such authority. As noted below, the Treaty qualified the United States commitment with a reference to the parties' constitutional process. The effect is to leave the allocation of power as it would have been in the absence of the treaty.

C. Case Law: The Delegation Doctrine

Since the founding of the Republic prominent members of Congress have believed that the Constitution limits the authority of Congress to transfer its war making power to the executive. In 1834, for example, President Andrew Jackson requested statutory authorization for reprisals against France in the event France failed to satisfy claims arising out of attacks on American shipping during the undeclared naval war between the two countries. The Senate Foreign Relations Committee, in a report apparently authored by Senator Henry Clay, recommended against Jackson's request:

Congress ought to retain to itself the right of judging of the expediency of granting [letters of marque and reprisal] under all the circumstances existing at the time when they are proposed to be actually issued. The committee are not satisfied that Congress can, constitutionally, delegate this right. . . . Congress ought to reserve to itself the constitutional right, which it possesses, of judging of all the circumstances by which such refusal might be attended and of deciding whether, in the actual posture of things as they then exist, and looking to the condition of the United States, of France, and of Europe, the issuing of letters of marque and reprisal ought to be authorized, or any other measure adopted.[30]

In 1859, President James Buchanan asked for congressional approval to use land and naval forces to guarantee the neutrality of Columbia and to protect the lives and property of American citizens in the area. Senator William Seward answered as follows from the Senate floor:

Could anything be more strange and preposterous than the idea of the President of the United States making hypothetical wars, conditional wars, without any designation of the nation against which war is to be declared; or the time, or place, or manner, or circumstance of the duration of it, the beginning or the end; and without limiting the number of nations with which war may be waged? No, sir. When we pass this bill we do surrender the power of making war or preserving peace in each of the States named, into the hands of the President of the United States.[31]

The Supreme Court, similarly, has long inveighed against the delegation of legislative power to the executive. "The general rule [of law]," Justice Story said in 1831, "is that a delegated authority cannot be delegated."[32] Sixty years later the elder Justice Harlan re-affirmed "[t]hat Congress cannot delegate legislative power to the President."[33] This precept, he said, is "universally recognized as vital to the integrity and maintenance of the system of government ordained by the Constitution."[34] Finally, during the New Deal, the Court actually twice struck down an act of Congress as violative of the delegation doctrine in *Panama Refining Co. v. Ryan*,[35] and *Schecter Poultry Corp. v. United States*.[36]

The "delegation" doctrine deriving from these cases has been relied on by a number of authorities who view as unconstitutional any treaty automatically committing the United States armed forces to hostilities. "[W]hat can't be done," the late Professor Alexander Bickel testified before the Senate Foreign Relations Committee, "is a generalized commitment. 'You, England or France, are our pals, you are our friends, and any time you are in trouble we will help you.' That can't be done."[37] "The attempt of Congress to transfer its power and responsibility to make war to the President," Professor Francis D. Wormuth wrote, "is constitutionally unauthorized and destroys the political system envisaged by the framers."[38]

Yet two objections might be made to those arguments: first, that the delegation doctrine is a constitutional dead letter; and second, that if it is alive it has no application in the realm of foreign relations. Each warrants examination.

No federal statute has been struck down through application of the delegation doctrine in 50 years. The reasons are not hard to guess. The doctrine smacks of substantive due process, admitting of limited possibility for principled application and permitting statutory invalidation for reasons having less to do with the Constitution than with gastronomically derived notions of public policy. It is guilty by association: like substantive due process, it is remembered largely as a tool of juridical reactionaries who sought to write Herbert Spencer's *Social Statics* into the United States Constitution.

Rumors of the doctrine's death have thus been frequently reported[39]—and are probably exaggerated. In the 1980 *Benzene Case*,[40] the plurality opinion of Justice Stevens, joined by Chief Justice Burger and Justice Stewart, relied upon the delegation doctrine on construing narrowly a federal statute conferring rule making authority on the Secretary of Labor.[41] Justice Rehnquist, concurring, argued that the statute should have been invalidated through use of the doctrine.[42] He repeated the opinion the following term in the *Cotton Dust Case* and was joined by the Chief Justice.[43] On at least two occasions Justice Brennan expressed a measure of approval for continued application of the doctrine.[44] It is of course one thing to use the doctrine as a canon of statutory construction and quite another to employ it as a criterion of validity; moreover, some justices willing to do the latter would doubtless disagree on the doctrine's applicability in a given case. Nonetheless, it is not farfetched to believe that in the right case, for the right purpose, the doctrine could indeed command a majority of the current Supreme Court.[45]

If the doctrine is still alive, does it have any application to statutes touching upon foreign relations? That question arose in *United States v. Curtiss-Wright*.[46] In *Curtiss-Wright*, Congress by law[47] had authorized President Franklin Roosevelt to prohibit the sale of arms and ammunition to countries engaged in armed conflict in the Chaco. The statute required that, before proclaiming the embargo, the President fulfill three conditions: first, he was required to consult with other governments of the region; second, he was required to secure that measure of their cooperation he deemed necessary; and third, he was required to find that an embargo would contribute to the reestablishment of peace in the region.[48] President Roosevelt issued such a proclamation[49] and defendant Curtiss-Wright was indicted for violating the statute authorizing the President's proclamation.[50] On appeal, Curtiss-Wright challenged the statute on the ground, *inter alia*, that it unconstitutionally delegated legislative power to the executive. Justice Sutherland, writing for six members of the Court, upheld the law on the notion that Congress may, in the realm of foreign affairs, "accord to the President a degree of discretion and freedom from statutory restriction which would not be admissible were domestic affairs alone involved."[51] The theory by which Justice Sutherland supported that conclusion—that the President's foreign affairs powers derive not from "affirmative grants of the Constitution" but from the "law of nations" and from its "investment of the federal government with the powers of external sovereignty . . . "[52]—is entirely *dicta* and has been widely and justly criticized as bad history, bad logic, and bad law.[53]

Its rationalizing theory apart, *Curtiss-Wright* does *not* hold that the delegation doctrine has *no* application to international relations; rather, the point is that it does not have *equal* application. The distinction is of obvious importance and often has been overlooked.[54] It might thus be argued, as Professor Bickel seemed to, that the case should be restricted to its facts, or at least not extended to "powers to go to war, or to use the armed forces. . . . "[55] One might also wonder why it was necessary to reach even that question. As Professor Bickel suggested, the Court could well have found simply that the standards encompassed in the law met delegation requirements.[56]

More important, the central policy reasons underpinning the delegation doctrine militate in favor of applying it to foreign affairs matters. "As formulated and enforced" by the Supreme Court, Justice Rehnquist wrote in his *Benzene* concurrence,[57] the doctrine "[f]irst, and most abstractly, ensures to the extent consistent with orderly governmental administration that important choices of social policy are made by Congress, the branch of our government most responsive to the popular will. . . . "[58] It would be hard to imagine a "choice of social policy" more important than the choice to go to war, or the choice, once the armed forces are involved in hostilities, to raise the ante as substantially as the use of nuclear weapons could entail. Moreover, the responsiveness of Congress (as opposed to that of the Senate and the President) to the popular will apparently represented the precise reason that the Framers placed the decision to go to war in congressional hands.[59]

Second, Justice Rehnquist wrote, "the doctrine guarantees that, to the extent Congress finds it necessary to delegate authority, it provides the recipient of that authority with an 'intelligible principle' to guide the exercise of the delegated discretion. . . . "[60] In this sense the doctrine is not unlike other provisions of the Constitution directed at curbing the exercise of "naked preferences"—the dormant commerce, privileges and immunities, equal protection, due process, contract, and eminent domain clauses.[61] The delegation decisions merely require, Justice Rehnquist wrote, that Congress "lay down the general policy and standards that animate the law, leaving the agency to refine those standards, to fill in the blanks, or to apply those standards to particular cases."[62] In so holding, the decisions require that the agency, or the President, adhere to broad principles of policy formulated by those constitutionally charged with their origination. The exercise of arbitrary power is precluded. If anything, this concern would seem particularly pertinent in the realm of foreign affairs. The President's powers in that field already are especially broad. The potential for abuse is therefore commensurately great. To add to that expanse of executive authority additional uncircumscribed discretion—discretion intended by the Framers to reside in the legislature—would be to write out of the Constitution any meaningful notion of separation of powers in the realm of foreign relations.[63]

The reasons for exempting foreign affairs powers from the operation of the delegation doctrine are thus less than compelling. This may explain why the Court appears in successive stages to have backed steadily away from the exception suggested by *Curtiss-Wright.*

The first major step was taken in 1952 with *Youngstown Sheet & Tube v.*

Sawyer,[64] the famous "Steel Seizure Case." Although the seizure had been justified by President Truman on the ground that the continued operation of the steel mills was necessary for the successful continuation of the war effort in Korea—and was therefore permitted under his sole powers as commander in chief—the Court rejected the argument and held instead that President Truman's action represented, in effect, an exercise of legislative authority. No examination was made of congressional enactments (such as defense authorization or appropriation acts) from which delegation might conceivably have been inferred. Nor was any reference made to powers that President Truman might have derived from the nation's "sovereignty" or from the "law of nations." Indeed, no reference whatever was made to *Curtiss-Wright*.

Six years later the Court moved further from Justice Sutherland's constitutional exegesis. In *Kent v. Dulles*[65] the Court invalidated a passport revocation as lying beyond the statutory authority of the Secretary of State. If the "power is to be delegated," the Court said, "the standards must be adequate to pass scrutiny by the accepted tests."[66] It referred expressly to *Panama Refining*[67] and completely ignored *Curtiss-Wright*.

The next passport case, *Zemel v. Rusk*,[68] represented a step backwards. In the face of a majority opinion upholding broad authority on the part of the Secretary of State, Chief Justice Warren relied upon *Curtiss-Wright* in noting that Congress—in giving the executive authority over matters of foreign affairs—"must of necessity paint with a brush broader than it wields in domestic areas."[69] The Chief Justice reiterated, however, that *Curtiss-Wright* did "not mean that simply because a statute deals with foreign relations, it can grant the Executive totally unrestricted freedom of choice."[70] Justice Black, dissenting, would have overturned the statute as an invalid delegation.[71]

In the two most recent passport cases, *Haig v. Agee*[72] and *Wald v. Regan*,[73] the Court again relied upon *Curtiss-Wright*. In neither case, however, was the breadth of the statutory delegation a determinative issue; *Curtiss-Wright* was cited for notions of generalized deference to the executive in matters of foreign affairs.

Taken alone, therefore, the passport cases might be read broadly to suggest that the foreign affairs exception carved from the delegation proscription by *Curtiss-Wright* remains good law. But it is hard to see why those cases must be read that broadly: that the Court will permit Congress wide latitude in delegating authority to the executive to limit the international travel of private citizens can hardly mean that the Court must necessarily uphold equally wide power to confer congressional war making power on the President. If one criterion represents, as Justice Rehnquist suggested, the magnitude of relevant social choices, the policy considerations are manifestly incomparable: that an aspect of the foreign commerce power happens to be delegable simply says little or nothing about the delegability of central elements of the war power.

That the passport cases should be read narrowly seems further suggested by two more far-reaching cases decided by the Court in 1981 and 1983. In *Dames*

& *Moore v. Regan*[74] the Iranian claims settlement agreement was upheld through the application of the analytical framework set forth by Justice Jackson in *Youngstown Sheet & Tube v. Sawyer*,[75] an approach that rejects the notion of "fixed" presidential powers on the premise that executive power fluctuates in conjunction or disjunction with whatever action is taken by Congress.[76] The majority opinion, authored by Justice Rehnquist, made no reference to *Curtiss-Wright* or to any notion of presidential power deriving from sovereignty or the law of nations.

More important, perhaps, is the Court's 1983 opinion in *Immigration and Naturalization Service v. Chadha*.[77] In invalidating use of the "legislative veto," the Court declined to permit Congress to affect the legal rights or obligations of executive branch officials unless Congress adheres strictly to constitutionally required procedures for the enactment of legislation. "Convenience and efficiency"—apparently considerations foremost on Justice Sutherland's mind in upholding the broad delegation in *Curtiss-Wright*—were said by Chief Justice Burger to be insufficient to save a statute "if it is contrary to the Constitution." "Convenience and efficiency," he wrote, "are not the primary objectives—or the hallmarks—of democratic government. . . . "[78] The Court's emphasis in the opinion on the need for adherence to "clumsy, inefficient, even unworkable" constitutionally required procedures raises serious question whether the pilings of *Curtiss-Wright* have not been swept away.

To whatever extent the delegation doctrine has continued vitality, therefore, no persuasive reasons have been advanced as to why it should not be applied to foreign affairs questions. And be it alive or not, the Framers' intent to include the House of Representatives in any decision to go to war would raise the most serious doubts about any treaty purporting to impose an "automatic" commitment on the United States to use armed force.

II. THE NATO TREATY

Perhaps because of the vexing constitutional questions raised by the delegation doctrine, the mutual security treaties entered into by the United States at the conclusion of World War II made clear that no party was committed automatically to come to the defense of any other party.[79] With regard to the United States, the legislative histories on this point underscored the treaties' text, and made clear in addition that none of the treaties was intended to confer upon the President any war making power that he would not have had in the treaties' absence. The NATO Treaty is the principal illustration of these truisms.

The NATO Treaty provides that "its provisions [shall be] carried out by the Parties in accordance with their respective constitutional processes."[80] The principle provision referred to is undoubtedly that of Article 5:

The Parties agree that an armed attack against one or more of them in Europe or North America shall be considered an attack against them all; and consequently they agree that, if such an attack occurs, each of them, in exercise of the right of individual or collective self-defense . . . , will assist the Party or Parties so attacked by taking forthwith . . . such action *as it deems necessary*, including the use of armed force, to restore and maintain the security of the North Atlantic area.[81]

The Treaty is thus clear that no nation is committed to introduce its armed forces into hostilities; it may do so if it deems such action necessary, but such introduction is not required. That this is the intended interpretation emerges from every level of consideration of the treaty in the United States.

The day the text of the proposed North Atlantic Treaty was made public, Secretary of State Dean Acheson addressed the nation. The Treaty, he said, "does not mean that the United States would be automatically at war if one of the nations covered by the pact is subjected to armed attack. Under our Constitution, the Congress alone has the power to declare war."[82]

In his letter transmitting the Treaty to President Truman, Secretary of State Dean Acheson again emphasized that the United States would reserve for itself the right to determine what action the Treaty required:

The obligation upon each Party is to use its honest judgment as to the action it deems necessary to restore and maintain . . . security and accordingly to take such action as it deems necessary. Such action might or might not include the use of armed force depending upon the circumstances and gravity of the attack. . . . Each Party retains for itself the right of determination as to whether an armed attack has in fact occurred and what action it deems necessary to take. . . .

This does not mean that the United States would automatically be at war if we or one of the other Parties to the Treaty were attacked. Under our Constitution, only the Congress can declare war. The United States would be obligated by the Treaty to take promptly the action which it deemed necessary to restore and maintain the security of the North Atlantic area. That decision as to what action was necessary would naturally be taken in accordance with our constitutional processes.[83]

This analysis was transmitted to the Senate by President Truman on April 12, 1949.[84]

Secretary Acheson re-emphasized the limited scope of the NATO commitment on the first day of hearings before the Senate Foreign Relations Committee.[85] Senator Connally questioned him about it:

THE CHAIRMAN: Is there or is there not anything in the treaty that pledges us to an automatic declaration of war in any event?

SECRETARY ACHESON: There is nothing in the treaty which has that effect, Senator.

THE CHAIRMAN: Those are matters still residing in the discretion and judgment of the Government and the Senate?

SECRETARY ACHESON: That is true.

THE CHAIRMAN: Even after the occurrence of events, we would still have that freedom, would we not?

SECRETARY ACHESON: That is true.[86]

Senator Vandenberg asked the same questions and got the same answers:

SENATOR VANDENBERG: Is there anything in the treaty which will lead automatically
    to a declaration of war on our part?
SECRETARY ACHESON: No, sir.
SENATOR VANDENBERG: The answer, of course, is unequivocally "No."
SECRETARY ACHESON: Unequivocally "No."[87]

Senator Donnell nonetheless continued to press Secretary Acheson on the scope
of the United States' obligation and the role of the President and Congress. In
response, Secretary Acheson commented further on the requirement that the
"provisions [be] carried out by the parties in accordance with their constitutional
processes." Those words, he said, "obviously mean that Congress is the body
in charge of that constitutional procedure."[88] In a response that would go directly
to the power conferred by the Treaty upon the President to use nuclear weapons,
Secretary Acheson said: "Article 5 . . . does not enlarge, nor does it decrease,
nor does it change in any way, the relative constitutional position of the President
and the Congress."[89]

   These critically important qualifications were elaborated at some length in the
Senate Foreign Relations Committee's report on the Treaty:

During the hearings substantially the following questions were repeatedly asked: In view
of the provision in article 5 that an attack against one shall be considered an attack against
all, would the United States be obligated to react to an attack on Paris or Copenhagen
in the same way it would react to an attack on New York City? In such an event does
the treaty give the President the power to take any action, without specific congressional
authorization, which he could not take in the absence of the treaty?
   The answer to both these questions is "No." . . .
   In the event any party of the treaty were attacked the obligation of the United States
Government would be to decide upon and take forthwith the measures it deemed necessary
to restore and maintain the security of the North Atlantic area. . . .
   Nothing in the treaty . . . increases or decreases the constitutional powers of either the
President or the Congress or changes the relationship between them.[90]

   These important limitations on the United States' commitment were re-affirmed
on the Senate floor by Senator Connally, the Chairman, in explaining the Treaty
to the Senate: "The treaty does not involve any commitment to go to war," he
said, "nor does it change the relative authority of the President and the Congress
with respect to the use of the armed forces."[91] Senator Connally reiterated the
qualifications set forth in the committee report[92] and addressed specifically the
charge that the Treaty was an "automatic" commitment:

While the treaty was being drafted rumors circulated about Washington that article 5
carried with it a commitment which would bind the United States automatically to go to
war in the event of an armed attack. I challenge anyone to find such a commitment. . . .

Not only must we ratify the treaty by constitutional processes, but it will be carried out under the provisions of the Constitution of the United States. The full authority of the Congress to declare war, with all the discretion that that power implies, remains unimpaired.[93]

Senator Connally noted that this was understood by all the signatories to the Treaty, and included in the record a portion of a British white paper setting forth the understanding of the United Kingdom.[94] Senator Vandenberg affirmed the correctness of Senator Connally's interpretation of the Treaty, at some length.[95]

Yet opposition arose, centering around the alleged vagueness of the Treaty's commitments and the possibility that it might draw the United States into foreign wars. Senator Jenner referred to the "garbled diplomatic gibberish"[96] and charged that even supporters of the Treaty were divided over the "wisdom of clarifying beyond question of doubt the real nature of the military commitments contained in the weasel-worded clauses of this treaty."[97] A senator could be inconsistent or kid himself, Senator Jenner said, but "let him not delude the American people."[98] He and Senator Donnell then engaged in an extended colloquy concerning what they saw as a "military alliance" which would "sabotage the United Nations" (and, conceivably, tie the United States to communist governments that might become members of NATO).[99] European signatories to the Treaty, Senator Donnell argued, had proceeded under the belief that the United States would be pledged to go to war if one of them were attacked; he entered in the record a statement to that effect by the Danish foreign minister.[100] Senator Watkins later complained that the Treaty "creates an obligation to defend our allies' territory in the event of an armed attack upon them."[101] It was this obligation that he opposed:

The historic and generally accepted American view, is that only Congress sitting at the time the armed attack occurs, has the power, when the attack is made on United States territory, to declare war and authorize the employment of the armed forces of the United States to repel such an attack.[102]

He therefore proposed a reservation, worded as follows:

The United States further understands and construes article 5 to the effect that in any particular case or event of armed attack on any other party or parties to the treaty, the Congress of the United States is not expressly, impliedly, or morally obligated or committed to declare war or authorize the employment of the military, air, or naval forces of the United States against the nation or nations making said attack, or to assist with its armed forces the nation or nations attacked, but shall have complete freedom in considering the circumstances of each case to act or refuse to act as the Congress in its discretion shall determine.[103]

Senator Connally described the reservation as a "complete repudiation of the treaty." Under it, he said, we would have "no obligations."[104] Senator Watkins responded by reading from a letter by Charles Evans Hughes to Senator Hale, wherein the late Justice wrote that article 10 of the Treaty represented an "illusory engagement." The United States, Hughes' letter said, "should not enter into a guarantee which would expose us to the charge of bad faith or having defaulted on our obligation. . . . Democracies cannot promise war after the manner of of monarchs."[105] The argument had little effect, however; one Senator proceeded to hail the Treaty as "the logical next step in the development of the conception of the Monroe doctrine. . . ."[106] Senator Connally entered in the *Congressional Record* a letter from Secretary of State Dean Acheson opposing the reservation, which, the Secretary of State said, would "not only raise doubts as to our determination in the minds of those who might be considering aggression, but would certainly raise the gravest doubts in the minds of our partners in the pact. . . ."[107] The reservation was defeated, 87 to 8.[108] The Senate then ratified the Treaty by a vote of 82 to 13.[109]

Defeat of the reservation might be viewed as Senate acceptance of its converse: that the Treaty did and should contain an "automatic" commitment to use armed force.[110] A reading of the Senate's will more consistent with the context in which the Watkins reservation was rejected, however, is that the reservation articulated a delicate but purposefully unexpressed element of the unanimous understanding of the signatories, and that a spelling-out of that element would have undermined the political force of the Treaty—thereby risking the possibility of renegotiation and throwing the solidarity of the alliance in jeopardy. Most Senators seemed to believe, in short, that the element of non-commitment in the commitment was clear enough. And a consensus appeared to have been reached between the executive branch and the Senate concerning the measure of specificity required to satisfy the demands of the Constitution as well as putative allies.

III. CONCLUSION

As Senator Stennis reminded the Senate during the confused debate on a subsequent treaty with South Korea, it is important to "keep our eye on the ball."[111] The issue is *not* what procedures are implied or required by the term "constitutional processes." Whether congressional approval is required before the President can introduce the armed forces into hostilities is a vast and complex question, far beyond the scope of this essay. Rather, the issue here is whether the NATO Treaty can and does serve as a supplementary source of authority on which the President can rely to introduce the United States armed forces into hostilities. This article shows that the Treaty is not such authority. Instead it leaves the war making powers of each branch precisely where those powers would have been in its absence. The NATO Treaty has no operative legal effect in altering the discretion that the President or Congress can exercise in meeting an armed attack on a treaty partner.

The dilemma confronting NATO Treaty negotiators was a real one. The primary purpose of mutual security pacts was to be deterrence of aggression.

Deterrence is effective, in international relations as in domestic criminal justice, only to the extent that it is swift and sure. Yet the negotiators were also compelled to assure that the pact comported with the deliberative decision making processes of the democracies they sought to preserve. Speed and certainty are not the hallmarks of democratic procedure—particularly as regards the decision to use armed force. The evolution of Anglo-American constitutionalism is in no small part a history of the decline of the war making power as a "prerogative" power, a history of its transfer to legislative authorities. To have disregarded that evolution would have been—at least in the United States—to have ensured the rejection of the pacts. An initial flirtation with "automatic" commitments, reflected in the ambiguous language of the proposed NATO Treaty, was thus quickly ended when the Treaty was taken up by the Senate.

So the negotiators wrote into the Treaty the fullest measure of commitment that their domestic legal and political systems would allow—which was zero. They rejected swift and sure deterrence in favor of the right to decide—to weigh the facts of each incident, to judge whether an armed attack actually had occurred, to assess whether the attack had been provoked, to determine whether a military response was the most propitious—to consider all the factors that go into an evaluation of what action is most appropriate. The United States could not have both, so it chose the latter. Its constitutional system may not have permitted the former, but the question was not faced. It declined to conclude automatic security commitments. It declined to empower the President to draw authority from those commitments. It promised that it would, in good faith, consider such assistance as it deemed appropriate if another party is attacked. But that is all it promised.

NOTES

1. North Atlantic Treaty, Apr. 4, 1949, T.I.A.S. No. 1964; 34 U.N.T.S. 243 (hereinafter cited as "NATO"). Current parties to the treaty are Belgium, Canada, Denmark, France, the Federal Republic of Germany, Greece, Iceland, Italy, Luxembourg, the Netherlands, Norway, Portugal, Spain, Turkey, the United Kingdom, and the United States. U.S. Dep't. of State, *Treaties in Force* 274 (Jan. 1, 1985).

2. NATO, art. 5.

3. Letter from Chapman B. Cox, General Counsel, Dept. of Def., to Jeremy J. Stone (Aug. 23, 1985).

4. *See* 131 Cong. Rec. H5079 (daily ed. June 27, 1985) (statement of Rep. Kemp) (Rio Treaty imposes solemn obligation of armed support in event of attack); *id.* at H5067 (statement of Rep. Foley) ("obviously an armed attack against any American state [which has signed the Rio Treaty] would give authority for the President to act"); *id.* at 5093 (statement of Rep. Hunter) (Rio Treaty vests full authority in President).

5. Or of any other mutual security treaty to which the United States is presently signatory. *See* Glennon, *United States Mutual Security Treaties: The Commitment Myth*, 24 Colum. J. Transnat'l L. 201 (1986).

6. S. Rep. No. 7, 96th Cong., 1st Sess. 31 (1979) (Taiwan Enabling Act).

7. U.S. Const. art. II, § 2, cl. 2.

8. *Id.*, cl. 11.

9. *Id.*, cl. 12.

10. *Id.*, cl. 13.

11. *Id.*, cl. 14.

12. Bas v. Tingy, 4 U.S. (4 Dall.) 37 (1800). Justice Chase had no doubt that it lay within the power of Congress to circumscribe executive discretion after authorizing the use of the armed forces in hostilities. He said:

Congress is empowered to declare a general war, or Congress may wage a limited war; limited in place, in object, in time. If a general war is declared, its extent and operations are only restricted and regulated by the *jus belli*, forming a part of the law of nations; but if a partial war is waged, its extent and operation depend on our municipal laws.

Id. at 43. *See also* Talbot v. Seeman, 5 U.S. (1 Cr.) 1 (1801), (upholding the power of Congress to wage "partial war").

13. Geofroy v. Riggs, 133 U.S. 258, 267 (1890). *See also* Holden v. Joy, 84 U.S. (17 Wall.) 211 (1872); Asakura v. Seattle, 265 U.S. 332 (1924).

14. Geofroy v. Riggs, 133 U.S. 258, 267 (1890). *Accord* Reid v. Covert, 354 U.S. 1 (1954).

15. S. Exec. Rep. No. 12, 95th Cong., 2d Sess. 65 (1978).

16. I M. Farrand, *The Records of the Federal Convention of 1787* 300 (1937 ed.) (hereinafter cited as "Farrand").

17. II Farrand 318.

18. *Id.* at 318–19.

19. I Benton *Abridgment* 650–51.

20. The historical events of which the custom consists must be similar. The act constituting the custom must be repeated more than once; the greater the number of times the act has been repeated, the more probative the custom. The period of time over which the act is performed is also relevant: the longer the time period, the more reason to view the time period as having the authority of custom. "Density" is also to be considered, which means the number of times an act has been repeated over the course of its duration. If repetition of the act is irregular, so that comparatively long periods of time occur in which the practice has not been followed, less reason exists for the act to take on the authority of custom. Finally, it must be asked whether the act has been performed during periods of normalcy, meaning that the act was not an aberration attributable to unique historical circumstances. These factors are discussed in Glennon, *The Use of Custom in Resolving Separation of Powers Disputes*, 64 B.U.L. Rev. 109, 129–33 (1984).

21. Henkin, *Foreign Affairs and the Constitution* 160 (1972) ("no treaty has ever been designed to put the United States into a state of war without a declaration by Congress"); Glennon, *supra* note 4.

22. 2 *Messages and Papers of the Presidents 1789–1897* 31–32 (J. Richardson ed. 1897) (Monroe in support of sending troops to Florida); W. H. Taft, *Our Chief Magistrate and His Powers* 86 (1938) (T. Roosevelt in support of sending troops to Cuba); 54 Dep't. State Bull. 474, 485 (1966) (State Department in support of sending troops to South Vietnam).

23. U.S. Const. art. II, § 3.

24. *See* Glennon, *Raising the Paquete Habana: Is Violation of Customary International Law by the Executive Unconstitutional?* 79 Nw. U. L. Rev. 321, 332 (1985).

25. *Id.* at 334. Madison referred to the President's power to execute "the national laws." 1 Madison, *The Constitutional Convention of 1787* 52–53 (Hunt ed. 1908).

26. *See* 54 Cong. Rec. 4273 (1917).

27. *Id.* at 4878–79.

28. *See, e.g., U.S. Commitments to Foreign Powers: Hearings on S. Res. 151 Before the Senate Comm. on Foreign Relations*, 90th Cong., 1st Sess. 205 (1967) (comments of Senators Fulbright and Ervin).

29. *See, e.g.,* United States v. Midwest Oil, 236 U.S. 458, 481 (1914); Myers v. United States, 272 U.S. 52, 163 (1926). *See generally* Glennon, *supra* note 20, at 137–40.

30. 7 Moore, *Digest of International Law* 128 (1906).

31. Cong. Globe, 35th Cong., 2d Sess. 1120 (1859).

32. Shankland v. Washington, 30 U.S. (5 Pet.) 390, 395 (1831).

33. Field v. Clark, 143 U.S. 649, 692 (1892).

34. *Id.*

35. 293 U.S. 388 (1935).

36. 295 U.S. 495 (1935).

37. *War Powers Legislation: Hearings on S. 731, S.J. Res. 18 and S.J. Res. 59 Before the Senate Comm. on Foreign Relations*, 92d Cong., 1st Sess. 565 (1971) (statement of Alexander M. Bickel, Professor of Law, Yale University).

38. Wormuth, "The Vietnam War: The President vs. the Constitution," in 2 *The Vietnam War and International Law* 799 (R. Falk ed. 1969). *See also* Lofgren, *War-Making Under the Constitution: The Original Understanding*, 81 Yale L. J. 672 (1972); Berger, *War-Making by the President*, 121 U. Pa. L. Rev. 29 (1972); Berger, *War, Foreign Affairs, and Executive Secrecy*, 72 Nw. U. L. Rev. 309 (1978); Casper, *Constitutional Constraints on the Conduct of Foreign and Defense Policy: A Nonjudicial Model*, 43 U. Chi. L. Rev. 463 (1976).

39. *See, e.g.,* Eastlake v. Forest City Enters., Inc., 462 U.S. 668, 675 (1978) (Marshall, J., concurring). *See generally* Schwartz, *Of Administrators and Philosopher-Kings: The Republic, the Laws, and Delegations of Power*, 72 Nw. U. L. Rev. 443 (1978).

40. Industrial Union Dept. v. American Petroleum Inst., 448 U.S. 607 (1980).

41. *Id.*

42. *Id.* at 687 (Rehnquist, J., concurring).

43. American Textile Mfrs. Inst. v. Donovan, 452 U.S. 490, 543 (1981) (Rehnquist, J., dissenting).

44. *See* California Bankers Ass'n v. Schultz, 416 U.S. 21, 91 (1974) (Brennan, J., dissenting); United States v. Robel, 389 U.S. 258, 272–73 (1967) (Brennan, J., concurring).

45. *See* Note, *Rethinking the Nondelegation Doctrine*, 62 B.U.L. Rev. 257, 311–20 (1982) (suggesting that recent Supreme Court decisions indicate the doctrine's resurrection).

46. 299 U.S. 304 (1936).

47. 48 Stat. 811.

48. *Id.*

49. 48 Stat. 1744.

50. *Curtiss-Wright*, 299 U.S. at 311.

51. *Id.* at 320.

52. *Id.* at 318.

53. *See, e.g.,* Levitan, *The Foreign Relations Power: An Analysis of Mr. Justice Suth-*

erland's Theory, 55 Yale L. J. 467 (1946); Lofgren, *United States v. Curtiss-Wright Export Corporation: An Historical Reassessment*, 83 Yale L. J. 1 (1973); Berger, *Presidential Monopoly of Foreign Relations*, 71 Mich. L. Rev. 1 (1972), *reprinted in* R. Berger, *Executive Privilege: A Constitutional Myth* (1944).

54. *See, e.g.*, Patterson, *In re The United States v. Curtiss-Wright Corporation* (pts. 1 & 2), 22 Tex. L. Rev. 286 (1944); Quarles, *The Federal Government: As to Foreign Affairs, Are Its Powers Inherent as Distinguished from Delegated?*, 32 Geo. L. J. 375 (1944).

55. *War Powers Legislation: Hearings on S. 731, S. J. Res. 18 and S. J. Res. 59 Before the Senate Comm. on Foreign Relations*, 92d Cong., 1st Sess. 555 (1971) (statement of Alexander M. Bickel, Professor of Law, Yale University).

56. "Whether this assumption was valid at the time," Bickel testified before the Senate Foreign Relations Committee, "is thoroughly questionable. . . . The [law] closely defined what the President was to do, and where he was to do it. . . . This was hardly delegation running riot. . . ." *Id.*

57. *Industrial Union Dept.*, 448 U.S. at 661 (Rehnquist, J., concurring).

58. *Id.* at 685.

59. *See supra* notes 15–19 and accompanying text.

60. *Industrial Union Dept.*, 448 U.S. at 686–87.

61. *See* Sunstein, *Naked Preferences and the Constitution*, 84 Colum. L. Rev. 1689 (1984).

62. *Industrial Union Dept.*, 448 U.S. at 675.

63. The third purpose of the doctrine—to provide standards for judicial enforcement—is less relevant because the courts have traditionally played a lesser role in foreign affairs. It is not irrelevant, however, for the "foreign affairs" cases decided by the Supreme Court are not so few as some might think. *See, e.g.*, M. Glennon & T. Franck, *United States Foreign Relations Law* (1980) (setting forth cases).

64. 343 U.S. 579 (1952).

65. 357 U.S. 116 (1958).

66. *Id.* at 119.

67. *Id.* at 199 n.95.

68. 381 U.S. 1 (1964).

69. *Id.* at 17.

70. *Id.*

71. *Id.* at 20–22 (Black, J., dissenting).

72. 453 U.S. 280 (1981).

73. 468 U.S. 222 (1984).

74. 453 U.S. 654 (1981).

75. 343 U.S. 579 (1952).

76. *Id.* at 634 (Jackson, J., concurring).

77. 462 U.S. 919 (1983).

78. *Id.* at 944.

79. *See generally* Glennon, *supra* note 5.

80. NATO, art. 11.

81. *Id.*, art. 5 (emphasis added).

82. Address by Sec. of State Acheson delivered on Mar. 18, 1949, over the combined networks of the Columbia and Mutual Broadcasting Systems, 20 Dep't. State Bull. 384–88 (Mar. 27, 1949).

83. 20 Dep't. State Bull. 532–36, 534 (Apr. 24, 1949).

84. President's Message to Senate Transmitting North Atlantic Treaty, 20 Dep't. State Bull. 599 (May 8, 1949).

85. *North Atlantic Treaty: Hearings on Exec. L. Before the Senate Comm. on Foreign Relations*, 81st Cong., 1st Sess. 11 (1949) (statement of Dean Acheson, Secretary of State).

86. *Id.* at 18.

87. *Id.* at 25.

88. *Id.* at 80.

89. *Id.*

90. S. Exec. Rep. No. 8, 81st Cong., 1st Sess. (1949).

91. 95 Cong. Rec. 8812, 8814 (1949).

92. *Id.* at 8815.

93. *Id.*

94. *Id.*

95. *Id.* at 8894–95.

96. *Id.* at 9553.

97. *Id.* at 9554.

98. *Id.*

99. *Id.* at 9564.

100. *Id.* at 9640.

101. *Id.* at 9900.

102. *Id.* 9899.

103. *Id.* 9904.

104. *Id.*

105. *Id.* at 9907.

106. *Id.* at 9911.

107. *Id.* at 9915.

108. *Id.* at 9916.

109. *Id.*

110. Justice Jackson argued in the *Steel Seizure Case* that rejection of an amendment by the Senate which would have authorized the seizure of the steel mills effectively represented legislative *disapproval* of such an act. Youngstown Sheet & Tube Co. v. Sawyer, 343 U.S. 579, 634 (1952) (Jackson, J., concurring).

111. 100 Cong. Rec. 779, 789 (1954).

6

Congressional Authority to Regulate the Use of Nuclear Weapons

Allan Ides

The image of the presidential finger gripping the nuclear trigger is perhaps somewhat simplistic. But it does reflect, more accurately than not, a fatalistic national concession that the ultimate decision on nuclear war rests on the shoulders of one somewhat isolated human being and his or her small coterie of self-selected advisors; a human being, who prior to the moment of consecration, will likely have had little or no experience in, and may possess only the most superficial knowledge of, nuclear weaponry, strategy, tactics and the ultimate consequences of a nuclear strike. For good or ill, we do not elect Presidents because of their special expertise in this delicate realm. The vagaries of presidential politics select the finger; we supply the trigger and our prayers. One cannot be faulted for wondering whether there exists a more sensible approach.

The Federation of American Scientists (FAS) has suggested one such approach, by proposing to, in effect, ban the first use of nuclear weapons and at the same time empower a committee of Congress to rescind that ban.[1] The proposal raises not only constitutional issues specific to itself, but more far-reaching constitutional questions regarding the relative roles of Congress and the President in the realm of nuclear war making. It is the purpose of this chapter to explore those issues, both the specific and the general.

In assessing these constitutional questions, the primary question is not whether presidential first use is unlawful, not whether this proposal is *the* appropriate constitutional response to nuclear weapons technology, nor whether the proposal

A substantially similar version of this chapter appeared in 13 *Hastings Constitutional Law Quarterly* 233 (Winter 1986). Reprinted with permission.

The author would like to express his gratitude to Tzivia Schwartz, Loyola Law School, '86, and Allyson Saunders, Loyola Law School, '87, for their invaluable research assistance.

is somehow necessary to establish the primacy of Congress over the President. Rather the inquiry is whether Congress, as the lawmaking branch of the national government, may take a more active role in the regulation of nuclear weapons use, and, more specifically, whether Congress could plausibly conclude that the Constitution is receptive to this proposal or some reasonable variation of it. If the threshold of constitutional plausibility is crossed, the decision whether to adopt such a proposal is classically political, *i.e.*, the choice is within the realm of discretion vested in the political branches, and particularly, in Congress.

The analysis begins with an examination of the structure of separation of powers with particular emphasis upon the legislative authority of Congress and the derivative authority of the President to execute the policies adopted by Congress. Next, the relationship between the structural principles and the division of authority in the war making context is considered. Last, objections that the device of committee approval of first use would violate presidential prerogative and the nondelegation doctrine are considered.

I. ALLOCATIONS OF CONSTITUTIONAL AUTHORITY

A. The Basic Structure

The legislative authority conferred by the Constitution is reposed in Congress.[2] That authority, which is in essence the power to make law, may be exercised over all matters enumerated in Article I, Section 8 of the Constitution, including the powers to create and support a military establishment and the power to declare war. This legislative or lawmaking authority is plenary. That is, the authority of Congress over these matters is complete. Thus, with respect to the powers over military affairs, Congress may create an army or decline to do so; Congress may fund a weapons system or ban basic research on that system; Congress may declare war or refuse to so declare. Moreover, Congress may select any means it deems appropriate to accomplish the ends it desires so long as those ends are consistent with the vast array of powers and procedures granted to the national government.[3]

There are only three limitations upon the pervasive and predominant lawmaking authority of Congress. First, Congress may not transgress negative restraints on governmental power such as those enumerated in the Bill of Rights or in Article I, Section 9. Next, Congress may not assume for itself the roles specifically assigned to executive and judiciary:[4] administration and enforcement of the laws enacted by Congress, and adjudication of matters arising under those laws and the Constitution, respectively.[5] Finally, Congress must, in general, abide the procedural limitations imposed by the Constitution upon the legislative process.[6]

The history of the British Constitution was in general a movement away from monarchy and autocracy toward representative government.[7] The Framers saw the government they designed as a further step in that progression, a grand experiment in representative democracy.[8] To place the lawmaking authority in either of the other branches would have been anathema to republicanism and a clear step backwards.[9] This philosophical perspective explains Madison's observation that, "[i]n republican government, the legislative authority necessarily predominates."[10] Or as one commentator has observed, "[N]o one doubted that the legislature was the most important part of any government."[11]

This is not to deny or disparage the power of the presidency. As a practical reality that power is enormous. The source of presidential power is not, however, an amorphous construct of constitutional law. Rather, the well spring of presidential power—aside from pure political clout—is positive law enacted by Congress; law that defines the scope of national policy and delegates appropriate authority to the President. In addition, as discussed below, the President derives practical power from the acquiescence of Congress in unilateral presidential initiative. In other words, the source of presidential power is the accumulated action and inaction of Congress, not the Constitution as it exists in the abstract. The President has no independent power to tax, spend, regulate, impose embargoes or to create a military establishment.[12] The President's seemingly unilateral authority over these matters is in fact based upon broad delegations, express and implied, by Congress.[13] The delegations may be stretched and contorted in any particular case, but such efforts to conform prior delegations to present action do not disparage the underlying principle. Indeed, they are designed to pay obeisance to it.

B. Judicial Affirmation of Basic Structure

Youngstown Sheet & Tube Co. v. Sawyer[14] affirms these basic structural principles. Just prior to the commencement of a nationwide steel strike in 1952, President Truman ordered the Secretary of Commerce to seize the nation's steel mills. Truman believed that the strike would seriously jeopardize the war effort in Korea. The mill owners immediately sought an injunction. They argued "that the President's order amounts to lawmaking, a legislative function which the Constitution has expressly conferred upon Congress and not the President."[15] In fact, the government did not claim that the President's order was authorized by any legislation. Rather, the government argued that the President's "action was necessary to avert a national catastrophe which would inevitably result from a stoppage of steel production, and that in meeting this grave emergency the President was acting within the aggregate of his constitutional powers as the Nation's Chief Executive and the Commander in Chief of the Armed Forces of the United States."[16]

Justice Black's opinion for the Court focused upon the government's concession that no act of Congress had authorized the action taken by the President. That being the case, the sole question was whether the Constitution authorized the seizure. Justice Black rejected outright the government's reliance on inherent powers of the Commander in Chief. The decision whether to permit such a taking of private property was a "job for the Nation's lawmakers, not for its military authorities."[17]

Justice Black rejected as well the government's argument that the vesting of "the executive power" in the President supported the seizure. "In the framework of our Constitution, the President's power to see that the laws are faithfully executed refutes the idea that he is to be a lawmaker. The Constitution limits his functions in the lawmaking process to the recommending of laws he thinks wise and the vetoing of laws he thinks bad."[18] That the President had overstepped those bounds by the seizure was evident. "The preamble of the order itself, like that of many statutes, sets out reasons why the President believes certain policies should be adopted, proclaims these policies as rules of conduct to be followed, and again, like a statute, authorizes a government official to promulgate additional rules and regulations consistent with the policy proclaimed and needed to carry that policy into execution."[19] The Court held that this lawmaking role assumed by the President was one to be performed by "Congress alone in both good and bad times."[20] An emergency did not alter the scheme of separation of powers.

Justice Jackson, concurring, proposed a three-tiered model of presidential authority. First, when the President acts with the express or implied authorization of Congress, his authority is at its apex. "In these circumstances, and in these only, may he be said . . . to personify the federal sovereignty."[21] Second, when the President acts in the absence of either a congressional grant or denial of authority, he acts within a zone of twilight in which authority is uncertain. Third, when the President acts in contravention of the implied or express will of Congress, his authority is at its nadir.

In essence, Justice Jackson's first and third categories are identical to Justice Black's overall model. In the first category, when Congress has authorized presidential action, the question is not one of separation of powers, but of national power. Accordingly, the inquiry focuses upon the enumeration of substantive powers, not upon the roles of the particular branches, and an affirmative grant of authority from Congress gives the President the power to act. In the third category, the President is free to act contrary to the will of Congress only in cases of exclusive executive power.[22] In all other circumstances, to sustain presidential action contrary to legislation would unite the lawmaking and law enforcement powers in one person, a situation quite at odds with the most fundamental constitutional principles. Writing in the *Federalist Papers*, James Madison stated:

The accumulation of all powers legislative, executive and judiciary in the same hands, whether of one, a few or many, and whether hereditary, self appointed, or elective, may justly be pronounced the very definition of tyranny. . . . The reasons on which Montesquieu grounds his maxim [on separation of powers] are a further demonstration of his meaning. "When the legislative and executive powers are united in the same person or body," says he, "there can be no liberty, because apprehensions may arise lest *the same* monarch or senate should *enact* tyrannical laws to *execute* them in a tyrannical manner."[23]

Similarly, Justice Jackson made it clear that he was quite reluctant to ever uphold such sweeping presidential prerogative: "Presidential claim to a power at once so conclusive and preclusive must be scrutinized with caution, for what is at stake is the equilibrium established by our constitutional system."[24]

The main difference between the majority and concurring opinions is Justice Jackson's recognition of a "zone of twilight," a zone which is not apparent in Justice Black's articulation of constitutional theory. Justice Jackson is plainly willing to permit the executive to take action when Congress has not expressly forbidden the action. But one must be careful to understand the extent of this seeming permissiveness. Justice Jackson explained the second tier as a practical reality, not as a constitutional doctrine: "[C]ongressional inertia, indifference or quiescence may sometimes, *at least as a practical matter*, enable, if not invite, measures on independent presidential responsibility. In this area, any actual test of power is likely to depend on the imperatives of events and contemporary imponderables rather than on abstract theories of law."[25] In other words, even though the Constitution may impose the responsibility upon Congress, a failure to exercise that responsibility will invite the executive to assume the dormant power. Justice Jackson goes on to observe, "But I have no illusion that any decision by this Court can keep power in the hands of Congress if it is not wise and timely in meeting its problems. A crisis that challenges the President equally, or perhaps primarily, challenges Congress. If not good law, there was worldly wisdom in the maxim attributed to Napoleon that 'The tools belong to the man who can use them.' We may say that power to legislate for emergencies belongs in the hands of Congress, but only Congress itself can prevent power from slipping through its fingers."[26]

Dames & Moore v. Regan [27] is an excellent illustration of the Jackson thesis. In that case, which involved a challenge to the agreement negotiated by the Carter administration for the release of the American hostages held by Iran, the Supreme Court engaged in a masterful exercise of statutory construction to find congressional support for the President's action. Some components of the agreement were well within the letter of the law; others were not. Particularly suspect was the suspension of claims against Iran pending in American courts. The Court found that although neither the International Emergency Economic Powers Act nor the Hostage Act provided "specific authorization" for the suspension of those claims,[28] the acts were relevant in indicating "congressional acceptance of a broad scope for executive action in circumstances such as those presented in this case."[29] This, coupled with a long history of congressional support for the presidential settlement of private claims against foreign powers and the absence of any specific prohibition, indicated a congressional affirmation of presidential authority under the circumstances.[30] In the words of the Court, "[c]rucial to our decision today is the conclusion that Congress has implicitly approved the practice of claim settlement by executive agreement."[31]

Thus, *Dames & Moore* underscores the view that the primary responsibility for unleashing national power rests in Congress. The zone of twilight exists only beyond the rim of congressional action and even then the extent of the zone is defined by the tacit position of Congress articulated in marginally relevant statutes and patterns of acquiescence.

Youngstown provides an important structural model for two reasons. First, both the opinion of the Court and the concurrence of Justice Jackson recognize that the lawmaking authority is vested in Congress and not in the President and that because of this ordering of responsibility the President takes his cue from Congress. Justice Jackson seems to accept the theoretical possibility of affirming presidential action taken contrary to the legislated will of Congress, but concedes the rarity as well as the difficulty of such theoretical possibilities and gives no examples.[32] *Youngstown* therefore depicts a model of congressional superiority based upon the lawmaking function of Congress.

Second, Justice Jackson alone recognized that as a practical matter, congressional failure to exercise its legislative responsibility may invite presidential intrusions upon the congressional turf. Here again primary constitutional responsibility rests in the hands of Congress. The question is whether Congress will exercise that responsibility or whether failing to do so will risk a loss of the authority.

C. Basic Structure and the Power to Make War

The basic structural framework described above is fully applicable to the war making context. Article I, Section 8 of the Constitution places considerable emphasis upon the war making capacity of the national government. Specifically, that article provides:

Congress shall have Power . . . to raise and support Armies, but no Appropriation of Money to that Use shall be for a longer Term than two Years . . . ; To provide and maintain a Navy; To make Rules for the Government and Regulation of the land and naval Forces; To provide for calling forth the Militia to execute the Laws of the Union, suppress Insurrections and repel Invasions; [and] to provide for organizing, arming, and disciplining the Militia and for governing such Part of them as may be employed in the Service of the United States . . .[33]

Of course, this language cannot be construed as granting Congress all governmental authority over these matters. The power is vested in the national government as a whole. Congress is given the legislative or lawmaking authority over these enumerated substantive matters. But, as indicated earlier, in our republican form of government, that legislative authority is quite significant. It is, in essence, a trigger device that must be activated before national power can be exercised. It defines the policy that the executive branch will execute. Without action by Congress there is no independent presidential war making power.

The practical power and responsibility vested in Congress by these clauses is quite extensive. Congress must make the initial determination of whether—or the extent to which—we should have any armed forces, the character of those forces and, it would seem, the general uses to which those forces may be applied. The power is, after all, to raise, govern and regulate. The President may participate in this determination through the executive branch's enormous powers of persuasion and through the exercise of the veto. In other respects, the executive power arises only upon affirmative action taken by Congress. If Congress fails to provide a particular weapons system, the President lacks the constitutional wherewithal to procure that system. He also lacks the general authority to use authorized forces or weapons in a manner inconsistent with specific congressional determinations. To conclude otherwise would be to permit the President to assume a lawmaking authority plainly reposed by the Constitution in Congress.

Of course, once the armed forces are created and once the arsenal is stockpiled, serious consideration must be given to Justice Jackson's zone of twilight. To the extent that Congress provides little or no guidance on the disposition of troops or on the uses of weapons, the executive will assume the power to dispose of those troops and weapons as he deems appropriate.[34] Patterns of congressional acquiescence in presidential action will further bolster practical executive power. This acquired power is not, however, irretrievable. Nothing in Justice Jackson's theory or in the Constitution prevents Congress from recapturing lost turf.[35]

II. ALLOCATIONS OF THE POWER TO MAKE WAR AS PERCEIVED BY THE FRAMERS AND THROUGH THE LOOKING GLASS OF HISTORY

A. The Power to Raise Armies

The predominant authority of Congress was a recurring theme in the *Federalist Papers*. This was particularly so with respect to the war making powers. In *The Federalist Nos. 24 and 26*, Alexander Hamilton responded to charges that the Constitution was deficient in that it permitted the national government to keep troops in time of peace and in that it vested the executive with plenary power to levy troops. Hamilton refuted the first charge on policy grounds—the need for some military establishment being a practical necessity—and the second by demonstrating that the Constitution vested no such authority in the executive.

[T]hat the whole power of raising armies was lodged in the *Legislature*, not in the *Executive*; that this legislature was to be a popular body, consisting of the representatives of the people periodically elected; and that . . . there was to be found . . . an important qualification even of the legislative discretion, in that clause which forbids the appropriation of money for the support of an army for any longer period than two years—a precaution which, upon a nearer view of it, will appear to be a great and real security against the keeping up of troops without evident necessity.[36]

The requirement that no appropriation for the army be for a period of more than two years was, according to Hamilton, designed to obligate Congress to actively oversee the armed forces and to determine at regular intervals "the propriety of keeping a military force on foot."[37]

Today the appropriations limitation does not operate in the precise fashion anticipated by Hamilton and the Framers of the Constitution. As a practical matter, a peacetime armed force equipped with a massive arsenal of nuclear weapons will be with us for the foreseeable future, regardless of whether the appropriation for those forces be for two years or for some other time configuration. However, the spirit of the restraint and the role it was intended to play in the structure of authority over military affairs is no less significant today than it was in 1787. It indicates a strong constitutional sense that Congress is to retain primary jurisdiction over the armed forces and to be a constant watchdog and regulator of military activity.

In a passage fraught with irony for contemporary readers, Hamilton disparaged the notion that the elected representatives of the people could successfully undermine this carefully structured system of constitutional authority and obligation.

Schemes to subvert the liberties of a great community *require time* to mature them for execution. An army so large as seriously to menace those liberties could only be formed by progressive augmentations; which would suppose, not merely a temporary combination between the legislature and executive, but a continued conspiracy for a series of time. Is it probable that such a combination would exist at all? Is it probable that it would be persevered in and transmitted along, through all the successive variations in the representative body, which biennial elections would naturally produce in both houses? Is it presumable, that every man, the instant he took his seat in the national senate, or house of representatives, would commence a traitor to his constituents and to his country? Can it be supposed, that there would not be found one man, discerning enough to detect so atrocious a conspiracy, or bold or honest enough to apprise his constituents of their danger?[38]

These observations indicate a firm constitutional sense of the responsibilities of Congress. It is not enough to create a war machine and then hand it to the President. Control over the uses to which the machine may be put is at the heart of congressional duty. In Hamilton's view, only a traitor to our republican system of government would tolerate an abdication of that responsibility.

B. The Power to Declare War and the Power of the Commander in Chief

During the Revolutionary War, the entire war making power was vested in the Continental Congress. The Articles of Confederation provided that the "sole and exclusive right and power of determining on peace and war" was the prerogative of Congress.[39] The commander in chief of the Continental Army was appointed by the Congress and fully answerable to it. The perception of the Framers, among them former Commander in Chief George Washington, was that Congress as a deliberative body had proved itself ill-suited to the task of conducting war.[40] As a consequence of this perception, the Framers lodged the power to conduct war in the President as commander in chief.[41] In the words of Hamilton,

Of all the cares or concerns of government, the direction of war most peculiarly demands those qualities which distinguish the exercise of power by a single hand. The direction of war implies the direction of the common strength; and the power of directing and employing the common strength, forms an usual and essential part in the definition of the executive authority.[42]

This power to direct the war effort did not, however, vest the President with the constitutional authority to override the more pervasive authorities of Congress, including the power of Congress to declare war. "The President's power as commander in chief . . . was simply the power to issue orders to the armed forces within a framework established by Congress."[43]

Again, turning to Hamilton,

The President is to be Commander-in-Chief of the army and navy of the United States. In this respect his authority would be nominally the same with that of the king of Great Britain, but in substance much inferior to it. It would amount to nothing more than the supreme command and direction of the military and naval forces, as first General and Admiral of the Confederacy; while that of the British King extends to the *declaring* of war and to the *raising* and *regulating* of fleets and armies; all which by the Constitution under consideration would appertain to the Legislature.[44]

It would seem that in Hamilton's view there was no major friction between the power of Congress to declare war and the power of the President to direct the war effort once declared. The potential conflict would be no more severe than one would expect to witness in the tension between the legislative and executive powers generally. Congress makes policy by declaring war; it also shapes that policy through the breadth of the declaration and through the design of the military apparatus it has created. The President, as commander in chief, executes the policy within the confines of the framework created by Congress. To each branch is granted the function most appropriate to the composition and general purpose of that branch.

The commander in chief power does give the President a limited authority to act unilaterally in emergency situations. Initial drafts of the Constitution had given Congress the power to "make war." The purpose, according to Madison's notes, was to make clear that the President, in his capacity as commander in chief, would have the authority "To repel sudden attacks."[45] The published records of the Federal Convention of 1787 indicate that the adopted language was not meant to dilute congressional policy making power, but rather was a recognition of a special instance of executive competence to represent the interests of the nation in directing the military. Just as a deliberative body cannot effectively conduct a war, such a body cannot be expected to make tactical decisions designed to fend off sudden attacks or to otherwise respond, short term, to equivalent emergency situations.[46]

Importantly, the recognition of a limited authority to repel sudden attacks was not meant to permit the executive to engage in full scale war in the absence of congressional participation in that decision. Certainly, there is nothing in the historical debates to suggest as much. Rather, the purpose was to permit the President to take immediate action in defense of the nation, leaving to Congress the authority to consider the appropriate long term response. Seen in this light, the power to repel sudden attacks is not an exception to the overall separation of powers framework. It is a responsible recognition of the relative functions of each branch.[47]Indeed, the power would likely have been implied even in the absence of Madison's notes and even if the "make war" language had been retained.

In fact, the Madison and Gerry motion to alter the "make war" language was made in part as a response to a suggestion by Pierce Butler that the entire power to make war be vested in the President.[48] Speaking to this suggestion, Gerry observed that he "never expected to hear in a republic a motion to empower the Executive alone to declare war."[49] Similarly, George Mason stated that he "was against giving the power of war to the Executive, because [he was] not [safely] to be trusted with it; or the Senate, because [it was] not so constructed as to be entitled to it. He was for clogging rather than facilitating war; but for facilitating peace."[50] There is no record of any support for the Butler position. In adopting the Madison and Gerry motion, the Framers rejected Butler's suggestion of broad executive war making authority.

The power to declare war is plainly a legislative function. Not only is that power listed among the enumerated legislative powers in Article I, Section 8, its exercise involves precisely the type of policy judgment that is the prerogative of the representative branch. This power has been the focal point of considerable debate. The issues have ranged from whether a particular conflict is a war within the technical meaning of the clause or whether a particular action taken by Congress amounts to the required declaration to the larger question of whether declarations of war are outmoded in the modern world.[51] Such inquiries are not without their validity, but they do not address the fundamental structural question now at issue. That question is whether the grant to Congress of the power to declare war alters or affirms the basic principle of separation of powers, a principle which gives Congress the predominant lawmaking role in our government. When viewed along with a proper understanding of the commander in chief's constitutional powers, the power to declare war plainly affirms that principle. If anything it underscores the proposition that Congress has the initial authority to define the nation's military establishment and to determine the immediate military policy to be prosecuted by that establishment.

C. A Modern Gloss

The Framers' language and intent aside, one cannot ignore the common perception that the modern presidency is a repository of war making authority that

transcends the basic framework described above.[52] To the extent that this perception is an observation of political reality, it cannot be denied; to the extent
that it assumes an alteration in constitutional structure, it is demonstrably wrong.

The distinction between power conferred by the Constitution and power conferred by Congress through the constitutional process must be kept in mind. The
former involves allocations of primary authority that can only be changed through
the amendment process. Thus, Congress will retain the constitutional power to
dominate the nation's war making policy so long as the Constitution is not altered
through that process. The latter involves power conferred by Congress through
the exercise of those allocated authorities. Such power can be delegated to the
President either expressly through legislation or impliedly through a combination
of general grants of authority coupled with acquiescence in patterns of presidential
initiative.

In this regard, the circumstances of many presidential military excursions—
most of which have been relatively minor in terms of presidential intrusion upon
congressional prerogative—indicate a congressional acceptance and endorsement
of the precise presidential initiative undertaken. For example, each time a President orders the military rescue of American citizens residing in a foreign country,
a lack of objection from Congress as a body contributes to the perception that
Congress, having conferred a military force upon the President, has implicitly
consented to or even endorsed such uses of that force. Future presidents can be
expected to act upon that implied consent. This seems to be the clear message
of *Dames & Moore*. Thus in the absence of specific legislation addressing the
point, presidential practice unobjected to by Congress may alter the political
allocation of power by creating a presumed consent to take limited initiatives in
the military context. Moreover, a practice long endured may require a specific
repudiation, albeit not a constitutional amendment, before the consent will be
deemed withdrawn.

With respect to larger military conflicts, the independent presidential war is
more myth than reality. As stated by Professor Louis Henkin:

[I]t is increasingly difficult to make an authentic case that the President has taken the
country into war without Congressional authorization in advance or ratification soon after.
Presidents cannot use the armed forces for long in substantial operations without Congressional cooperation; surely any action that can properly be called war depends on Congressional appropriations and other forms of approval, expressed or implied. Presidents who
fought these wars inevitably sought Congressional approval and invariably obtained it.[53]

Thus, although President Polk may have ordered troops to cross the Rio Grande,
Congress crossed the Rubicon when it expressly endorsed the President's action
and declared war on Mexico.[54] More recently, in the Korean War, although
Congress did not expressly declare war, it plainly supported the war effort by
appropriating substantial funds toward accomplishment of the articulated goals.[55]
More recently still, Congress, through the Gulf of Tonkin Resolution, approved

our initial military involvement in South Vietnam and then sustained its massive escalation by enormous military appropriations.[56]

But the executive branch gains no constitutional power superior to Congress by taking action with which Congress explicitly or implicitly agrees.[57] Willingness to support the President's policy objectives does not necessarily indicate support for a broad interpretation of the commander in chief's constitutional powers. And, of course, Congress is free to rescind or alter its delegations to the President.[58]

In discussing the constitutionality of the War Powers Resolution, Professor Louis Henkin observed, "Congress can surely proscribe for future uses of force in situations amounting to war. As regards hostilities 'short of war,' it may be that, although the President can use force if Congress is silent, Congress can forbid or regulate even such uses of force, if only on the ground that they might lead to war."[59] In other words, the longstanding silence of Congress in the face of presidential military initiative grants the President leeway to act under similar circumstances in the future. That silence does not, however, preclude Congress from altering the course of power by taking specific action to limit seemingly independent presidential initiative in the military context.

Moreover, even if one assumes that the presidential initiatives described above, including Vietnam, were undertaken in direct contravention of congressional will, at most this indicates a violation of basic constitutional principle. Certainly, violations of the Constitution cannot be considered an acceptable form of amendment. Those usurpations of congressional prerogative would serve to indicate a need for a resurgence of congressional oversight, not a further abdication of responsibility.

Finally, regardless of whether one accepts any theory of congressional acquiescence or how one reads the historical account, the FAS proposal involves a practice that has not been "usurped" by the President. Indeed, it involves a practice that has been consistently exercised by Congress each year as part of the legislative process—namely, the determination of the shape, size and fighting potential of the military establishment.[60] The annual budget battles over defense appropriations and authorizations are a constant reminder of this very important and unrelinquished power of Congress.[61]

III. THE REGULATION OF NUCLEAR ARMS

A. The Lesser Powers of Arsenal Control

Extrapolating from the general principles discussed above, it should be quite clear that Congress, as the nation's lawmaking institution, possesses considerable authority over the nation's nuclear arsenal. A consideration of that authority begins with the obvious proposition that if it were not for Congress, there would be no nuclear arsenal.[62] If Congress had chosen to reject development of nuclear weapons technology, there is nothing in the Constitution that would have permitted the President to override that decision. Nor, as indicated above, is there any history of a presidential practice that would indicate to the contrary. It is, accordingly, beyond cavil that Congress may refuse a presidential request for a weapons system.

Similarly, nothing in the Constitution, other than the practical effect of a veto, would prevent Congress from eliminating or drastically reducing the present nuclear arsenal. The Constitution does not require that the President, as Commander in Chief, be armed with the best weapons; indeed, it does not require that he be armed with any weapons at all.

Arguably, this greater power to determine whether to arm the President would include the lesser power to legislate selectively and in increments with respect to particular types of armaments.[63] Thus, Congress may refuse to fund a particular weapon system, but at the same time provide a sufficient appropriation to permit basic research on the efficacy of that system. And, consistent with the Constitution, Congress could prohibit or limit certain avenues of research or testing.[64] The President would not be free to purchase the system merely because research had been funded nor would he be free to extend the research to specific avenues forbidden by Congress. Moreover, once a system is adopted, Congress need not give the President complete discretion over the use of that system. Congress could stockpile a certain weapon on the express condition that the weapon not be used until such time as Congress passed legislation permitting its use. Similarly, Congress could go a step further by giving the President the discretion to use a weapon, but only upon the occurrence of a particular event.

An example of congressional regulation of a weapon system is found in Chapter 32 of title 50 of the United States Code entitled, "Chemical and Biological Warfare Program."[65] The pertinent sections of the code limit the testing, transportation, deployment, storage and disposal of chemical and biological weapons. Similarly, section 111 of the Department of Defense Authorization Act, 1985,[66] provides: "[N]one of the funds appropriated pursuant to authorization of appropriations in this title may be used for procurement of binary chemical munitions, including advanced procurement of long-lead components or for the establishment of a production base for such munitions." There is no legitimate constitutional objection to this type of modified or limited delegation. Congress can give all, nothing at all, or something in between.[67]

Turning to the question of nuclear weapons and applying the above principles, it seems that Congress possesses the constitutional wherewithal to do any of the following things:

1. Create a nuclear arsenal (or expand upon the current one);

2. Refuse to create a nuclear weapons arsenal;

3. Eliminate the current nuclear stockpile;

4. Limit the nuclear arsenal to particular types of weapons (e.g., defensive only or offensive only);

5. Purchase a weapons system, but refuse to provide the practical means for use of the system;

6. Purchase the system and the practical means to use it, but absolutely forbid use of the system in the absence of implementing legislation; or

7. Purchase the system and the practical means to use it, but permit use only upon the occurrence of specific events.

This is not to argue the wisdom of any of the above alternatives; it is to suggest that the implementation of any one of them falls squarely within the constitutional authority of Congress to make basic policy determinations regarding the nation's nuclear weapons system.

If these seven possibilities are within the power of Congress to implement, what can be said of the FAS proposal which appears to take a middle course between giving the President total control over the nuclear arsenal and denying the President any such control? It would appear that the overall desuetude of the nondelegation doctrine coupled with the deference accorded the political branches in matters involving foreign relations[68] would permit Congress to grant the President the unfettered discretion to use nuclear weapons in the exercise of his powers as commander in chief. Similarly, as explained above, nothing in the Constitution or in any historical gloss upon it requires Congress to grant the President the authority to use such weapons. This, too, is within the political discretion of Congress. That being the case, one would think that a middle ground between these constitutional extremes would be equally acceptable.

But this intuition is not without its difficulties. Even though Congress may regulate the use of nuclear weapons, it must be careful in so doing to avoid methods that invade the province of the executive branch or which otherwise may violate certain structural limitations found in the Constitution. A middle ground approach, which I believe the committee proposal is, must be carefully defined to avoid those pitfalls.

Apropos of this, the proposal may be objected to on grounds that it invades the province of the commander in chief by impinging on his authority to conduct war. It is clear that the commander in chief possesses the specific authority to conduct war once declared and to conduct military operations in any emergency amounting to a sudden attack.

Nevertheless, a blanket prohibition on the first use of nuclear weapons is constitutionally unobjectionable. Although the prohibition does affect the commander in chief's ability to engage in military activities by refusing to grant him plenary power over a particular weapon system, it does not invade the President's constitutional prerogative to conduct war within the confines of the military apparatus created by Congress. Such a prohibition is no more intrusive upon that domain than limitations on the number of troops, restrictions on the size of the Navy, or refusals to approve a new line of jet fighters, all of which are decisions plainly within the congressional policy-making prerogative.[69] Constitutionally the prohibition on first use stands on the same footing as these examples.

On the other hand, one can conceive of congressional regulations on the use of weapons, both nuclear and non-nuclear, that would transgress the commander in chief's constitutional authority to conduct war. The distinction between what is permissible and what is not lies in the difference between the creation of policy and the actual execution of that policy. While there may be examples in which the distinction is amorphous, some guidance can be gleaned from more obvious cases. For example, Congress would overstep the boundaries that separate the legislative from the executive were it to require the commander in chief to seek congressional approval or committee approval of daily war plans, or more particularly, of daily weapons usage. This is precisely the type of situation the commander in chief clause was designed to prevent. Congress, under the example given, is not defining policy, but is administering the operations that implement policy. The President would be correct in challenging such an invasion. Thus, if the proposed congressional committee has the power to review or approve tactics in the context of ongoing military operations, it treads upon the executive prerogative to conduct the operations of war.

On the other hand, if the role of the committee is to act as a surrogate of Congress in the determination of policy questions, the likelihood of interference with the constitutional prerogatives of the President is diminished, if not eliminated completely. My understanding of the proposal is that the committee's function is limited to the latter; namely, the committee may determine the policy of Congress with respect to the first use of nuclear weapons. If that policy decision permits a first use, the President, as commander in chief, may then determine whether such a use is an appropriate military response. In other words, the committee grants the President the flexibility to exercise the option of first use.

If the above understanding is correct, it would seem that the device of committee approval of first use would not violate the separation of powers. Surely just as Congress is free to ban first use of nuclear weapons, Congress could pass legislation rescinding such a ban. The committee does no more. It exercises a plainly legislative function in rescinding a ban on first use. From the perspective of the President's constitutional authority to conduct war, whether the committee or Congress as a whole exercises the approval function is a constitutional irrelevancy.[70] In neither case is the province of the executive branch invaded.

B. The Delegation Problem

This characterization of the committee's authority should insulate the proposal from a separation of powers challenge. It does, however, give rise to a second potential objection.[71] In permitting a committee to exercise the authority to rescind a ban on first use, Congress may have improperly delegated its institutional responsibility to legislate in the war making context. Certainly, the committee is given the authority to determine the nation's policy with respect to the first use of nuclear weapons. This is usually a job for Congress. Moreover, a presidential request for first use would likely arise only under circumstances of an imminent or ongoing military conflict. Considering the strategic effect of using even a tactical nuclear weapon, approval of a request for first use might be tantamount to a declaration of war,[72] which the Constitution carefully vests in the Congress as a whole.[73] As a consequence, this excessive delegation objection is not frivolous.

The argument that the entire Congress must participate in the creation of policy is not easily refuted.[74] However, when one considers the power to declare war in the context of modern technology and a potential instantaneous nuclear exchange, the opportunity to proceed in the traditional manner is evanescent at best. Split-second timing and secrecy may be of the essence. Because of these factors, the President, at the grace of Congress, now has the practical authority to use nuclear weapons in any manner he deems consistent with his power as commander in chief. While this state of affairs may satisfy the very limited legalistic norms of nondelegation in the foreign affairs context, it does strain severely congressional responsibility over the war powers. Certainly it does nothing to advance the constitutional virtue of full consideration by both houses of Congress on the question of war. There would seem to be good constitutional sense to the notion that Congress should be free to create an option that falls somewhere between this current negation of responsibility and an unrealistic insistence that Congress as a whole answer the first use question in the context of an ongoing conflict. The proposal may present that option.

The necessary and proper clause states, "Congress shall have the power . . . [t]o make all Laws which shall be necessary and proper for carrying into Execution the foregoing Powers . . . "[75] One of those "foregoing Powers" is the power to declare war. If the development of nuclear technology has advanced to a point where the power to declare war cannot be effectively exercised in the historical fashion, the necessary and proper clause would seem to provide ample authority to Congress to devise some reasonable method for exercising that power. Such flexibility has long been an accepted part of constitutional jurisprudence.

In *McCulloch v. Maryland*,[76] Chief Justice John Marshall observed:

But it may with great reason be contended, that a government, entrusted with such ample powers, on the due execution of which the happiness and prosperity of the nation so vitally depends, must also be entrusted with ample means for their execution. The power being given, it is the interest of the nation to facilitate its execution. It can never be their interest, and cannot be presumed to have been their intention, to clog and embarrass its execution by withholding the most appropriate means.[77]

In applying and explaining this principle, Chief Justice Marshall stated that Congress was free to "exercise its best judgment in the selection of measures, to carry into execution the constitutional powers of the government," and to "avail itself of experience, to exercise its reason, and to accommodate its legislation to circumstances."[78] Of course, the accommodations must be consistent with the general structure and limitations of the Constitution. But the structure of the Constitution need not be interpreted as a straitjacket.

With this interpretation of the necessary and proper clause in mind, adoption of the committee proposal appears to be well within the bounds of constitutional reason and structure. It provides a limited but workable method through which Congress may exercise its constitutional responsibility over potential nuclear war while at the same time not completely disarming the nation in the face of unforeseen circumstances. The Framers adopted a structure of government based on the presumption that Congress would retain authority over the war making decision; legislation adopted by Congress that tends to advance that aim, especially when perfect realization of the Framers' goal is impossible, can hardly be said to be beyond the pale of the necessary and proper clause.

It should also be made clear that the role of the committee extends beyond the approval or denial of the first use option. The committee will exercise an oversight function on matters that may affect the potential use of nuclear weapons. Fulfillment of this function will further preserve the congressional prerogative by informing Congress of the need to adopt specific measures to ensure that the nation retains effective military options other than the nuclear one. Thus, while the proposal does create a narrow exception to the traditional legislative process, it also reaffirms the importance of that process.[79]

I would add the following gloss to the proposal. The committee should not be empowered to approve first use unless it finds that Congress as a whole is unavailable to decide on the first use question, either because of the short notice upon which the decision must be made or because of an overriding need for absolute secrecy due to an immediate military crisis. Such a gloss limits the authority of the committee to the narrow purpose for which it was created—to act as a surrogate for Congress under circumstances in which the national security prevents Congress from addressing a question requiring an immediate response.

Finally, the committee is not merely a convenient, "useful 'political invention,' " which the Court held insufficient to ignore constitutional limitations in *Chadha*.[80] The committee is essential to ensure that constitutional structure be honored to the fullest extent possible. Rather than rearranging the relative roles of each branch, it preserves them.[81] Without the committee, the congressional responsibility goes to the President by default. An otherwise legitimate objection to alterations based on convenience should not be used to prevent a narrow modification based on stark necessity.

"To employ means necessary to an end, is generally understood as employing any means calculated to produce the end, and not as being confined to those single means, without which the end would be entirely unattainable."[82] If Congress deems creation of this committee vital to the exercise of one of its most important functions, nothing in the Constitution should prevent its implementation.

IV. CONCLUSION

If Congress can, consistent with the Constitution, conclude that the decision on first use should be delegated to the President, there should be no constitutional basis for claiming that a similar delegation to its own committee is somehow excessive. Certainly the delegation to the President undermines the bicameralism requirement to a greater extent than committee approval. In any event, the necessary and proper clause gives Congress the authority to make the choice between these two constitutional alternatives.

NOTES

1. *See* Stone, *supra* Ch. 1.

2. U.S. Const. art. I, § 1.

3. McCulloch v. Maryland, 17 U.S. (4 Wheat.) 316 (1819); U.S. Const., art. I, § 8, cl. 18 (providing Congress with the power, "To make all Laws which shall be necessary and proper for carrying into Execution the foregoing Powers, and all other Powers vested by this Constitution in the Government of the United States, or in any Department or Officer thereof").

4. United States v. Klein, 80 U.S. (13 Wall.) 128 (1871); Myers v. United States, 272 U.S. 52 (1926); Buckley v. Valeo, 424 U.S. 1 (1976).

5. U.S. Const., art. II, § 1; art. III, § 2.

6. U.S. Const., art. I, § 7; Immigration and Naturalization Service v. Chadha, 462 U.S. 919 (1983).

7. *See generally* D. Keir, *The Constitutional History of Modern Britain: 1485–1951* (8th ed. 1966); W. Stubbs, *The Constitutional History of England* (1979); E. Wade & A. Bradley, *Constitutional Law* (7th ed. 1965).

8. *See* A. Koch, *Power, Morals, and the Founding Fathers: Essays in the Interpretation of the American Enlightenment* 103–21 (1961).

9. *See* G. Wood, *The Creation of the American Republic* 105–73 (1969) (hereinafter cited as "Wood").

10. *The Federalist No. 51*, at 350 (J. Madison) (J. Cooke ed. 1961).

11. Wood, *supra* note 9, at 162.

12. The Constitution does vest the President with a few narrowly drawn independent powers. Article II, section 2 grants the President the authority to "require the Opinion, in writing, of the principal officer in each of the Executive Departments, upon any Subject relating to the Duties of their respective offices," and "the Power to grant Reprieves and Pardons." The former involves the internal operations of the executive branch; the latter was considered at the time of the adoption of the Constitution to be a quintessential executive prerogative. *See* Schick v. Reed, 419 U.S. 256 (1974); Grupp, *Some Historical Aspects of the Pardon in England*, 7 Am.J.Legal History 51, 55 (1963). Article II, section 3 imposes the duty upon the President to "receive Ambassadors and other public Ministers." This ministerial function (*see* L. Henkin, *Foreign Affairs and the Constitution*

41 & n.* (1972) has been suggested as an independent authority to recognize foreign sovereigns. But neither the language of the Constitution nor the ratification debates (*see The Federalist Papers No. 69*, at 468 (A. Hamilton) (J. Cooke, ed. 1961)) support that conclusion. Moreover, the Supreme Court has never resolved a conflict between Congress and the President on this issue. *Cf.* Goldwater v. Carter, 444 U.S. 996 (1979); United States v. Pink, 315 U.S. 203 (1942); United States v. Belmont, 301 U.S. 324 (1936). Finally, the President has the power to remove officers of the executive branch. Myers v. United States, 272 U.S. 52 (1926). *But see* Humphrey's Executor v. United States, 295 U.S. 602, 625 (1935) (no power to remove officers of independent regulatory agency).

13. For example, while the current embargo imposed upon trade with Nicaragua was instigated by the executive branch, the legitimacy of the embargo derives from specific statutory delegations of authority from Congress. Executive Order 12513, May 1, 1985, 21 *Weekly Compilation of Presidential Documents* 566 (1985).

14. 343 U.S. 579 (1952).

15. *Id.* at 582.

16. *Id.* A number of commentators have assumed that *Youngstown* is a domestic separation of powers case, implying that some other structure of separation may apply in the foreign policy context. However, the Supreme Court expressly relied upon *Youngstown* in *Dames & Moore v. Regan*, 453 U.S. 654 (1981), which quite plainly involved separation of powers in the field of foreign affairs. In addition, nothing in the text of the Constitution indicates that the separation of powers would take on a different meaning in the foreign policy context. Article I, section 8 grants Congress the power to regulate interstate commerce as well as the power to regulate commerce with foreign nations. The President's independent powers over foreign commerce are no more extensive than the President's independent powers over interstate commerce. Both derive from the President's power to administer the laws passed by Congress.

17. *Youngstown*, 343 U.S. at 587.

18. *Id.*

19. *Id.* at 588.

20. *Id.* at 589.

21. *Id.* at 635–36 (Jackson, J., concurring).

22. *See supra* note 12.

23. *The Federalist Papers No. 47*, at 325 (J. Cooke, ed. 1961).

24. *Youngstown*, 343 U.S. at 638.

25. 343 U.S. at 637 (emphasis added).

26. *Id.* at 654.

27. 453 U.S. 654 (1981).

28. *Id.* at 676.

29. *Id.* at 677.

30. *Id.* at 686.

31. *Id.* at 680.

32. Both the power to pardon and the power to remove executive officers have been defined as exclusively presidential. Myers v. United States, 272 U.S. 52 (1926) (power to remove); United States v. Klein, 80 U.S. (13 Wall.) 128 (1871) (power to pardon). *See supra* note 12. Thus, Congress may not legislatively limit the exercise of those powers.

33. U.S. Const. art. I, § 8, cls. 12–16.

34. For a discussion of this phenomena, *see* Ides, *Congress, Constitutional Respon-*

sibility and the War Power, 17 Loy. L.A.L. Rev. 599, 616–42 (1984) (hereinafter cited as *Constitutional Responsibility*).

35. *Powell v. McCormack*, 395 U.S. 486 (1969), involved a challenge to the exclusion of a member of Congress. In determining that this member's right to be seated had been violated, the Supreme Court refused to give constitutional credence to prior exclusions that had been based on similar factors. "The relevancy of prior exclusion cases is limited largely to the insight they afford in correctly ascertaining the draftsmen's intent. Obviously, therefore, the precedential value of these cases tends to increase in proportion to their proximity to the Convention in 1787." *Id.* at 547. In a similar vein, the Court stated "[t]hat an unconstitutional action has been taken before surely does not render that same action any less unconstitutional at a later date." *Id.* at 546–47. Similarly, in *United States v. Midwest Oil Co.*, 236 U.S. 459 (1915), the Court strongly suggested that although a presidential pattern of practice had been acquiesced in sufficiently long to give rise to an implied grant of authority, an express rejection or "dissaffirmance" of that authority by Congress would rescind the implied grant. *Id.* at 471, 474–75, 479–83. *Dames & Moore v. Regan*, 453 U.S. 654 (1981), is to the same effect.

36. *The Federalist No. 24*, at 153 (A. Hamilton) (J. Cooke ed. 1961).

37. In *The Federalist No. 26*, Hamilton stated:

The legislature of the United States will be *obliged* by this provision, once at least in every two years, to deliberate upon the propriety of keeping a military force on foot; to come to a new resolution on the point; and to declare their sense of the matter, by a formal vote in the face of their constituents. They are not *at liberty* to vest in the executive department permanent funds for the support of an army; if they were even incautious enough to be willing to repose in it so improper a confidence.

Id. at 168. *See also* 2 M. Farrand, *The Records of the Federal Convention of 1787* 326–27, 330 (1966) (hereinafter cited as *Farrand*).

38. *The Federalist No. 26*, at 169 (A. Hamilton) (J. Cooke ed. 1961).

39. Articles of Confederation art. IX.

40. *See, e.g.*, 1 J. Marshall, *Marshall's Life of Washington* 214 (2d ed.); J.T. Flexner, *George Washington, In the American Revolution* 90–97, 487–88, 547–48 (1967); Henkin, *supra* note 12, at 33, 50.

41. Art. II, § 2 provides: "The President shall be Commander in Chief of the Army and Navy of the United States, and of the Militia of the several States, when called into the actual Service of the United States . . . "

42. *The Federalist No. 74*, at 500 (J. Cooke ed. 1961).

43. A. Schlesinger, Jr., *The Imperial Presidency* 6 (1973). *See also* Henkin, *supra* note 12, at 50 ("There is little evidence that the Framers intended more than to establish in the President civilian command of the forces for wars declared by Congress (or when the United States was attacked) . . . ").

44. *The Federalist No. 69*, at 456 (J. Cooke ed. 1961).

45. Farrand, *supra* note 37, at 318–19 ("Mr. Madison and Mr. Gerry moved to insert '*declare*,' striking out '*make*' war; leaving to the Executive the power to repel sudden attacks.").

46. One must be careful not to impose a rigid, legalistic interpretation on the phrase "repel sudden attacks." In the first place, the wording is Madison's, not the Convention's. It expresses his sense, apparently shared by others, that the President would be free to take some limited emergency military action in the absence of specific authorization by

Congress. Moreover, a rigid interpretation of the phrase would seem quite inconsistent with the intent of the Framers to grant the President some flexibility in emergency situations when Congress was not available to consider the appropriate military response. The phrase "repel sudden attacks" is instructive in that it underscores the limited scope of both the power and the appropriate presidential response as perceived by one of the most respected and influential members of the Convention.

47. *See* Bickel, *Congress, the President, and the Power to Wage War*, 48 Chi.-Kent L. Rev. 131, 132 (1972).

48. Farrand, *supra* note 37, at 318.

49. *Id.*

50. *Id.* at 319. *See also id.* (statement of Mr. Elsworth).

51. *See, e.g.*, Wallace, *The War-Making Powers: A Constitutional Flaw?*, 57 Cornell L. Rev. 719, 741–44 (1972).

52. *See Constitutional Responsibility*, *supra* note 34, at 616–20.

53. Henkin, *supra* note 12, at 100–101.

54. *See* 1 Stat. 9, 29th Cong., 1st Sess. (May 13, 1846) (An Act providing for the Prosecution of the Existing War between the United States and the Republic of Mexico); 1 Stat. 17, 29th Cong., 1st Sess. (1846) (Supplemental Act). Indeed, a member of Congress who took President Polk at his word might easily have concluded that United States troops had been subjected to unjustified aggression by the Mexican military forces. *See* H. S. Commager, *Documents of American History 310–11* (Polk's Message on War with Mexico, May 11, 1846) (1963).

55. *See, e.g.*, General Appropriation Act, 1951, Pub. L. No. 81–759, Chap. X (1950); Department of Defense Appropriation Act, 1952, Pub. L. No. 82–179 (1951); Department of Defense Appropriation Act, 1953, Pub. L. No. 82–488 (1952); Mutual Security Act of 1951, Pub. L. No. 82–165, § 301 (1951); Mutual Security Act of 1953, Pub. L. No. 83–118 (1953); Mutual Security Act of 1954, Pub. L. No. 83–665, § 132 (1955). *See also* Henkin, *supra* note 12, at 89–123, 107 n.43; *Constitutional Responsibility*, *supra* note 34, at 624–31.

56. Henkin, *supra* note 12, at 101–02.

57. Dames & Moore v. Regan, 453 U.S. 654 (1981); United States v. Midwest Oil Co., 236 U.S. 459 (1915).

58. *See supra* text accompanying notes 26–31; United States v. Midwest Oil Co., 236 U.S. 459 (1915).

59. Henkin, *supra* note 12, at 103.

60. For example, the Defense Department Authorization Act, 1985, Pub. L. No. 98–525, 98 Stat. 2492 (1984), places limitations on the procurement, research, development, testing and evaluation of weapons and weapon systems. *See* §§ 101–113, 201–207. One specific limitation is found in section 110 which limits the number of operational MX missiles that may be purchased by the executive branch. Another is found in section 111 which states, "None of the funds appropriated pursuant to authorizations of appropriations in this title may be used for procurement of binary chemical munitions, including advanced procurement of long-lead components or for the establishment of a production base for such munitions." Still another occurs in section 205 which defines the policy governing the testing of anti-satellite warheads.

61. *See, e.g.*, *Cong. Q.* 2241–46 (November 14, 1981); *id.* at 1155–59 (May 15, 1982); *id.* at 3107–10 (December 25, 1982); *id.* at 2513–16 (November 26, 1983); *id.* at 2361–65 (September 29, 1984); *id.* at 2441–45 (October 6, 1984); *id.* at 2628–32

(October 13, 1984); *id.* at 2733–36 (October 20, 1984); *id.* at 3145 (December 22, 1984); *id.* at 1798–99 (September 14, 1985).

62. *See supra* note 60.

63. *Cf.* United States v. Midwest Oil Co., 236 U.S. 459 (1915) ("It is only necessary to point out that, as the greater includes the less, the power to make permanent reservations includes power to make temporary withdrawals.").

64. *See, e.g.*, The Department of Defense Authorization Act, 1984, Pub. L. No. 98–94, 97 Stat. 614, § 206 (1983) (prohibition on research and development of small mobile missile); The Department of Defense Authorization Act, 1985, § 205 (1984) (limitation on testing of anti-satellite warheads); 50 U.S.C. § 1520 (1982) (limitation on use of human subjects for testing of chemical or biological agents by Department of Defense).

65. 50 U.S.C. §§ 1511–1520 (1982).

66. Pub. L. No. 98–525, 98 Stat. 2492 (October 19, 1984).

67. It has been suggested that Congress' power to regulate the use of chemical weapons may be more extensive than its power to regulate the use of nuclear weapons. The theory is that since chemical weapons are made unlawful by treaty, Congress may enforce the treaty by appropriate legislation. *See infra* Ch. 7 Part III (comments of Professor John Norton Moore). There is no treaty counterpart for nuclear weapons. Therefore, according to the argument, Congress may not be free to regulate the use of nuclear weapons. However, if the constitutional argument against the regulation of nuclear weapons is based upon a perceived invasion of the President's constituional prerogative, Professor Moore's theory must be wrong. There is no doctrine of alteration of constitutional structure by treaty. *Cf.* Reid v. Covert, 354 U.S. 1 (1957). Certainly a pure act of legislation which derives from specific grants of authority in Article I, section 8, is deserving of the same constitutional respect that legislation enforcing a treaty would be afforded. If Congress may regulate and limit the procurement and use of chemical weapons, it may do the same with respect to nuclear weapons regardless of whether that legislation is attached to a treaty.

68. *See* United States v. Curtiss-Wright Export Corp., 299 U.S. 304 (1936).

69. *See supra* notes 59–61 and accompanying text.

70. From a policy perspective, placing the approval power in a committee actually enhances presidential flexibility and power since the committee can meet in secret and vest the President with first use capability without announcing the new policy to the enemy.

71. An additional set of objections to the proposal derives from the characterization of committee approval as a legislative veto, void under a mechanical reading of *Immigration and Naturalization Service v. Chadha*, 462 U.S. 919 (1983). These objections are explored elsewhere in this collection. *See infra* Part III of this book.

72. Stone, *supra* Ch. 1, at text preceding note 10.

73. As James Madison observed at the Federal Convention:

Despotism comes on mankind in different shapes. Sometimes in an Executive, sometimes in a military, one. Is there danger of a Legislative despotism? Theory & practice both proclaim it. If the Legislative authority be not restrained, there can be neither liberty nor stability; and it can only be restrained by dividing it within itself, into distinct and independent branches. In a single house there is no check, but the inadequate one, of the virtue & good sense of those who compose it.

1 Farrand, *supra* note 37, at 254 (remarks of James Wilson). *See also The Federalist Nos. 22 & 51* (J. Cooke ed. 1961).

74. *See, e.g.*, Immigration and Naturalization Service v. Chadha, 461 U.S. 919, 944–59 (1983).

75. U.S. Const. art. I. § 8, cl. 18.

76. 17 U.S. (4 Wheat.) 316 (1819).

77. *Id.* at 408.

78. *Id.* at 415–16, 420.

79. Although not a perfect analogy, the Select Committee on Intelligence of the United States Senate operates in a similar fashion. *See* Senate Resolution 400, 94th Cong., 2d Sess. (1976); Miller, *Infra* Ch. 12. Among other things, the purpose of that committee is "to provide vigilant legislative oversight over the intelligence activities of the United States to assure that such activities are in conformity with the Constitution and laws of the United States." However, while 50 U.S.C. § 413(a)(1) (1982), requires the President to keep both the Senate Select Committee on Intelligence and the Permanent Select Committee on Intelligence of the House "fully and currently informed" on new and ongoing intelligence activities, fulfillment of this duty is not a condition precedent to the initiation of intelligence activity. *Id.* By contrast, the device of committee approval proposed by the FAS would operate as a condition precedent to presidential action. This distinction is justifiable since upon notification of an intention to use nuclear weapons the committee would not likely have the luxury of reporting to Congress on the need for an appropriate legislative response.

80. 462 U.S. 919, 945, 959 (1983).

81. *Id.* at 953–54 n.16.

82. *McCulloch*, 17 U.S. (4 Wheat.) at 413–14.

7

Debate: Allocating Nuclear War Powers Under the Constitution

In the following excerpts from a panel discussion of "Allocating Nuclear War Powers Under The Constitution," the contributors and the editor are joined by Paul Warnke, lawyer and former Director of the United States Arms Control and Disarmament Agency, chief negotiator at the SALT talks (1977–78), and Assistant Secretary of Defense; Professor Arthur L. Berney of Boston College Law School; William Miller, President of the American Committee on U.S.-Soviet Relations and former Chief of Staff to the Senate Select Committee on Intelligence; Raymond Celada of the Congressional Research Service, Library of Congress; and Robert L. Turner, President of the United States Institute for Peace and former Acting Assistant Secretary of State.

I. WHAT WAR IS AUTHORIZED BY A CONVENTIONAL ATTACK ON NATO?

MR. RAVEN-HANSEN: Professor Moore, you argue that the President's command authority pursuant to constitutionally authorized war cannot be restricted by Congress. It seems to me that begs the question of which constitutionally authorized war he is fighting. You yourself have said of the Indochina war, assuming it was constitutionally authorized, that the President was not authorized to order the bombing of Beijing.

I would like to know whether it is your contention that a first use of nuclear weapons during conventional war in Europe is distinguishable from an attack on Beijing during the Indochina war. To put it differently, which war is authorized by Congress in the case of conventional attack on the NATO nations?

MR. MOORE: We have to look at a number of the elements in the setting. There has been constitutionally an attack on the United States forces. Secondly, under the NATO treaty, quite apart from any question of what it authorizes, the NATO treaty by law, with Congress participating, said that an attack on the NATO area would be an attack on the United States of America.

Now those are features that are part of the context that have to be taken into account in a massive conventional attack against Europe. I think we also have to take into account that we are dealing with a setting—when we talk about a first use of nuclear weapons—that would only be an extraordinary *in extremis* situation in which the choice to the United States is the loss of the democracies of Western Europe. That is an enormous cost to the United States. That is the reason, despite the enormous uncertainties and dangers of use of nuclear weapons, that NATO has wanted the potential, at least for deterrence, of being able to say that the United States may use nuclear weapons. That is why it has not ruled out the question of the use of a U.S. strategic strike, as opposed to a battlefield nuclear weapon or an intermediate nuclear weapon.

So my answer is there is nothing in the Constitution, given a central front NATO attack, that says the President of the United States may not respond with some of the United States' strategic forces, as well as a Pershing II, for example, or as well as a battlefield nuclear weapon.

Now let me go to the question of the area restriction—the notion of the President having a nuclear strike capability against Beijing as part of the Vietnam War. The answer why that clearly was not under the authority of the President is that the United States was not at war with Beijing. Beijing had not attacked the United States.

The second setting is one that deals with the use of chemical weapons and dum-dum bullets. Frankly this is an area where there are good, fair counterarguments to some of the doubts that I have been presenting of the scope of the Congress' power to limit the commander in chief power. But there is a difference, though I am not sure that it is decisive. I myself have argued that Congress has had the power to limit in that area. The difference is that, in this area, we are talking about weapons that are internationally agreed as illegal. The President is restricted from using these weapons, or required to use the weapons in a particular way, because the United States concludes that it is the international law view of the United States Government that these are international legal obligations by treaty or otherwise. A chemical no first use ban falls into that and the dum-dum bullets do, and the others do.

Now I don't say that that is the necessary total answer. I am not saying, on this occasion, that I think it is absolutely certain Congress has no power to interfere in that second hypothetical. I am saying there are a variety of very fundamental doubts. I do not regard these particular examples as necessarily resolving those doubts.

MR. GLENNON: Is it your position, Professor Moore, that the NATO Treaty, taken in and of itself, would authorize the President to use nuclear weapons?

MR. MOORE: No. There is no need for the NATO Treaty to authorize any use of nuclear weapons or initiation of coercion. In the setting of an attack on

NATO involving U.S. forces I see no question whatsoever that the President has the authority to conduct hostilities, including the use of nuclear weapons, unless Congress has in fact acted in some fashion to tell the President that he cannot do certain things—and, another large "if," if those congressional actions are constitutional.

II. THE LIMITS OF A POWER TO REPEL ATTACK

MR. RAVEN-HANSEN: One argument that I think I heard Professor Moore make is that when the Russians have attacked in a conventional scenario in Europe, we are in a state of de facto war and we don't need the NATO Treaty to authorize the President to respond because he has the "repel the attack" authority that most of us would concede from reading the Framers' history. The question is what is the scope of the repel the attack authority? The "repel" gives the sense of a defensive measure, so one argument is that it's strictly whatever you need to defend against immediate attack.

Secondly, one could argue that, given the structure of the Constitution, the limit to "repel the attack" is that the President can only do what's necessary to preserve the status quo until Congress can convene. There is other language in the Constitution that suggests this same model of decision making. For example, there is a provision about the state legislatures which states that the executives of state legislatures can call out the militia if the legislatures do not have time to meet and, basically, that the executive can act only until the legislature does have time to meet.

A third way to look at the "repel the attack" power is to look at other provisions in the Constitution for congressional support of a war. The "repel the attack" right is clearly limited in duration because ultimately the attack is starved unless Congress raises and supports armies and appropriates monies to keep them in the field. This was particularly true at the framing of the Constitution, when there was no serious military stockpile and no large standing army, and it took a long time to reach the area of hostility. No unilateral presidential initiative, even of a defensive sort, could long continue without further authorization from Congress. Maybe there is a durational limit to "repel the attack."

The question is which of those limits, if any, is there to the "repel the attack" power?

MR. MOORE: Once you ask the question of the scope of the President's commander in chief power, absent any congressional limitation on that power, I think the answer is reasonably simple. That is that he can use the minimum force necessary to achieve effective defense. The purpose of the commander in chief power is to enable the President of the United States to defend against attack.

If there were simply the occasion of some tiny attack not involving either NATO and the Warsaw Pact, or central issues in Europe, and the President simply decided to use the occasion of some very minor attack to use nuclear weapons or wage a conventional attack, obviously that would be a gross distortion of the commander in chief power.

It really is a matter of using force necessary to achieve effective defense. I do not see any area limitation written into the Constitution, and I don't see any nuclear weapons threshold or other weapons threshold automatically written into the Constitution. Remember, the only time this issue realistically arises—and any other setting is just simply not there in the real world—is a case in which there is a massive conventional attack against NATO which the West as a whole has reason to believe it is not going to be able to stop. And the stake for the West as a whole is, "Do we accept the loss of all of Europe and its democracies?"

And that setting is the only one in which you would seriously talk about some kind of use of nuclear weapons in this setting. Whatever the fringe cases are, it is a paradigm setting. Under the Constitution, absent Congress trying to intervene and saying you can't do it, the President does have the authority as commander in chief to make the decision in that setting.

III. ANTECEDENT LIMITS ON THE COMMANDER IN CHIEF

MR. IDES: In my paper I suggest that the President's power to repel sudden attacks is essentially to preserve the status quo so that Congress will be free to exercise its larger authority to determine whether we ought to proceed with a full-scale war. But I think this "repel sudden attacks" question is not at issue here. It's "repel sudden attacks" within the confines of the weapons and the military policy granted to the President by Congress, and it seems to me Professor Moore concedes that.

The question is not how broad is the power to repel sudden attacks in a vacuum, but how and to what extent can Congress narrow it by saying you cannot use certain weapons when you are attacked by conventional weapons?

MR. RAVEN-HANSEN: As I understood Professor Moore, he suggested that Congress has the power to prohibit the use of dum-dum weapons, or chemical weapons, because international law is the backup. That suggests that Congress has less power to fetter the commander in chief than does international law. Are you suggesting that the President is bound in his choice of weapons by international law but that Congress cannot, absent the backup of international law, similarly bind him?

MR. MOORE: Part of the answer to that is that Congress is given certain additional power in the international law area. I don't regard it as decisive, but Congress does have the power to punish offenses against the law of nations, for example, and presumably an illegal use of weapons is an offense against the law of nations. If Congress can punish an offense against the law of nations, it seems fairly reasonable under that power they do have the ability to limit the commander in chief power.

I don't regard that issue as necessarily a decisive one in favor of the other side. I admit that it is an issue that somewhat cuts on that side of the equation. I continue to regard this issue constitutionally as unclear. I have cited a whole set of scholars and Supreme Court language that have taken the position that that is unclear.

So far the only argument that I have heard collectively as to why Congress has the power to pass the legislation under discussion—and it may, I am not sure on this point—but the only argument that I have heard on the merits is the argument that because Congress can prevent the President from having an army altogether, or prevent the President from having nuclear weapons altogether, it can conditionally create limitations on uses of the forces. Well, that is the classic *petitio principii* logical fallacy of begging the question. Precisely the issue before us is whether those questions are different. That is precisely the one that in *Ex Parte Milligan* Chief Justice Chase said was different, and it is certainly something that proves too much if we were to use that as a general basis of power.

Let me just give you an example. Congress, of course, has the power to prevent the creation of armies. So can it simply pass a law establishing a committee which said that henceforth all of the individual tactical judgments and determinations, or at least the major tactical judgments and determinations—as to whether we're going to attack Pork Chop Hill or whether we're going to evacuate Khe Son—will be made by a congressional committee? Now if Congress, solely as a matter of having the authority not to provide an army or weapons to fight, can do that, then it can solely, on that basis, decide in the absolute core areas, where I think there would be no debate that Congress can't act.

So the only argument that's been advanced so far to define the congressional power is one that I regard as not resolving the issue one way or the other.

MR. IDES: I'm glad we're finally getting to what I think is the issue here. The constitutional provisions I would rely upon are all the provisions in Article I giving Congress the power to raise and support an army, navy, govern and so forth. The simple question I would like to ask Professor Moore is could Congress refuse to fund the MX missile? And I think the answer is quite clearly yes.

My next question is could Congress appropriate funds for the MX missile, but say we're just going to stockpile it and you can't use it? I think if I know his response to that then I think we can start talking about what the constitutional issues are here.

MR. MOORE: I think that does raise exactly the same issue that is posed by the question of area restrictions. I don't know the answer to that, just as I have said I don't know the answer to the generic issue.

But I would say there are a variety of substantial doubts. If Congress provides a particular weapons system, then it seems to me there is a significant doubt as to whether it has the constitutional power to place constraints on the use of it in other than settings where it's illegal. Now again I'm not saying that I know the answer as to what the Court would do on that. I think the other cases are clear.

MR. IDES: Maybe there is no right and wrong answer and, if that's the case, then it is up to Congress to make the political judgment of whether it will do it or not. Maybe this is a classically political question. And if that's the case then I think yes, we can raise doubts on both sides of the issue. Then it is up to individual Members of Congress to determine whether they are fulfilling their constitutional obligations in voting for the measure.

You have said that there are substantial doubts about this. But frankly I'm completely confused as to what those doubts are. Congress could stockpile a weapon, in exercise of their powers under Article I, coupled with the very potent "necessary and proper" clause. It could say it wants to stockpile the weapon because it thinks it is sufficiently important that it be available, should it determine that it ever wanted to give the President power to use it, because it knows it will take ten years to put together the stockpile and wants it ready. I would be astounded if the Court, or a substantial number of commentators, would say that Congress couldn't do that.

MR. RAVEN-HANSEN: And if Congress has stockpiled the weapons with the intent that the President can use it, why can't it change its mind? Suppose it says we changed our mind about the stockpile; now we don't want you to use it.

MR. WARNKE: Is there any doubt that a President of the United States would be bound by a treaty that banned first use of nuclear weapons, assuming, of course, that the United States were a signatory to the treaty? Second, if in fact the President would be bound, is there any doubt that Congress could enact legislation implementing that treaty by placing restrictions on the sole discretion of the President to use nuclear weapons? And then, third, if the treaty would be valid, and if Congress could pass implementing legislation, is it somehow less the law of the land if the Congress on its own initiative passes legislation saying that the President may not indulge in the first use of nuclear weapons? Is it different somehow for chemical weapons? I mean, we store chemical weapons for deterrent purposes, even though we are bound not to use them first—and really the only issue we face now is whether we should modernize that deterrent by going to some sort of binary form.

MR. MOORE: I think the answer to the first part, Mr. Warnke, is no. Certainly we could have a treaty that would be binding on the President on no first use of any particular weapon system. Secondly, of course, Congress can enter into a law that would implement that treaty within the United States. Thirdly, yes, there may be a distinction between that case and the setting where Congress simply on its own says to do that.

And that is precisely the point that I have been making all along. In the international law setting, the treaty is an international law issue. That is like the no first use of chemical weapons. That does fall under the specific additional area where Congress is given specific power under the Constitution of the United States relating to the law of nations.

Again, I am not arguing that the solution in all of these cases is that Congress doesn't have the power. I am simply saying, even on this starting point proposition, there is a great deal of doubt. I certainly believe those two cases continue to present the doubt and that question is really a variant of exactly a point that has come up in a number of other contexts.

MR. BERNEY: My answer is clearly yes to all three of Mr. Warnke's questions. If Congress passes such a law the President has the power to veto it. If he vetoes it, and it is overridden, he has expended his constitutional power. And if then that law becomes law under the Constitution, he is bound by it and has been involved in it.

MR. GLENNON: Who seriously can doubt that the Geneva Protocol of 1925, which bans the use of chemical and biological weapons, is constitutional? Why is the ban on the use of chemical and biological weapons any different from a treaty which would ban a first use of nuclear weapons? I don't see the distinction.

MR. IDES: As I understand Professor Moore's potential objections to the stockpiling with limitations, they are structural objections that the Congress would be somehow invading the province of the presidency. I think his answer to the questions put by Mr. Warnke essentially proves the case in favor of the constitutionality. Because it would be astounding if a treaty could alter the structure of our government, whereas a statute passed by Congress, either with the President's signature or over his veto, could not. If a treaty could do it, *a fortiori*, the structure of our government could be tampered with—if you will—under the "necessary and proper" clause by Congress. So his doubts, which he still hasn't explained, and I don't know what they are, must have vitiated in the course of answering this question on the treaty.

MR. MOORE: It is not a matter of a treaty being able to alter the Constitution in any particular setting. Of course it can't do that. *Reid v. Covert* tells us that that cannot be done constitutionally. The point that makes the example different is that it is an area that Congress has greater ability over, or at least reasonably clear ability to enact legislation. That is, there is a specific grant of power in the Constitution to deal with a setting relating to international law and offenses against the law of nations. So it is not a matter of altering it. It comes back to the issue of what areas of power they have.

Now the second point on this. Let's assume for a moment that others believe very strongly, which is obviously the case, that in fact Congress does have the power to move forward in this particular case. We have also heard that the Congress has, in the exercise of the individual representatives' judgment in passing this legislation, a right to make its own reasonable judgments about the constitutional requirements. That is absolutely correct.

The problem on the other side is that the President also has such a duty. He is sworn to uphold the Constitution of the United States and to protect his powers under the doctrine of separation of powers. And one of the things that troubles me about the proposal, generically and specifically, to be quite frank, is that whatever the answers to these things, I rather think there is going to be a great deal of fuzziness about them. If there is a great deal of fuzziness about the answers to these things as to precisely where the line is to be drawn, then what we may be doing is fusing a constitutional crisis that would go off precisely at the time when the nation could least afford it. That is, we are really significantly lessening crisis stability.

In a particular setting, after it passed this law, the committee might decide that the weapons would not be used. The President looks at it, and in his determination says the act is unconstitutional and that, in fact, he is going to use nuclear weapons. He does. He uses one nuclear weapon. The other side then is contemplating how it is going to respond in that particular case. Suddenly it sees a constitutional crisis with every member of that committee seeking the impeachment of the President of the United States in the middle of that use. I regard that as one of the most serious problems here—even if there is a significant uncertainty in dealing with the legal issue—of the effect on crisis stability.

IV. FIRST USE: POLITICAL OR COMMAND DECISION?

DR. STONE: On this question of whether the committee should be involved in operational command decisions, Professor Moore presumes that it is clear what the factual situation is going to be: "a massive Soviet attack on all of Western Europe, and the impending loss of all the Western democracies." He makes it seem as if there really isn't any political question here—that we are talking about a scenario so well defined that it isn't even necessary for a special congressional committee to talk about it if we had one.

But his other comments reflect the true fact that there is a big spectrum possible. There are fights over Berlin. There are revolutions in which the West Germans are helping the East Germans and the Soviets cross the line only for a short distance saying, "It is true we fired on your troops, but this is not an attack on America. Don't use nuclear weapons first. We don't declare war on you and if you do use nuclear weapons we will respond in kind." The Russians would make out of any crisis a very specific political problem, one impossible to predict in its precise dimensions.

Now the President does have power to repel attacks under the Constitution. This meant, in the last century, arming ships so that they could fire back when fired upon. But it didn't mean then, and I don't think it means now, that the President has the authority to march on Paris or blockade French ports if he couldn't stop the immediate firing on our ships by French ships.

So here again I'd say the "repel the attack" power means you can let the army fire back. But if you are going to try to do something to decide the whole conflict, then it requires more than "repel the attack" rights. It requires more than saying war "exists" because our armies have been fired upon. It cries out for a rather precise discussion of what exactly has happened—of which the committee is capable if it were convened.

This is why Professor Ides is right that, in the use of nuclear weapons, there is a highly political judgment here as to whether to start a general nuclear war. Controlling this matter is not really getting into the operational chains of command, so much as it's trying to decide whether a conflict in Central Europe should be escalated to the level of general war. The first nuclear weapon used— although the President might justify it as an attack on Soviet tanks—would in fact be a gross political decision to face the Russians with the choice of either continuing the war, and going to nuclear war, or giving up on the advance.

This is such a gross choice, that I don't think anybody could maintain, it is simply a question of operational command. This is a question of the whole scope of the war. Congress is being left out of a decision to concede, compromise, or try to halt Soviet forces in the center of Germany or whether, on the other hand, to risk everything.

So I wonder, Professor Moore, if you are so sure that first use would only be used *in extremis*.

MR. MOORE: I certainly accept the point as a very critical and important point, that the essence of any decision to use nuclear weapons first is an enormously important, critical political and military decision. There is no doubt about that. I have no quarrel with it.

I don't believe, however, that that gets you to the constitutional conclusion that somehow it is a "new" war. The Constitution, as far as I can tell, simply does not draw that line. You may want to advocate a constitutional amendment to do that. I have substantial uncertainty with respect to the question of whether Congress has the power involved. That's an issue maybe you can persuade me on. I would like to hear continuing argument about that. But there are two areas where I differ very strongly and believe the constitutional issue is clear.

One of those is *Chadha*. The second is the difference between Congress dealing with a general law on the one hand, as in a no first use policy enacting that the President has no ability to order first use, which I think is the arguable constitutional issue—and the difference of moving from that setting to real time, placing the decision in the operational chain of command. This is where your point is particularly telling. Can Congress do something in this whole area that really does take account of context, in the specifics, as a check in a variety of enormously complex cases? Congress really does have difficulty with broad general policies ahead of time. It is no doubt one of the reasons Congress so far has not found no first use attractive in the nuclear area.

But if Congress is going to, in a particular case, look at precisely every option available to the President under real time battlefield conditions—as to exactly which weapons system should be used and how—it seems to me it is placing itself in the operational chain of command. There is a very substantial policy reason behind why the Framers of the Constitution of the United States didn't want Congress in the operational chain of command.

MR. IDES: I think the language Professor Moore uses about the operational chain of command is very seductive. But I think he is doing the same thing he accuses me of, begging the question. The question is, are they in the operational chain of command? For the purposes of his statement he has suggested that he would concede for the moment that Congress could ban first use of nuclear weapons. I would assume that he would say that the President would certainly be free to go to Congress in the whole, and ask Congress to rescind the ban, even though we were under attack at the time. The President might tell Congress, or a committee of Congress that would report to Congress as a whole, that the reason I need to rescind the first use ban is because I need to use these weapons for military reasons.

I am not sure how the proximity in time necessarily places what I think is a quintessentially legislative act into the chain of command. Congress is not being asked: "Should I use these weapons? How should I use these weapons? Is this the best weapon to use?" Congress is being asked: "Do you think the situation is sufficiently serious that I should have the discretion to determine whether to use these weapons?" And that is a policy judgment, and that is the kind of judgment Congress makes.

So again I think it just boils down to the real problem of asking a committee to do it.

V. AREA AND USE RESTRICTIONS AND THE APPROPRIATIONS POWER

MR. MILLER: We all recall the amendments during the Vietnam War which were aimed at area limitation. It was a conscious series of amendments of the containment type to exclude the war, initially from Thailand and Laos and certainly China, but specifically Thailand and Laos in the first instance, and then after the Cambodian incursion, from Cambodia as well, and then the process was extended to Vietnam itself conditional upon the safe withdrawal of forces. You are not maintaining that that activity was in any way unconstitutional?

MR. MOORE: That's a good question. I'm glad you're asking it as a question. First let me give a little bit of background and then a specific answer on the Cambodia resolution, and also that restricting the ability of the President to come out of Vietnam in a forced withdrawal.

MR. MILLER: I should add, before you go on, that an important element in those amendments was the particular use of force. The bombing was one aspect of it. So in a way, this is analogous to our discussions on other kinds of weapons systems.

MR. CELADA: Weren't they tied to a restriction on funds as well—no money shall be spent for?

MR. MILLER: Yes, the use of the appropriations power.

MR. MOORE: First on the general point, this question of the area restriction as opposed to the nuclear issue, which is a new one, has been debated substantially throughout American history, and one can find arguments on both sides of the equation.

I would simply point out the evidence on the other side of the equation, saying the Constitution did not give Congress that power. Mr. Miller, in the record of the North Carolina Constitutional Convention, objected to the Constitution on the grounds that it did not give the Congress of the United States the power to control the movement of the armed forces of the United States.

The second point, we know in one of the debates that Charles Evans Hughes—

MR. MILLER: In time of war?

MR. MOORE: In time of war, precisely. We know that Charles Evans Hughes, one of our great Justices, specifically took the position there was no such power on the area limitation setting. We have at least four different scholars that have spoken to that point and taken that view, including Quincy Wright, which I think frankly did one of the best pieces in 1922 on the overall control of foreign relations in general.

Now the appropriations power does not, under the Constitution of the United States, serve as an independent basis for establishing conditions under the separation of powers—I underline "under the separation of powers"—which Congress does not otherwise have. If it did, then the reality is there would never be any separation of powers. Congress could always attach whatever measure it sought to deal with solely on an appropriations measure. There would simply be no separation of powers.

That is no different than the setting in which it cannot unconstitutionally attach a provision on discrimination or denial of due process to an appropriation measure. There are opinions of the Attorney General, by the way, that take exactly that same position on the appropriations power in the separation of powers area generally.

I personally believe, although I realize many scholars have different views on this, that the area limitations on President Nixon—during the course of a hostility in which there were 40,000 DRV troops attacking United States troops from Cambodian territory before the United States incursion—were unconstitutional partly because of the area of restriction, but partly because it went beyond that to directing the commander in chief what to do in the battle. I also regard the provision saying the President could not have the authority—any reasonable period of time, in essence—to withdraw the forces from Saigon after the war was terminated as unconstitutional. Does the President constitutionally have an unimpairable commander in chief power to pull the forces out in a reasonable period of time? I think the answer to that is yes. In that context, congressional action was flatly unconstitutional.

I might add that the War Powers Resolution didn't add a bit to it because Congress tried to give him the authority under the War Powers Resolution. As Bob Turner shows very well in his study, Congress failed miserably in that. They worked for three weeks trying to get something out. The House finally went away for the weekend and the President had no authority in the final crunch.

He simply went ahead and did it on his own. There was not a single member of Congress that said the President of the United States had done something wrong or unconstitutional in that case.

MR. RAVEN-HANSEN: If the Congress decides to appropriate no further funds whatsoever for the continuation of hostilities, under your theory is the President allowed to go to the Treasury himself, and once it's empty, to raise revenues directly? I mean, where is the outer limit?

MR. MOORE: Well, there is a real world checks and balance problem. At some point when the President does not have money the President cannot operate. Things don't work. It's a checks or balance setting. That, however, is not an argument for saying that the appropriations power is a basis for doing things, under either separation of powers or the Fourteenth Amendment, that you could not otherwise do under the Constitution.

So I don't think that solves the problem any more than the "necessary and proper" clause. In fact, I regard those two powers as sort of the classic myth systems in talking about the separation of powers, and where the line should be drawn, in terms of bootstrap arguments for Congress.

MR. RAVEN-HANSEN: It seems to me that appropriations were the ultimate check that the Founders placed on the President's power to commit to hostilities on his own. Hamilton said schemes to subvert the Constitution take time to execute. If the reality today is that schemes don't take time to execute, and you can do it in a matter of hours, doesn't that authorize and require the development of a new check that will serve in place of the ultimate check?

You are saying that my extreme hypothetical is a checks and balances question, and I agree with that wholeheartedly. But I say that this particular check is completely ineffective in a nuclear war era because of the speed with which we can destroy the world. And so the issue is whether there is constitutional authority, in any of the branches, but particularly in Congress, to devise a narrowly framed alternative check to preserve the original balance.

MR. GLENNON: Professor Moore's theory on the power of the purse, I think, is a radical one. It has no support in the constitutional text, which expressly assigns to the Congress the power over the purse. It provides that no appropriations may be drawn from the Treasury except in consequence of law. It has no support in the case law. The Supreme Court has never overturned any congressional funding limitation. It has no support in the intentions of the Founding Fathers. The letter from Jefferson to Madison in 1789 says we have already given one effectual check to the dog of war by transferring the power of letting him loose from the executive to the legislative body, from the body that spends to the body that pays. Finally, the theory is in essence one that would rob the spending power—rob the power over the purse—of any substantive content.

MR. RAVEN-HANSEN: You reminded me of another section, the two-year limit on appropriations for standing armies. It seems an odd Constitution that limits the supporter of the army, Congress, and leaves the President, who normally has to have that congressional support, with no limit.

MR. TURNER: There's no question that the President can't fight but with the army that Congress gives him. And if Congress decides to give him no money, he has no army and he can't fight. But a different question is whether Congress can, by putting conditions on appropriations bills, seize control of the independent powers given to the President as commander in chief and so forth.

This issue came up in 1826. Daniel Webster made a brilliant statement on the House floor when somebody tried to limit the power of an executive delegation going to negotiations to discuss certain subjects, and Webster got up and said, if this was our money we could put any condition we wanted on it, but we are agents of the people just as the President is an agent of the people. His powers come from the Constitution and we cannot properly use our power of the purse to control him.

Professor Glennon said there are no court cases on this. There are several that are very appropriate. The commander in chief power, and the pardon power, are found side-by-side in Article II, Section 2 of the Constitution. When Congress tried to misuse its power, a very clear power, to set the jurisdiction of inferior courts to deny the President his pardon power in *United States v. Klein*, the Court said you could completely destroy the Court of Claims if you wanted, but you can't so define its jurisdiction as to deprive the President of his pardon power. In *United States v. Lovett*, when Congress claimed its power of the purse was a plenary power and could not be subject to review, the Supreme Court said you cannot put restrictions on a funding bill that violate the Constitution, in this case a bill of attainder.

Let me give you just one analogy. What would happen if Congress were to pass a funding bill for the Supreme Court of the United States—clearly the Court can't work without money—saying no funds in this bill may be expended if and after such time as the Supreme Court holds any of the following listed bills to be unconstitutional? Now if the Congress, by its appropriations power, can completely gut the President's independent powers as commander in chief, why can't they do the same thing to the other co-equal branch of the Supreme Court?

MR. GLENNON: My one-sentence answer is the Supreme Court's statement in *Martin v. Hunter's Lessee*—that a power is subject to abuse is no argument against the existence of the power.

III.

THE FORM OF CONGRESSIONAL PARTICIPATION

8

War Making Under the Constitution and the First Use of Nuclear Weapons

Stephen L. Carter

In an era when most thinking people are worried about the risk of nuclear cataclysm, nearly any proposal intended in good faith to reduce that risk will carry with it an immediate surface appeal. None of us wants a nuclear war. Consequently, we hope fervently for the success of any reasonable proposal intended to avoid the horror. So I am not surprised to find that any number of thoughtful people are attracted by The Federation of American Scientists (FAS) proposal that a committee of members of the Congress—what I will call a ''crisis committee''— be established and granted what is in essence a veto over presidential decisions to use nuclear weapons when no adversary has yet employed them.[1]

Such a presidential first use of nuclear weapons would turn a conventional conflict into a nuclear one;[2] it could move the world from a moment of relative peace to the moment of Armageddon. In harsher but still accurate terms, a President who makes a first use of nuclear weapons starts a nuclear war. Almost anything aimed at preventing that outcome will sound like a good idea. But the ideas that sound best to one expert or another are not always easy to fit into the constitutional scheme. The ''good idea'' embodied in the crisis committee proposal, involving delegation to a committee of a power that rests in the whole Congress if it exists at all, should be particularly troubling to students of constitutional structure.

There is something eerie and disquieting in discussing the prospect of nuclear holocaust in terms so legalistic. But if the United States is to remain a nation under the rule of law in general, and under the rule of our received constitutional law in particular, then these terms are surely the appropriate ones.[3] And when

The author wishes to acknowledge Enola Aird, Harold Koh, Henry Hansmann, Peter Raven-Hansen, Allan Ides, and Jeremy Stone for beneficial discussions of these matters.

cast in this fashion—as simply a legislative proposal that must pass constitutional muster—the suggestion for a veto-carrying crisis committee does lose much of its luster. Indeed, although there are certainly clever arguments available in favor of the proposal's constitutionality, none of them is as simple and straightforward as the argument against it. The "crisis committee" idea is almost certainly unconstitutional.[4]

In explaining my conclusion, I will defend three propositions:

(1) In the absence of congressional action restricting his freedom, the President may decide whether to make a first use of nuclear weapons when, in his judgment, the nation's security so requires.

(2) The Congress may, through affirmative legislation, restrict the President's ability to make this first use.

(3) Should the Congress choose to exercise its authority to restrict the President, it may do so only through means that permit it to exercise its war power by manifesting its consent or its refusal of consent. These means may include explicit limitations on the power and probably some forms of the controversial legislative veto. These means may not, however, contain a delegation to anyone else of the consent manifestation authority. In particular, the Congress may not, consistent with the constitutional structure, delegate its consent authority to the proposed crisis committee.

I. CONSTITUTIONAL ANALYSIS AND THE WAR POWER

A. The Crisis Committee Proposal

As I understand the FAS proposal, the fundamental rule, legislatively enacted, would be this one: The President is not permitted to make a first use of nuclear weapons unless he first obtains the assent of a majority of the members of the crisis committee. Thus the proposal would grant to a legislatively created entity the authority to veto a decision by the President, the titular commander in chief, on the use of American armed forces.[5]

As described in Dr. Stone's essay, the crisis committee would comprise "the speaker and minority leader of the House of Representatives, the majority and minority leaders of the Senate, and the chairman and ranking members of the Senate and House committees on armed services, the Senate Committee on Foreign Relations, the House Committee on International Relations, and the Joint Committee on Atomic Energy."[6] Given its composition, this committee may accurately be termed a committee of the Congress. The veto authority, in other words, would be in the hands of leading members of the Congress, and in that sense would be a veto wielded by a creature of the legislature.[7]

The crisis committee proposal, then, possesses two noteworthy features. It grants to an entity other than the full Congress the authority to veto a presidential decision on use of the armed forces, and it constitutes that entity as a legislative committee. I will contend that both these features, however well intentioned they might be, would do violence to the system of balanced and separated powers of which the shared war power forms a part. With this background in mind, I now move on to consider the nature of the war power shared by the President and the Congress.

B. The Structure of the War Power

The Constitution divides between the President and the Congress the various powers needed to make and sustain warfare. Under Article II, Section 2, the President is the commander in chief of the armed forces of the United States.[8] The Constitution gives no explicit clue on the powers attendant on this title and says no more in Article II about the military. Article I grants the Congress three relevant powers: the discretion whether to declare war,[9] the authority to raise and support armies,[10] and the right to promulgate rules and regulations to govern the armed forces.[11] On the content of these powers, too, the document offers no further detail.

Unlocking the meaning of these clauses begins with an understanding of their nature. The constitutional clauses establishing the war making power are what might be called ''structural'' provisions—constitutional language concerned with the distribution of authority among the branches of the federal government and the way those branches ought to operate, rather than with the protection of individual rights against government oppression. As a general proposition, structural provisions tend to be significantly more concrete (or more easily rendered so) than the sections of the Constitution intended to guarantee fundamental rights. In part for this reason, I have argued elsewhere that the legislative history of the document's structural provisions may yield important clues in working out precisely how their language should be construed.[12] But in searching for these clues, a scholar ought not be blinded by a literalism so sweeping that it makes a difference, in Paul Brest's splendid example, whether the automobile that struck the jogger and led to the banning of vehicles in the park was a blue Ford or a white Chevy.[13] At the same time, the history is vital to understanding the structure of the federal government and the system of balanced and separated powers, the key to governance under the American Constitution. As I argue in detail in other work, the rules for construing these structural provisions should be fashioned with the conscious goal of preserving that system.[14] A rule requiring inquiry into history when a court faces a question on the interaction of the branches of the federal government is a sensible means for pursuing this goal. The inquiry, however, will yield less an answer than a picture of an answer; rendering it concrete will still require an act of creative imagination on the part of the interpreter. Thus when I urge a search in the history for clues, I mean nothing more ambitious than an effort to determine how the Framers hoped the government they created would function. Absolute precision would be impossible; a pretense that it has been discovered should be worrisome; but gaining a sense of the original scheme for operation of the checks and balances should help lend meaning to the structural provisions meant to implement it.

Obviously, the history of the Constitution will yield nothing related to nuclear weapons, and I suppose one could argue that as the authors of Articles I and II could not possibly have anticipated the development of these terrible devices, their views are quite irrelevant in divining what restrictions the Constitution permits Congress to place on their use.[15] The problem is that an approach that rejects any use of the history when the world has developed in a way the authors of the document could not have imagined, would place few limits on what the courts might do, and certainly might quickly vitiate substantial chunks of contemporary constitutional doctrine. By far, the more prudent course is to examine the language and the structure and then, if the distribution of authority remains unclear, to study the history of drafting and ratification for whatever light it might shed. One cannot reasonably expect to find in the history all the answers, and the background of the provisions on the war power is such that one cannot really expect to find very many of them. Nevertheless, the history is a good place to start; even if it does not solve the problem, it might get the inquiry headed in the right direction.[16]

Unfortunately, the legislative history of the war power may charitably be described as thin. Under the Articles of Confederation, the Congress possessed "the sole and exclusive right and power of determining on peace and war."[17] The draft federal constitution presented at the Philadelphia Convention by the Committee on Detail granted the Congress the authority to "make war."[18] The Convention voted to alter this wording, vesting in the Congress instead the obviously narrower power "to declare war."[19] The delegates made this change after a debate that Madison's notes record only in fragments and for reasons that the other historical materials leave obscure.[20]

There is more, but not much more, in other parts of the historical record.[21] So in the vision of those who wrote and ratified the Constitution, how narrow was the congressional war power, and how broad the President's? Despite the devoted efforts of legions of scholars to unpack the history of these clauses,[22] I fear that the honest truth is a modest one: the legislative history of the war making power teaches almost nothing concrete about the Framers' understanding, except, perhaps, that whatever the scope of the war making power under the Articles of Confederation, some slice of it was taken and given to the President. How great a slice the history does not say.

Careful analysis of the constitutional structure, however, does point toward an answer. If the division of the war power is considered as part of a larger and integrated system of checks and balances, and if one accepts as an interpretive principle that no provision of the document should be read in a way that renders another provision meaningless, then at least the framework of the distribution of power begins to emerge.

The President is commander in chief. Of what? Of "the Army and Navy of the United States"—and presumably of the Air Force as well, although the strict student of language and history might perhaps find this point troubling. And does the Constitution reveal what the Army and Navy are? Well, not quite, but it does state that the Congress possesses the power to raise and support armies and provide and maintain navies and to make rules and regulations for both land and naval forces.[23] Consequently, I think few would quarrel with the conclusion that the armed forces which the President commands are the ones that the Congress raises and supports. Certainly this was the position pressed by Alexander Hamilton in *The Federalist*,[24] and while this conclusion may seem to be quite an obvious one, the argument is worth reviewing because of what it says about the nature of the shared power over the armed forces.

Unless there is a Platonic essence called "army," a thing that exists beyond the definition given it by the Congress, then the most sensible understanding of the constitutional language is surely that the Congress can raise the army it wants; no other army exists for the President to command. If the Congress says the army shall consist of no more than one million soldiers, I see no way that the President can recruit instead one million and two. If the Congress says the army shall have no more than two thousand tanks, the President possesses no authority to purchase three thousand instead.

To this I would add what might at first seem quite a large jump: if the Congress says the army shall not make war on Canada, the President cannot decree instead that it shall. The leap is actually quite a small one. Nothing in the language or structure of the Constitution suggests a distinction between rules limiting the number of tanks and limiting the theaters of operation.[25] One might, I suppose, try to argue that restrictions on the number of soldiers or amount of equipment are limits on what the armed forces shall *be*; stipulations on where or how these forces can fight are limits on what the armed forces may *do*. But that difference— if it is a difference—is merely semantical. After all, one could always respond that the rule prohibiting war making against Canada is also a restriction on what the armed forces shall be: they shall not be the sort of armed forces that fight a war with Canada, just as they shall not be the sort of armed forces that include psychopathic criminals or violate treaties or purchase more tanks than three thousand.

In the absence of constitutional support for the distinction, there is no reason to import it into constitutional law merely because it sounds good; not, at least, without doing violence to the structure of balanced and separated powers that the Constitution envisions. On the contrary, restrictions that flow logically from the congressional authority to raise and support armies, and to regulate them as well, are quite clearly authorized by the language of the document and its scheme of checks and balances on the war making power that it creates. Restrictions of this nature—restrictions through which the Congress effectively says "We have created this army, not that one"—I will refer to as *definitional*. For the reasons I have set out, these definitional restrictions should nearly always be ruled constitutional.[26]

Because the Congress is constantly redefining the roles of all the parts of the federal government, this discussion suggests that the Congress could, if it chose to do so, place definitional restrictions on the armed forces even after the conflict to which it objects has already begun. The President might order American forces to invade Canada, and the Congress could subsequently enact legislation providing, in effect, that American armed forces are not permitted to make war on Canada. This view of presidential war authority as sensitive to variations in congressional sentiment, as expressed through definitional restrictions and explicit permissions, also makes structural sense. It is wholly consistent with a view of the system of checks and balances as dynamic and shifting, yet at the same time providing real constraint on the exercise of power within the federal government. On this understanding, the Framers wisely created a system that is flexible enough to permit the nation to defend itself to the utmost if attacked, but is at the same time sufficiently durable to enable the Congress, if it so chooses, to prevent one individual from thrusting the nation into a war.

The powers to raise and support armies and to make rules to regulate them ought to be read in a way that yields substantive content. If the Congress cannot place restrictions on the military forces which in its discretion it brings into being, then there seems little point in vesting in that body the power to create the forces in the first place.[27] Certainly the commander in chief clause should be read as placing some limits on the restrictions from which the Congress can choose, and I will presently investigate where those limits might lie. For the moment, however, it ought to be enough to say that the congressional power to raise and support armies makes sense only if it implies a concommitant power to place definitional restrictions on those armies.

Similarly, preservation of the system of balanced and separated powers demands that the congressional authority to declare war be read to possess substantive content. One view holds that a formal declaration of war is simply a means of altering certain aspects of the relationships among nations, and that the declaration is thus in essence a mere formality, having nothing to do with the ability of any nation (including this one) to commit troops to battle.[28] Perhaps because any other policy would violate the United Nations Charter, no nation has formally declared war on any other nation since the 1956 Middle East conflict.[29] So in the modern era, at least, all nations apparently fight without declaring war. The United States has done so many times.[30] Advocates of a strong presidential war making power might conclude from this that once the Congress has created the armed forces (and assuming no relevant restrictions in their charters), the President as commander in chief may commit these forces at times and for reasons of his own choosing. This presidential authority would not be unbridled: the President would be subject to the usual panoply of balances and checks, including the electoral checks and the congressional power over the purse.[31] The President's war making authority could not, however, be reduced by a call upon the congressional power to declare war.

But this argument for a narrow congressional war power seems not quite consistent with the history and does indeed leave the power to declare war devoid of important meaning.[32] If so much of the war power was meant to shift to the

President that the Congress was left to clear up a few legal formalities and determine the amount of funding, then it is remarkable that so little was said about it, either in debate or—far more important—in the constitutional text establishing this radically different organization. If, moreover, one believes as I do that the entire panoply of powers of the President and the Congress should be read as performing a mutual checking and balancing function, it is quite a difficult move to read one of the most explicit of these powers out of the system of balanced and separated powers.

Certainly the Supreme Court has never endorsed so broad a construction of the President's authority as commander in chief. No matter what the scope of that independent authority—a matter in some dispute—the Court has never ruled that the President may use the armed forces in a manner inconsistent with the congressional will as expressed through definitional legislation.[33] On the contrary, the Court's decisions over the years have included as a consistent theme a healthy respect for the power of the Congress to place limits on that authority.[34] For example, advocates of a strong independent presidential war making power often place reliance on *Martin v. Mott*[35] for the proposition that the President possesses inherent authority to call forth the militia to repel invasion. As the Court noted in its opinion, however, the authority in question had been delegated to the President by the Congress.[36] The Justices never discussed the President's discretion to resist congressional restrictions. Even in the *Prize Cases*,[37] frequently cited as demonstrating judicial approval of President Lincoln's order to seize ships trading with the Confederacy, the Justices made express reference to the subsequent congressional ratification of the President's action.[38] To be sure, the Congress did not directly authorize the President's actions in advance, but that is somewhat beside the point if the question is one of *power*: the Justices sustained the presidential orders because the Congress had not countermanded them. The cases, in sum, are consistent with and, in fact, offer affirmative support for the view that the President's commander in chief power can be limited by the Congress in the exercise of its own war powers. They lend no support at all to the opposite proposition.

All of this machinery was a bit more than 150 years old when the destruction of Hiroshima and Nagasaki marked the dawn of the atomic age. The major wars and minor skirmishes the nation fought during that century and a half lent to the distribution of the war making power far more definition than the Constitution itself ever offered. Few of the Nation's wars have been declared. Over the years, the Presidents have assumed the authority to order American forces into combat around the world, and although there have been some exceptions, the Congress has generally acquiesced in the practice.[39] Of course, historical practice ought not by itself be taken as establishing a constitutional rule.[40] If the Constitution represents no more than an accumulation of practical experience, it might as well be an unwritten one.[41] On the other hand, what people of good will do in resolving their political conflicts—the way, in short, that the powers actually are exercised—should at least be taken as demonstrating *plausible* constructions of the disputed constitutional provisions. Thus if the President, for example, decides that the power to terminate treaties, not assigned specifically by the language or structure of the Constitution, belongs to him, and if the Congress acquiesces in his exercise of the power, a court rightly hesitates before telling both coordinate branches that they are wrong.[42] Similarly, if Presidents repeatedly send American forces to fight and the Congress does not raise an objection, a court should pause before decreeing that congressional permission is needed.[43]

But at the same time, a conclusion that congressional permission is unnecessary need not reduce to a conclusion that the Congress cannot interpose an objection. What the Congress gives, the Congress can take away: Congressional acquiescence, however longstanding, should never change the meaning of the Constitution.[44] If the Congress possesses authority in a particular field, its failure to exercise the authority means simply that the power is dormant, not that it is dead. If the system of checks and balances is to be preserved in a form approximating the original understanding, then the congressional privilege to try to revive its slumbering authority is inalienable.[45] Only the force of political reality, not the order of a constitutional court, should restrict the Congress in its efforts to regain a power properly its own.

C. The Congress Acts: The War Powers Resolution of 1973

Does the FAS proposal try to recover a power that the Congress might otherwise lose? To understand why it does not, it is fitting to begin with the analysis of the best-known congressional effort to regain a measure of control over the decision whether to fight: The War Powers Resolution of 1973.[46] That Resolution places a number of limitations on the ability of the President to commit troops in the absence of congressional enabling legislation. The two most important provisions for the purposes of understanding the crisis committee proposal are Section 5(b), which requires the President to withdraw the troops after sixty days if congressional permission is not received,[47] and Section 5(c), authorizing the Congress to compel him by concurrent resolution to withdraw the forces at once.[48] In contrast to the definitional restrictions I have already discussed, these might be termed *procedural* restrictions on the President's war making power, because rather than requiring him to use the armed forces only in particular ways, they command him instead to move through a particular process of legislative approvals before he may do what he desires to do.

As a general proposition, procedural restrictions are far more likely than definitional restrictions to run afoul of the independent authority that the President possesses as commander in chief. It is one thing to define the way in which armed forces can be used and leave the details to the President's discretion. It is something else to try to reserve the right, without enacting additional legislation, to alter those definitional restrictions at will. Consequently, the argument for constitutionality of Sections 5(b) and 5(c) of the Resolution may not be immediately obvious. The case for their constitutionality, however, while arguably somewhat subtle, is actually quite straightforward. Because an understanding of the constitutional status of these provisions is crucial to any analysis of the crisis committee proposal, I will attempt a summary of the longer argument I have presented elsewhere in favor of their validity.[49]

The restriction contained in Section 5(b) of the War Powers Resolution, the one limiting the amount of time for which the President, if he acts independently, may commit troops, presents by far the stronger case for constitutionality. Although on its face a procedural restriction and thus suspect under the analysis in this paper, the Section 5(b) time limit may more properly be considered a definitional restriction and thus presumptively constitutional. True, the section in terms requires the President to seek legislative approval for his use of the armed forces, but that is actually quite a formalistic view. The better approach would construe Section 5(b) as defining the armed forces as forces able to fight for up to sixty days. If the President wishes to do more, then he must do what he always must do when he wants to ignore a congressional statute: he must go to the Congress and seek amendment. In providing that the President may, with congressional approval, ignore the sixty-day limitation, Section 5(b) is simply stating the obvious: a successor Congress may alter the acts of a predecessor Congress.[50] The important substantive content of Section 5(b) is the time limit, not the requirement for congressional approval of an extension. The value of this distinction will presently be clear.

Section 5(c), which requires the President to withdraw the forces if the Congress by concurrent resolution so directs, contemplates a legislative veto. The provision is thus immediately suspect under the rule of *Immigration and Naturalization Service v. Chadha*,[51] wherein the Supreme Court ruled quite rightly that as a general proposition, legislative vetoes are not a permissible weapon for the Congress to use in its struggle with the President for power.[52] A case can be made, however, that the War Powers veto is quite different, because of the peculiar nature of the war power shared by the President and the Congress.[53] The War Powers veto, I have said in the longer version of this argument, should be viewed as a means through which the Congress is able to indicate its assent or non-assent to a presidential act plunging the United States into what the Congress considers a state of war.[54] The veto is permissible because the United States may not under the Constitution fight a war in the absence of congressional acquiescence. A declaration of war makes congressional permission explicit. When the Congress declines to take a position, the President's discretion provides a constitutionally sufficient justification for continuing hostilities. But by adopting a concurrent resolution disapproving a particular use of troops, the Congress is in effect stating that the conflict has reached the point at which a congressional declaration of war is necessary and that the declaration, if solicited, would be refused. In this view, both the Congress and the President must concur if the United States is to engage in what either considers a war. If the Congress expressly refuses its approval, then the United States may not fight one.

Any other result should seem troubling if the system of checks and balances is to be preserved in something approximating its original form. Even in deciding to use troops—some would say *especially* then—the President ought to be subject to a congressional check. If the views of the Framers are important, one might reason as follows: Why would the drafters of the Constitution go to all the trouble that they did to save for the Congress a tiny, largely irrelevant bit of authority? For if the power to declare war is not part of a system intended to balance the President's commander in chief power, then it is hard to see what balances there are—as well as what the power to declare war realistically could have been intended to do.[55]

This may sound simple, but the demonstration of the constitutionality of the War Powers Resolution need not be a complicated one.[56] The rule is clear: although the Congress may restrict the President's discretion, it may do so only in ways that permit it to manifest its consent or lack of consent to a presidential action that involves using armed forces for more than protection against a sudden assault on American territory. The War Powers Resolution does no violence to the system of checks and balances, because it retains for the Congress no more than that body is given under the Constitution. The legislative veto it contains is no more than a device for signaling a lack of legislative consent to the fighting of a war—a consent in the absence of which the conflict cannot proceed. For reasons that I will explain, it seems to me quite difficult to justify the crisis committee as a means for manifesting this consent or its absence.

II. THE CONSTITUTION AND THE CRISIS COMMITTEE

A. The President and Nuclear Weapons

From the dawn of the Republic until enactment of the War Powers Resolution in 1973, all three branches of the federal government implicitly accepted presidential authority to order American forces into combat as he chose, except when the Congress acted affirmatively to limit his discretion. Even today, the War Powers Resolution permits broad presidential action without explicit congressional authorization.[57] And even those who doubt the constitutionality of presidential orders sending American troops abroad in the absence of express congressional permission generally concede the President at least a power to order the armed forces to respond to sudden attacks.[58]

Whatever the proper scope of presidential discretion in the use of the armed forces, the constitutional rule must be the same whether the forces are nuclear or conventional. If the President's discretion to use American armed forces is as broad as I have suggested, then he has the same discretion in using nuclear forces. If the President's authority is limited to repelling attacks, then he can use nuclear weapons to repel attacks if in his judgment the action is necessary. Some have contended that this reasoning is too simplistic, that special constitutional analysis is needed when the weapons involved are nuclear ones,[59] or even that nuclear weapons are themselves unconstitutional,[60] but neither of those views can find substantive support in the Constitution, its history, or the legal culture that has grown up around both. We cannot wish nuclear weapons away, and we cannot excise them through judicial fiat either.

True, a thermonuclear warhead is not merely a larger bomb. It is a weapon of almost unimaginable destructive power. That practical and frightening observation is, however, devoid of constitutional significance. That a thermonuclear conflagration would be the last war this unhappy planet would ever endure is virtually beyond peradventure.[61] But the President's ability to provoke a conflict that would destroy life on earth does not lead to the conclusion that the Constitution ought to be given a fresh construction, taking that ability into account. Avoiding that conflict demands hard political choices, and if we are all luckier than we often have been, the Congress and the President, working together to create a foreign affairs and national security policy, will make some of them. But the urgent necessity for political solutions to the nuclear conundrum does not alter the meaning of the structural provisions establishing the system of balanced and separated powers. And under those provisions, unless the Congress acts, the discretion to use or abuse all American armed forces rests with the President of the United States.

B. What the Congress Can Do

Even if the Constitution does not by its own force limit the circumstances in which the President may use nuclear weapons, it hardly follows that the Congress can place no limits. On the contrary, as I have argued above, the Congress may exercise a power even after letting it lie dormant for centuries. If in its exercise of the war power, the Congress chooses to place restrictions on the circumstances in which the President may employ thermonuclear weapons, nothing in the commander in chief power prevents it from doing so. Naturally the President's prerogatives as commander in chief will shape the *types* of limits that are constitutionally permissible, but within certain broad areas that I will outline, the discretion of the Congress is essentially unbounded, except by the same political reality that restricts other congressional activity.

The Congress could, first of all, enact simple legislation circumscribing the President's discretion by defining the scope and mission of the forces the Congress has brought into being. "No nuclear weapons may be employed until an adversary has used them," a statute might read, or, "No first use of nuclear weapons in the Middle East." The Chief Executive might find these statutes frustrating, they might be quite short-sighted, but as definitional restrictions, they are plainly valid exercises of the congressional authority to raise and support armies.[62] The President, as I have noted above, is commander in chief only of the forces the Congress actually creates, and the Congress is always free to say what those forces are and what they are for.

Even should the Congress add, as it has in the War Powers Resolution, the proviso that the President may seek legislative approval for exceptions to its rule, the result is the same. A clause noting that the President may come to Congress to alter its restriction is less a statute of law than a statement of the obvious. The Congress may always enact fresh legislation making exceptions to old legislation, and the President may always ask for it. Thus whether framed as absolute prohibitions or as prohibitions on acting without congressional approval, restrictions of this sort on the President's use of nuclear weapons ought to be considered constitutionally permissible.

Second, and far more important in evaluating the crisis committee proposal, the Congress may require the President to obtain its consent before taking certain specified actions, at least when those actions bring about a result—a state of war—that the Congress has the right to prevent. As a corollary, the Congress may provide for alternative means by which the lack of consent may be made manifest, as long as the alternative means actually do that. This is the point of my earlier discussion of Section 5(c) of the War Powers Resolution. In the war powers context, a legislative veto may indeed be the best means for demonstrating the non-existence of this consent, because, as I have explained, a Congress that would veto a war is not a Congress that would declare one. Thus the Congress could certainly preserve for its members an opportunity to veto the President's decision to make a first use of nuclear weapons. I emphasize, however, that the *only* permissible legislative veto of a presidential use of armed forces is one which signifies that the Congress as a whole refuses its consent to a continuation (or a beginning) of hostilities. Nothing less than a concurrent resolution or a resolution of a single House can logically manifest this lack of *congressional* consent, because no one but the Congress is the Congress.

C. What the Congress Can't Do

The congressional war power is broad, but not unlimited. As the Supreme Court has explained: "[T]he phrase 'war power' cannot be invoked as a talismanic incantation to support any exercise of congressional power which can be brought within its ambit."[63] In particular, the war power will not support the FAS proposal for a crisis committee with a veto over the President's decision to make a first use of American nuclear forces.

As I have argued already, the legislative veto available under section 5(c) of the War Powers Resolution is likely constitutional precisely because it is a *legislative* veto, performing a signaling function; it represents a means for conveying information, the information being the congressional refusal to consent to hostilities. The committee veto cannot possibly convey the same information; it gives no information concerning the preferences of *the Congress as a whole*. At best, a committee veto shows that a majority of a selected group of individuals disagree with what the President proposes to do. If the committee is not a congressional committee, then its opinion is constitutionally meaningless. If the committee is a committee of the Congress, then its veto is theoretically subject to congressional override and consequently cannot possibly signify the lack of congressional consent. If the fourteen-member committee envisioned in the FAS proposal were to vote 14–0 to halt a presidential action, no information about congressional consent or lack of consent would be transmitted. The entire Congress might still be split 521–14 in favor of what the President proposes to do. That such a result is unlikely hardly alters its constitutional significance: as long as there exists the possibility that the Congress and the committee disagree, no signaling function is performed by the committee's vote. If the committee's vote does not in fact indicate a lack of congressional consent to the use of weapons, then there is no constitutional reason for the President to respect it.

This difficulty cannot be cured by permitting the President to appeal an adverse decision to the entire Congress.[64] It is not the responsibility of the President to ascertain whether the Congress does or does not consent; it is instead the responsibility of the Congress, if it wishes to play a role, to create a method through which its refusal to consent may be made manifest. The crisis committee proposal is no first step toward congressional consent. It is an obstacle to that ascertainment. If the Congress wishes to reserve the right to approve all presidential first uses of nuclear weapons, then it may do so, but the right that is reserved must be the right of the entire Congress. If the Congress decides instead that requiring the President to come to Capitol Hill for approval of his decision to use nuclear weapons is too unwieldy, then it is better off sticking to definitional restrictions that require no subsequent congressional action.

In this sense, the congressional slice of the war power is nondelegable. This follows not from the traditional and hoary doctrine against delegation of legislative powers,[65] but rather from the simple proposition that only a refusal by the entire Congress to consent carries constitutional significance, and therefore, that the power to grant or refuse consent is one that must be exercised (if at all) by the Congress as a whole.[66] The President may make war without congressional authorization because he is the commander in chief of the armed forces the Congress has created. The Congress may limit his discretion or countermand his decision to fight, because the Congress holds ultimate power to decide whether a war should be fought. To place a committee between them, giving to it a little bit of the power of each branch, finally makes a shambles of the war making structure so painstakingly created at the end of the eighteenth century. Over the past two centuries that structure has been sufficiently strong to serve as a wall against tyrannical use of the armed forces, but sufficiently flexible to permit the swift application of military force when the President deems it necessary and the Congress does not object. It is a structure in which the Congress is far better equipped to establish policy through definitional restrictions than to try to manage it through procedural ones. That structure should not be brushed aside without an argument far better than "It's a good idea."

III. CONCLUSION: THE WAR POWER IN A NUCLEAR AGE

The crisis committee proposal, noble intentions or no, would probably be held constitutionally infirm in the unlikely event that it were enacted over presidential veto and subsequently challenged in the courts. Yet if the Congress is not permitted to restrain presidential power in this fashion, so the argument might be pressed, the United States will continue on its present course, lurching ever closer to nuclear war.

I am not as convinced as some that that is so plainly where we are lurching. Deterrence through the fact, not the theory, of mutually assured destruction, even if considered morally obscene, has so far kept the nuclear peace. Even if our lurch is toward war, the underlying contention that nuclear weapons are so devastating in their potential for destruction that all measures to limit their use should be deemed constitutional is reminiscent of *Korematsu v. United States*[67] and various cases involving the free speech rights of organizations and individuals deemed subversive.[68] There the government argued essentially that it is sometimes necessary to subvert the Constitution in order to save it, and was rightly condemned for its argument.[69]

The point pressed by proponents of the crisis committee proposal is quite similar. If we do not control the use of nuclear weapons, the argument runs, there will be no Constitution to preserve. That much strikes me as indisputable. But if we violate the Constitution because it seems like a good idea, then the thing that we have preserved is not the Constitution. The United States protected by unconstitutional committees of the Congress is much like the United States protected by locking up every one who is a potential threat to its safety or closing every newspaper that advocates its destruction. It is, perhaps, a physically safer society, but it is not the same society. A constitutional democracy is based on its Constitution. If nuclear weapons can be controlled only by violating that Constitution, then perhaps our constitutional democracy in this nuclear age has become a political dinosaur, ready for extinction.

I doubt that we have gone so far. The Congress can and should take the lead in reducing the likelihood of nuclear war, but should do so through the setting of long-term policy, the thing that the Congress does best. The Congress should not, however, try to involve itself in the day-to-day operations of the military; that is what the executive branch exists to do.

The FAS proposal for a crisis committee goes back many years.[70] The policy of the United States and its NATO allies to use nuclear weapons in the last resort to halt a conventional attack by forces of the Warsaw Pact—whether a wise one or a foolish one[71]—goes back even further. At this point in our history, the executive branch has chosen not to forswear the first use of nuclear weapons and the Congress has not sought to change this position by law. Putting aside for a moment the notion of a crisis committee, the Congress has not even enacted definitional restrictions on the first use of nuclear weapons.

The Congress as a whole, if it wishes to set the defense policy of the United States, may interpose substantive definitional barriers to the use of nuclear weapons. If the members prefer involvement in the management of a crisis, they may retain—but they may not delegate—a veto over the use of those weapons. One may of course object that as a matter of common sense, no rational Congress ought to reserve a full legislative veto over first use, because if the United States is ever called upon to decide whether to use its nuclear arsenal, the exigencies of time are likely to be such that plenary legislative consideration would be an obstacle.[72] But should the Congress be persuaded by this argument, then its members would merely be affirming what I think the Framers understood long ago: there can be only one commander in chief. The Congress may decide what and how much he may command, but having made the decision, may not appoint coadjutors.

Does this mean that the Congress should give the President completely free rein in the first use of nuclear weapons? That is a policy question beyond the scope of this paper. The Constitution limits the policies that the Congress can make, but only the members, in their wisdom, can choose among the permissible policies. Perhaps the strictures of the Constitution are such that the Congress cannot select a constitutionally valid scheme that will reduce the risk of nuclear war and that only the unconstitutional crisis committee proposal will do. But if our options are so limited, then we are already far too late.

NOTES

1. *See* Stone, *supra* Ch. 1. Dr. Stone refers to his proposed entity as a "planning committee," but I believe my own phraseology better captures its purpose. Dr. Stone's essay is largely concerned with demonstrating the theory stated in his title, but I consider that the less important part of what he has to say.

2. The "first use" of nuclear weapons, which is the expenditure of any nuclear weapon for a hostile purpose, should be distinguished from a "first strike," which is a pre-emptive and massive strategic attack.

3. Nor should the terms of constitutional argument be altered because of a perception of the importance of the issue involved. *See infra* notes 67–69 and accompanying text.

4. Obviously, were the crisis committee proposal enacted as law, litigation would be unlikely until the crisis was upon us. Nevertheless, it is difficult to do positive constitutional analysis other than by predicting what a hypothetical court would do if faced with a proposed piece of legislation. To instead engage in normative analysis— essentially to write a brief in favor of the proposal or against it—is a useful exercise, but should not be couched in terms purporting to show that the object of the analysis "is" or "is not" constitutional. *See* Carter, *The Morgan "Power" and the Forced Reconsideration of Constitutional Decisions*, 53 U. of Chi. L. Rev. 819 (1986) (hereinafter cited as Carter, *Constitutional Decisions*).

5. Although the proposal in terms concerns only American forces armed with nuclear weapons, I consider the generic description correct because, as I explain in text, I do not accept the proposition that constitutional analysis ought to vary with the type of armament involved. *Cf.* Rostow, *Great Cases Make Bad Law: The War Powers Act*, 50 Tex. L. Rev. 833 (1972) (arguing that constitutional analysis ought not to vary with the popularity of the armed conflict involved). *But cf.* Miller, *Nuclear Weapons and Constitutional Law*, 7 Nova L. J. 21 (1982).

6. Stone, *supra* Ch. 1 n. 21.

7. This facet alone might render the Stone proposal unconstitutional after *Bowshar*

v. Synar, 106 S. Ct. 3181 (1986), decided only after this paper was finished. *See infra* note 66.

8. U.S. Const. art. II, sec. 2.

9. *Id.*, art. I, § 8, cl. 11.

10. *Id.*, art. I, § 8, cls. 12, 13.

11. *Id.*, art. I, § 8, cl. 14.

12. *See* Carter, *Constitutional Adjudication and the Indeterminate Text: A Preliminary Defense of Muddling Through*, 94 Yale L. J. 821, 853–65 (1985) (hereinafter cited as Carter, *Indeterminate Text*); Carter, *The Political Aspects of Judicial Power: Some Notes on the Presidential Immunity Decision*, 131 U. of Pa. L. Rev. 1341, 1353–56 (1983) (hereinafter cited as Carter, *Judicial Power*).

13. *See* Brest, *The Misconceived Quest for the Original Understanding*, 60 B.U.L. Rev. 204, 209–13 (1980).

14. *See* Carter, *Indeterminate Text*, *supra* note 12, at 855–63; Carter, *Judicial Power*, *supra* note 12, at 1373–84. Obviously, one may quibble with the notion that the court or anyone else ought to "fashion" the rules for interpretation, but it is difficult to escape the force of the critical argument that even the choice of interpretive rules, not just the interpretation itself, reflects the values of the interpreter. *See* Tushnet, *Following the Rules Laid Down: A Critique of Interpretivism and Neutral Principles*, 96 Harv. L. Rev. 781 (1983). My suggestion is aimed at encouraging the courts to select rules that place comprehensible limits on the exercise of federal power, not at demonstrating that the rules have been pre-selected by some authoritative Master Interpreter. It is less than clear, moreover, that those who wrote the Constitution had any particular interpretive scheme in mind; in particular, although reliance on the fact may be hopelessly paradoxical, there is some reason to think that the Framers did not consider their concrete conceptions to be binding on future interpreters. *See* Powell, *The Original Understanding of Original Intent*, 98 Harv. L. Rev. 885 (1985). Consequently, if the interpretive rules are not our own inventions, I am not sure whose inventions they are supposed to be.

15. This form of argument is sometimes pressed by my first-year Constitutional Law students when confronted with the argument that because the Constitution makes explicit mention of an Army and a Navy, the Air Force must be unconstitutional under the maxim *expressio unius est exclusio alterius*. This matter was raised, but apparently not taken seriously, when the Air Force was established as a separate branch of the armed forces in 1947. *See* H. Chase & C. Ducat, *Edward S. Corwin's The Constitution and What It Means Today* 111 & n.337 (14th ed. 1978).

16. Then again, it might not. *See* Brest, *supra* note 13; Munzer & Nickel, *Does the Constitution Mean What It Always Meant?*, 77 Colum. L. Rev. 1029 (1977).

17. Articles of Confederation, art. IX, sec. 1.

18. II M. Farrand, *Records of the Federal Convention of 1787* 182 (1937 ed.) (hereinafter cited as *Records*).

19. *Id.* at 318–19.

20. *The Federalist Papers*, for example, merely reiterate the point without extensive discussion. Madison, in *The Federalist No. 41*, explains the necessity of vesting in the Congress the authority to declare war in part by reminding the reader that "[t]he existing Confederation establishes this power in the most ample form." This argument does not reveal why the power under the Constitution is less than the power under the Confederation. An additional clue is found in *The Federalist No. 74*, wherein Hamilton contends that the President must be commander in chief because "the power of directing and employing

the common strength forms a usual and essential part in the definition of executive authority.''

Although the precise reasoning of the delegates at the Convention is unclear, the prevailing view at the time was apparently that the decision under the Articles of Confederation to grant to the legislature plenary authority over the conduct of war had been an error. *See* I *Records supra* note 18, at 89 (comments of P. Butler); *id.* at 97 (comments of E. Gerry); W. Reveley, *War Powers of the President and Congress* 55–63 (1981); Rostow, *supra* note 5, at 844–51. Contemporary students of the war power are often quick to claim that the delegates intended to grant to the President only a narrow authority to repel ''sudden attacks''; anything more would require congressional authorization. *See, e.g.,* Ides, *supra* Ch. 6, text accompanying note 45. That is one possible reading— and quite a weak one—of a small excerpt from Madison's notes on the Convention. Detailed studies of the history, however, have cast doubt on this view of what the Framers intended. *See* W. Reveley, *supra*, at 82–85; Lofgren, *War Making Under the Constitution: The Original Understanding*, 81 Yale L. J. 672, 675–77 (1972). *See also* Carter, *The Constitution and the Prevention of Nuclear Holocaust: A Reaction to Professor Banks*, 13 J. Legis. 901, 906–07 (1986). It is at least peculiar, moreover, to give so much weight to a few pages of notes never available to the ratifiers, when the ''sudden-attack-only'' theory was not advanced in any important way in the ratification debates.

21. For a somewhat equivocal analysis of the sparse historical record, see W. Reveley, *supra* note 20, at 100–15.

22. For examples of scholarship defending a relatively broad conception of presidential authority, see, *e.g.,* Emerson, *The War Powers Resolution Tested: The President's Independent Defense Power*, 51 Notre Dame L. Rev. 187 (1975); Turner, *supra* Ch. 4; Rostow, *supra* note 5. For examples of scholarship defending a relatively broad conception of congressional authority, see, *e.g.,* A. Sofaer, *War, Foreign Affairs and Constitutional Power* (1976); Berger, *Warmaking by the President*, 121 U. Pa. L. Rev. 29 (1972); Carter, *The Constitutionality of the War Powers Resolution*, 70 Va. L. Rev. 101, 116– 26 (1984) (hereinafter cited as Carter, *War Powers*); Eagleton, *The August 15 Compromise and the War Powers of Congress*, 18 St. Louis U.L.J. 1, 6 (1973).

23. *See* U.S. Const. art I, § 8, cls. 12–14.

24. *See The Federalist No. 69* (Hamilton) (J. Cooke ed. 1961).

25. *But see* Emerson, *supra* note 22, at 213 (implying that latter is beyond congressional power, but offering no substantial argument to support the distinction).

26. I say ''nearly'' always because, as with other constitutional provisions, the congressional war power conveys no authority to violate any independently established constitutional right. Consequently, the Congress could not provide that only white troops could serve as officers or that no Roman Catholic pilots could fly planes. The Congress may however provide that only men and not women shall be drafted, and may perhaps provide in addition that women are not permitted to serve in certain combat-ready positions in the armed forces. *See* Rostker v. Goldberg, 453 U.S. 57 (1981).

27. One might argue, as Hamilton did in *The Federalist No. 69*, that vesting the power to raise armies in the Congress is a check on what might otherwise be an implied executive authority to raise them himself, but unless one considers it likely that the Congress would not provide for a standing army, a check of this nature is virtually meaningless.

28. *See* Rostow, *supra* note 5, at 850–51.

29. *See* Turner, *supra* Ch. 4. *Cf. The Federalist No. 25*, at 161 (A. Hamilton) (J.

Cooke ed. 1961) (defending ability of the Congress to raise armies in time of peace because "the ceremony of a formal denunciation of war has of late fallen into disuse").

30. Historical instances of independent presidential war making have been collected in, *e.g.*, L. Fisher, *Constitutional Conflicts Between Congress and the President* 284–99 (1985); W. Reveley, *supra* note 20, at 116–69; Rostow, *supra* note 5, at 851–70.

31. One critic has argued that even the power of the purse is not sufficient to permit the Congress to interfere with the President's prerogatives as commander in chief. *See* Emerson, *supra* note 22, at 213.

32. The Supreme Court has long held that the congressional war power authorizes far more than "victories in the field," *Stewart v. Kahn*, 78 U.S. (11 Wall.) 493, 507 (1871), and can be used in peacetime "to treat all the wounds which war inflicts on our society," *Woods v. Miller*, 333 U.S. 138, 144 (1948). How far can this power be carried? *See* Ashwander v. TVA, 297 U.S. 288, 327–28 (1936) (establishment of Tennessee Valley Authority is valid exercise of war power).

33. For a more detailed discussion than the one in text, *see* Carter, *War Powers*, *supra* note 22, at 118–26.

34. *See*, *e.g.*, Madsen v. Kinsella, 343 U.S. 341, 348 (1952) (President as commander in chief may create military tribunals unless the Congress prohibits him); Santiago v. Nogueras, 214 U.S. 260, 265 (1909) (President as commander in chief may administer conquered territories only until the Congress makes him stop); Fleming v. Page, 50 U.S. (9 How.) 603, 614–15 (1850) (same).

35. 25 U.S. (12 Wheat.) 19 (1827).

36. *Id*. at 29.

37. 67 U.S (2 Black) 635 (1862).

38. *Id*. at 670–71.

39. *See* W. Reveley, *supra* note 20, at 116–30, 135–61.

40. Carter, *War Powers*, *supra* note 22, at 121–26.

41. I am of course using the term in a way quite distinct from the meaning popularized by the work of Thomas Grey. *See* Grey, *Do We Have an Unwritten Constitution?* 27 Stan. L. Rev. 703 (1975); Grey, *Origins of the Unwritten Constitution: Fundamental Law in American Revolutionary Thought*, 30 Stan. L. Rev. 843 (1978).

42. *See* Goldwater v. Carter, 444 U.S. 996 (1979).

43. Judicial hesitation is not the same as judicial capitulation. For a discussion of what I mean by hesitation, see Carter, *Constitutional Decisions*, *supra* note 4.

44. For an arguably contrary argument, see Youngstown Sheet & Tube Co. v. Sawyer, 343 U.S. 579, 610–11 (1952) (Frankfurther, J., concurring).

45. *See* Bickel, *Congress, the President and the Power to Wage War*, 48 Chi.-Kent L. Rev. 131, 146 (1971); Black, *The Working Balance of the American Political Departments*, 1 Hastings Const. L. Q. 13, 20 (1974).

46. 50 U.S.C. §§ 1541–1548 (1976 & Supp. V 1981) (hereinafter cited as War Powers Resolution).

47. War Powers Resolution, Sec. 5(b), 50 U.S.C. § 1544(b) (1976).

48. *Id*. Sec. 5(c), 50 U.S.C. § 1544(c) (1976).

49. *See* Carter, *War Powers*, *supra* note 22, at 112–33. For convenience, I omit the citations to specific pages of the longer argument.

50. Stated as constitutional principle, the claim that an earlier Congress cannot bind a subsequent one may be a strong argument against legislation on the Gramm-Rudman-

Hollings model. *See* Kahn, *Gramm-Rudman and the Capacity of Congress to Control the Future*, 13 Hastings Const. L. Q. 185 (1986).

51. 462 U.S. 919 (1983).

52. *Id*,. at 944–59. *See* Carter, *Judicial Power*, *supra* note 12, 15 1365–66, 1390–93 (explaining structural reasons for unconstiutionality of most legislative vetoes).

53. *See* Carter, *War Powers*, *supra* note 22, at 129–33.

54. *Id.* at 116–18, 126–28.

55. But *see* Rostow, *supra* note 5, at 851–55; Turner, *supra* Ch. 4 (both suggesting narrower constructions).

56. For more complicated arguments, see, *e.g.*, W. Reveley, *surpa* note 20, at 225–62; Berger, *supra* note 22.

57. Some critics have objected, in fact, that the War Powers Resolution cedes *too much* authority to the President. Friedman, *Waging War Against Checks and Balances— The Claim of an Unlimited Presidential War Power*, 57 St. John's L. Rev. 213, 218–23 (1983).

58. Some scholars believe this "sudden attack" power to be the beginning and the end of the President's independent war making authority, but the evidence for that claim is weak. *See supra* note 20. The "sudden attack" approach, moreover, may not be a limitation on presidential power at all. To take a single recurring example, can the power to *repluse* sudden attacks be read to include a power to *prevent* sudden attacks? A negative answer seems silly, but a positive answer opens the way for quite a considerable expansion of power. Stumbling down the slippery slope, one may ask whether the President must wait to attack until the troops of an adversary are actually massed on the border, ready to invade the United States, whether it is enough that they are in transit to the invasion points, or embarking for such transit, or in training for the invasion, or simply on the drawing board in the enemy's presidential palace—or perhaps in the enemy's ideological vision.

59. *See* Stone, *supra* Ch. 1.

60. *See* Miller, *supra* note 5.

61. Even a "limited" nuclear exchange, intended only to strike military targets, might essentially destroy the United States. *See* Daugherty, Levi, and von Hippel, *The Consequences of "Limited" Nuclear Attacks on the United States*, Int'l Security 3 (Spring 1986). For a lyrical and tragic vision of the aftermath of a more extensive attack, see J. Schell, *The Fate of the Earth* (1982).

62. *See* notes 23–45 *supra* and accompanying text.

63. United States v. Robel, 389 U.S. 258, 263–64 (1967).

64. If the President must choose whether to appeal to the entire Congress, then the committee, not the Congress, is plainly exercising the veto, and there is no indication of congressional sentiment. The obvious alternative would be to empower the committee only to render an opinion to the President, and then to recommend to the entire Congress a veto of the President's decision. Perhaps there would be no time for the Congress to act, but as I indicated at the outset, some appealing ideas are constitutionally impermissible.

65. The nondelegation doctrine generally conjures images of a judicial effort to decimate the New Deal, *see*, *e.g.*, Schechter Poultry Corp. v. United States, 295 U.S. 495 (1935); Panama Refining Co. v. Ryan, 293 U.S. 388 (1935). Justice Rehnquist has more recently advocated its use to narrow the discretion of contemporary administrative agencies as well. *See* American Textile Mfrs. Inst. v. Donovan, 452 U.S. 490, 543–48 (1981)

(dissenting opinion); Industrial Union Dep't v. American Petroleum Inst., 448 U.S. 607, 671–88 (1980) (concurring opinion).

66. Although the Supreme Court has in the post–New Deal era been quite generous in permitting the Congress to delegate authority to executive officers and independent agencies, *see, e.g.*, National Cable Television Ass'n v. United States, 415 U.S. 336 (1974); Yakus v. United States, 321 U.S. 414 (1944), the Justices have recently made plain that the Congress may not delegate legislative authority to an employee of the Congress. *See* Bowsher v. Synar, 106 S. Ct. 3181 (1986). Unless a distinction between delegation to an employee of the Congress and delegation to a committee of the Congress is shown to hold constitutional significance, the decision in *Synar*, handed down after this paper was completed, may well blow the FAS proposal out of the water.

67. 323 U.S. 214 (1944).

68. *See, e.g.*, Schenck v. United States, 249 U.S. 47 (1919); Debs v. United States, 249 U.S. 211 (1919).

69. *See e.g.*, Rostow, *The Japanese American Cases—A Disaster*, 54 Yale L.J. 489 (1945) (condemning government's position in *Korematsu*); Kalven, *Professor Ernst Freund and Debs v. United States*, 40 U. Chi. L. Rev. 235 (1973) (similar condemnation of position in *Debs*).

70. The FAS proposal was first presented legislatively in 1975. *See* Raven-Hansen, *supra*, Introduction, text accompanying notes 2–4.

71. *Compare* Bundy, Kenna, McNamara & Smith, *Nuclear Weapons and the Atlantic Alliance*, 60 Foreign Affairs 753 (1982) (advocating an American pledge of no first use) *with* Kaiser, Leber, Mertes & Schulze, *Nuclear Weapons and the Preservation of Peace*, 60 Foreign Affairs 1157 (1982) (defending the status quo).

72. *See* War Powers Resolution, Sec. 5(b) (3), 50 U.S.C. § 1544 (b) (3) (1976) (excusing presidential compliance if the Congress "is physically unable to meet as a result of an armed attack upon the United States").

9

First Use of Nuclear Weapons: The Constitutional Role of a Congressional Leadership Committee

William C. Banks

Assuming that Congress may constitutionally participate in a first use decision, the issue is how. One way would be for it to prohibit first use by the President unless both houses in full pass an expedited emergency resolution approving it. It may, however, be unrealistic to involve the whole Congress in such a shared decision. Urgency and expediency may not require a decision in minutes, but the nation may be irretrievably damaged if days must pass for the Congress as a whole to debate and then decide the first use question.[1] While various other ways of sharing the first use decision exist,[2] the Federation of American Scientists (FAS) has proposed to prohibit presidential first use absent a prior declaration of war unless a select joint committee of Congress approves such use. Ironically, compared to the more extreme alternatives to the present uncertain constitutional calculus—an absolute bar to presidential first use or an expedited two-house approval requirement, both of which are perhaps unwise or unconstitutional alternatives—committee approval has the most serious constitutional problems after the 1983 Supreme Court decision in *Immigration and Naturalization Service v. Chadha*.[3] *Chadha* declared unconstitutional the legislative veto, whereby "legislative" action was taken by less than the full bicameral Congress.[4]

Committee approval would not apparently comply with the "single, finely wrought and exhaustively considered procedure,"[5] which the *Chadha* Court found to be the constitutional prescription for any exercise of legislative power.

Copyright © 1986 *Journal of Legislation*. Copies of the full text of this article, which appeared in Volume 13, Number 1, may be purchased by writing the *Journal of Legislation*, Notre Dame Law School, Notre Dame, IN 46657. Reprinted with permission.

The author would like to thank Daan Braveman and Peter Raven-Hansen for helpful suggestions on early drafts of this chapter, and Richard Thomas, a second-year law student at Syracuse, for his invaluable research assistance.

Avoiding the full bicameral deliberative process, the committee approval mechanism would allow Congress to act without the necessary "cumbersomeness and delays"[6] which the Framers intended as a check upon the "hydraulic" tendencies of the legislative branch vis-a-vis the other branches and upon that branch's own propensity[7] for unwise and hasty action.[8]

This article explores these alleged constitutional infirmities of the first use committee, and concludes for three reasons that neither *Chadha* nor the Constitution precludes the first use proposal. First, the committee "veto" proposed by FAS is not a legislative veto and is thus not *a fortiori* unconstitutional after *Chadha*. Second, whether or not the committee mechanism is characterized as a legislative veto, it does not suffer the formal constitutional defects which caused the Court to invalidate the INS veto. Nor, finally, would it violate separation of powers principles on which the Court could, and perhaps should have premised its *Chadha* decision.[9]

Like a few other unique exercises of the legislative power,[10] the committee approval mechanism is an integral component of an overall effort to define or clarify conflicts or ambiguities in the Constitution regarding the allocation of power between the elected branches. This clarification of the constitutional prescription for a first use decision is not ordinary legislation.[11] It defines the Constitution's terms and "delineates structures and processes,"[12] reminds the President of his limited war powers, and should therefore be viewed as "quasi-constitutional in nature."[13]

I. THE FIRST USE COMMITTEE APPROVAL MECHANISM IS NOT A LEGISLATIVE VETO

Generally a legislative veto may be defined as "an effort by Congress, by one house of Congress, or even by a single committee or chairman to retain control over the execution or interpretation of laws *after* enactment."[14] More specifically the veto is a "clause in a statute which says that a particular executive action . . . will take effect only if Congress does not nullify it by resolution within a specific period of time."[15] The legislative veto has three essential elements: "1) statutory delegation of power to the executive; 2) exercise of that power by the executive; 3) power reserved by the Congress to nullify that exercise of authority."[16]

Judge Breyer has characterized the veto's function "as a legislative compromise of a fight for delegated power."[17] "[S]ometimes," he says, "the veto compromises "important substantive conflicts embedded deeply in the Constitution."[18] But while Judge Breyer's functional characterization would likely include the first use committee approval mechanism as a legislative veto, that mechanism does not fit his fuller definition.

First, the committee mechanism does not involve any initial statutory delegation to the executive. Instead, the proposal contains an initial prohibition: "so long as no nuclear weapons have been used by others, the President shall not use nuclear weapons. . . . ''[19] In a pre-*Chadha* decision, the D.C. Circuit recognized in just such a prohibition a distinction between a statutory delegation followed by a committee veto and an initial prohibition followed by a committee authorization.[20] *AFGE v. Pierce* involved a HUD appropriations measure which provided that none of the appropriated funds "may be used prior to January 1, 1983, to plan, design, implement, or administer any reorganization of the Department without the prior approval of the Committees on Appropriations.''[21] The court recognized that the spending condition is not "naturally" characterizable as a "legislative veto in the usual sense. . . . [T]he directive is nothing more or less than a grant of legislative power to . . . [a] committee. . . . ''[22] In other words, the D.C. Circuit recognized that the provision contained an initial prohibition rather than a delegation, followed by a resolution of approval rather than disapproval. Such a provision is not a legislative veto. Functionally, the committee approval proposal is like a statute that prohibits the President from using nuclear weapons when they have not been used by others and authorizes a committee to rescind the prohibition.[23]

Second, the FAS proposal does not provide for a subsequent resolution of disapproval or a nullification of previously delegated authority. Unlike the legislative veto, the committee action here would be a subsequent resolution of approval, not disapproval. Further, the approval would be initiated by the President, much as he might seek a joint resolution of approval from Congress. This committee approval procedure, therefore, does not involve any withdrawal of authorization, but rather a new authorization, a lifting of a "congressionally-imposed restriction.''[24]

Since the committee approval mechanism involves neither an initial delegation of power to the President, nor a subsequent withdrawal of delegated power without presentment, it should not be characterized as a legislative veto and is not unconstitutional *per se* after *Chadha*.

II. THE FIRST USE COMMITTEE APPROVAL MECHANISM DOES NOT VIOLATE ARTICLE I

Chadha was based on form and form alone—Article I's literal requirements for bicameral congressional approval and presentment of proposal legislative action to the President for his veto or approval. The committee first use approval mechanism offends neither bicameralism nor presentment.

A. Bicameralism

The first component of the *Chadha* holding is the bicameralism requirement of Article I, sections 1 and 7.[25] Acknowledging that the one-house veto was a convenient and efficient device,[26] the Court found it nonetheless inconsistent with the Framers' conscious decision to "impose burdens on governmental processes that often seem clumsy, inefficient, even unworkable" in order to check "arbitrary governmental acts."[27] It is clear that a committee approval procedure, while involving members of both houses, nevertheless offends bicameralism "in the more significant sense . . . since neither house itself is fully involved in the legislative act."[28] The procedure would not apparently assure "that the legislative power would be exercised only after opportunity for full study and debate in separate settings."[29]

At first view, these objections would seem fatal to the committee release device. However, there are two bases for excepting the FAS proposal from formal bicameralism requirements. One basis is the Court's own approach in separation of powers cases.[30] While in a few recent cases the Court has tended to opt for the simple if often unrealistic approach to separation of powers which precludes one branch from sharing tasks that resemble those of another,[31] it has generally taken a more flexible approach in its infrequent decisions of separation issues. Especially in areas of shared powers, such as the war powers, Justice Jackson's famous formula for resolving conflicts between the branches has guided the Court.[32] By this formula, in this "twilight zone" of shared powers, if the Congress acts, it wins.[33]

This functional approach was applied in 1981 in *Dames & Moore v. Regan*,[34] where the Court declared that the Congress had acted through an implicit delegation by acquiescence to legitimate the President's curtailment of American claims against Iran in the wake of resolving the hostage crisis.[35] This past term, the Court again departed from its formalistic approach to separation of powers in *Thomas v. Union Carbide Agricultural Products Co.*,[36] proclaiming "practical attention to substance rather than doctrinaire reliance on formal categories."[37] Thus, the popularity of formalism to decide separation cases may be waning. Moreover, the formalistic approach of *Chadha* is especially unlikely to apply to war powers, in the allocation of which the courts have steadfastly refused to· become involved.[38]

Second, the bicameralism requirement has considerably less relevance in the foreign affairs context than in the domestic context, and even less in the context of the war powers and a first use decision. Two of the important concerns which led the Framers to adopt the bicameral requirement of Article I are relevant to the committee mechanism.[39] The first, and perhaps the most important, was the fear of legislative hegemony. The Court in *Chadha* relied upon James Wilson's comments during the convention debates and Hamilton's observations in *The Federalist Nos. 22 and 51* to the effect that legislative tyranny was greatly to be feared and only to be averted by dividing the legislative power to make its exercise more difficult and cumbersome.[40]

While the Court's emphasis upon this concern may fit the INS veto provision at issue in *Chadha*, it exemplifies the pitfalls of stating broad constitutional principles based on an extreme case. Although it is true *generally* that the Framers believed "that the powers conferred on Congress were the powers to be most carefully circumscribed,"[41] it is also true that in the area of war powers the legislature was not the branch whose potential for tyranny was most feared. It was the executive, not Congress, whose potential for abuse of war power was discussed at the convention[42] and examined in *The Federalist*.[43] The careful attention paid the "declare war" language by the Framers[44] demonstrates their concern that the President's powers be checked so that, absent a declaration of war, he would only be able to commit troops in response to "sudden attacks."[45]

In the usual case, then, bicameralism serves to check *the President* in the exercise of the war powers. Indeed, the "sudden attacks" exception would release the President from the bicameralism check in exigent circumstances not unlike those from which the Congress would seek an exception in the first use proposal. Furthermore, since the ratification of the Constitution, history has demonstrated that the legislative branch has not evidenced inherent "hydraulic pressure . . . to exceed the outer limits"[46] of foreign affairs and war powers; indeed, quite the opposite has been true.[47] Thus, the concern about curbing the legislative powers, which in part motivated the Framers' decision to require bicameral action, is of limited relevance in the foreign affairs and war powers context.

A second purpose for which the Framers adopted the bicameralism requirement was to assure "that the legislative power would be exercised only after opportunity for full study and debate in separate settings."[48] The *Chadha* opinion quotes Justice Story's characterization of the Framers' fears concerning the propensity of the legislative branch for hasty and ill-considered action: "If [a legislature] feels no check but its own will, it rarely has the firmness to insist upon holding a question long enough under its own view, to see and mark it in all its bearings and relations to society."[49] Thus, the Framers opted for a time-consuming "step-by-step, deliberate and deliberative process."[50]

Again, however, the exercise of legislative power in the area of war powers, and more particularly a first use decision, is distinguishable. It is true that the Framers saw the requirement of approval by both houses[51] as part of a " 'system [which] will not hurry us into war.' "[52] Nevertheless, the reality of modern warfare demands that certain decisions to commit or not to commit America into hostilities be made with greater dispatch than other legislative decisions. Consequently, in modern times, even when Congress does adhere to strict bicameralism in making emergency national security decisions, it often does not and *cannot* "insist upon holding a question long"[53] under its view.[54] As the Supreme Court has recognized, an appreciation that one important purpose of the Constitution is to "provide for the national defense"[55] should foster an attitude of realism concerning matters of national safety and the appropriate period and form of legislative deliberation.

More importantly, the concern that the allocation of powers between the Congress and the President "not hurry us into war" may be best served by excepting the first use context from the formal bicameralism requirement. In the present uncertain political and constitutional climate, the absence of explicit legislation on the first use context makes it possible that the President may unilaterally choose to initiate a nuclear attack. Because such a decision would most assuredly be an act of "war,"[56] the elasticity retained by the "emergency" clause in the War Powers Resolution is inadequate to assure a congressional role in the first use decision.[57] Assuming that the Congress would not impose the first use prohibition without the release mechanism, the release mechanism furthers the bicameralism purpose by providing at least some debate and perhaps restraint that would otherwise not exist.

In any event, it is important to remember that a procedure such as the committee approval mechanism in the first use proposal does not give the power to one " 'man, or a single body of men, to involve us in such distress,' "[58] which was the Framers' greatest fear. The FAS proposal is a realistic way of insuring that at least representatives of two different branches—the President and a committee composed of elected leaders of *both* houses—must concur before the nation can be involved in the distress entailed by a first use of nuclear weapons. The Framers' concern that "nothing but our national interest can draw us into a war"[59] is realistically honored and the *Chadha* majority's interest in dividing power and insuring fuller deliberation[60] is met, even though bicameralism in the strict sense is and probably cannot be followed.

B. Presentment

The second of two "formal" concerns which guided the *Chadha* Court's decision is the Article I, section 7, clause 3 requirement that every act of legislation be presented to the President for his approval.[61] The legislative veto did not fulfill this requirement because the veto had the effect of altering statutorily created authority without presenting the proposed alteration to the President.[62]

Unlike the legislative veto, however, the committee approval procedure would not be producing legislation without the participation of the President.[63] By definition, any exercise of the approval mechanism would be an affirmative act initiated by the President. Without the affirmative authorization from the committee, the original statutory prohibition on first use would still be effective. The committee approval device is merely the procedure by which the President obtains a release from the prohibition. The President could "veto" the first use authorization simply by not requesting it or by not acting upon it, that is, by not employing nuclear weapons despite the authorization. Thus, the committee approval procedure is consistent with *Chadha's* formal concern about presentment.

III. THE FIRST USE COMMITTEE APPROVAL MECHANISM PROMOTES THE SEPARATION OF POWERS

Generally the principle of separation of powers has been interpreted to prohibit arrogations of power to one branch of government which disrupt the proper balance between the coordinate branches,[64] or prevent one of the branches from accomplishing its constitutionally assigned functions.[65] The committee approval mechanism neither invades an executive function nor prevents Congress from doing its assigned functions. In fact, if anything, it promotes the purposes of the separation of powers.

A. No Arrogation of Executive Functions

Unlike most legislative vetoes, the committee approval procedure is not an arrogation of the executive function of the "execution or interpretation of laws *after* enactment."[66] While the joint committee would be exercising "discretion" in deciding whether to lift the congressionally imposed prohibition on first use, this discretion is properly characterized as congressional deliberation of the kind that would accompany any exercise of Congress' own war powers. Furthermore, the lifting of a congressionally imposed prohibition on first use could hardly be considered an executive function.

There is, of course, the additional separation of powers question as to whether or not the proposed first use legislation would intrude upon any Article II war powers of the President. This question, however, goes to initial prohibition on first use,[67] not the mechanism of its subsequent repeal. A committee repeal of the prohibition does not derogate from presidential power, but enhances it.

One way to decide whether the usurpation threat central to our separation of powers is present in the first use proposal is to ask whether Congress would want to grant first use power without the opportunity to check it.[68] If the answer is "no," the proposal grants power to the President that he would otherwise not be granted. This analysis focuses on the trade-off between the efficiency gained by the shared power arrangement and the chance that formal constitutional prescriptions for preventing tyranny are being violated. As Justice White said, dissenting in *Chadha*, the use of a veto-like device in the war powers area allows Congress to "transfer greater authority to the President . . . while preserving its own constitutional role."[69]

B. No Disruption of Legislative Functions

It is unlikely that the imposition of these new responsibilities upon selected members of the Congress would "interfere with their ability to perform their constitutionally-required duties."[70] Although the committee's deliberations would necessarily be secret and sensitive, and perhaps quite taxing, the episodic nature of the committee's function assures that the members' other legislative work would be accomplished. Thus, even if the committee is given the unlikely characterization of performing an "executive" function, the separation of powers interest in getting the business of government done is not offended.[71]

C. Promotion of Purposes of Separation of Powers

The separation of powers is far from a unitary concept. At least three discrete versions of separation were considered by our Framers, and there is evidence that all three—forestalling tyranny, insuring the government's legitimacy, and promoting efficiency—animated the separation which found its way into the Constitution.[72] Because there is no explicit reference to a separation rule in the Constitution,[73] the search for its requirements in a given instance is often elusive, particularly when the potentially competing dictates of the fear of tyranny and need for efficiency point toward opposite outcomes to a separation controversy.[74] But when the multiple purposes of the separation of powers are kept in view, the committee approval mechanism may, unlike the *Chadha* veto and perhaps other vetoes of administration, actually enhance the goals of separation of powers.

The avoidance-of-tyranny rationale which is often manifested in what is called "our system of checks and balances" would be enhanced by this check on the President, especially when otherwise none might exist. Indeed, support for the committee approval mechanism may be found in one of the most important separation disputes—*Youngstown Sheet & Tube Co. v. Sawyer*.[75] In holding that President Truman's seizure of the steel mills, without statutory authority, exceeded the President's constitutional power, the Court relied on evidence that Congress had recently considered, but then rejected, the idea of granting him the authority he had exercised. Thus, where the powers in question are concurrent, in the "zone of twilight," congressional intent to curtail presidential action may be effectively expressed by measures short of legislation. As long as the Congress has power to control the President in such an area by statute, allowing a less formal expression of congressional intent helps to insure that some check on presidential power exists.[76] While it is true that *Youngstown* did not look to a committee for its evidence of congressional intent, this recourse is not in principle different from looking to the vagaries of judicially reconstructed legislative history to ascertain why Congress did not enact legislation.

Furthermore, for these same reasons the committee approval mechanism legitimizes the exercise of war power by the government as a whole.

Finally, the release mechanism may also substantially further the efficiency values which loomed large at the Constitutional Convention.[77] History reveals that efficiency, getting the important work of government accomplished effectively, was as important to the Framers as either of the other reasons for separating powers.[78] While the decided cases are more often remembered for denying or downplaying this efficiency value in separation disputes,[79] their infrequency is strong evidence that the efficiency value is out there encouraging accommodation and cooperation among the branches. In the context of the shared war powers, the committee release mechanism may be the most effective way to make a first use decision, as compared to a unilateral decision by the President or full bicameral action by the Congress. On this view of the mechanism, the whole government gains in effectiveness and loses nothing.[80]

IV. CONCLUSION

Given the risks of human fallibility in a one-person decision and the risks to the survival of the nation from a nuclear war, good sense suggests the sharing of a first use decision. The urgency which requires immediate and therefore unilateral executive decision to fire nuclear weapons second in retaliation for a nuclear attack is not present in the same degree in a first use scenario. Furthermore, since the conflict into which nuclear weapons would be introduced would be one hitherto fought with conventional weapons, any lost time in ordering first use would not necessarily threaten the continued survival of the nation in a way that a nuclear attack could. The committee would involve the Congress in a most important national decision, yet meet the need for speed and secrecy. It is a compromise between letting the President decide for himself and involving the full Congress, but it may be more effective than either of the polar alternatives. The committee could engender the tough and independent criticism of the technical reports and factual or political assumptions which would be leading the President to favor the nuclear attack. As a result, no single President, too deeply involved, could drag the nation to a nuclear holocaust. For the first time, Congress would necessarily be a part of the decision-making process of nuclear weapons use issues.

NOTES

1. Strategic questions are addressed in Stone, *supra* Ch. 1 and Moore, *supra* Ch. 3.

2. Options include requiring some form of congressional consultation instead of approval or some form of presidential consultation with designated executive branch officials before first use.

3. Immigration and Naturalization Service v. Chadha, 462 U.S. 919 (1983).

4. *Id.* at 958–59.

5. *Id.* at 951.

6. *Id.* at 959.

7. *Id.* at 948–50.

8. *See* Consumer Energy Council of Am. v. Federal Energy Regulatory Comm'n, 673 F.2d 425, 463 (D.C. Cir. 1982), *aff'd*, 463 U.S. 1216 (1983) (discussing value of President's veto in checking hasty or unwise legislative action).

9. *See generally* Strauss, *Was There a Baby in the Bathwater? A Comment on the Supreme Court's Legislative Veto Decision*, 1983 Duke L. J. 789, 812–15 (1983).

10. *See* War Powers Resolution, 50 U.S.C. §1541 (1982); Congressional Budget and Impoundment Control Act of 1974, 31 U.S.C. §1403(a)-(c) (1976); International Emergency Economic Powers Act, 50 U.S.C. §1706(b) (1976 & Supp. V 1981).

11. Early authority for the distinction may be found in the Supreme Court's 1798 decision in *Hollingsworth v. Virginia*, 3 U.S. (3 Dall.) 378 (1798), which held that the proposed eleventh amendment need not be presented to the President because presentment "applies only to the ordinary cases of legislation. . . . " *Id.* at 381 n.*. Because Article I requires presentment of "Every Order, Resolution or Vote" of the Congress, *Hollingsworth* supports the notion that some legislation is not of that species. I do not wish to rely on *Hollingsworth* for too much, although Professor Carter has argued convincingly from *Hollingsworth* for the existence of a category of "extraordinary legislative power" in his attempt to save the legislative vetoes in the War Powers Resolution from *Chadha*.

See Carter, *The Constitutionality of the War Powers Resolution*, 70 Va. L. Rev. 101, 129–32 (1984).

12. G. Gunther, *Constitutional Law* 361 (1985).

13. *Id.*

14. B. Craig, *The Legislative Veto: Congressional Control of Regulation* 1 (1983) (emphasis added).

15. Breyer, *The Legislative Veto After Chadha*, 72 Geo. L. J. 785 (1984).

16. *Id.* at 786.

17. *Id.* at 787.

18. *Id.*

19. *See* Raven-Hansen, *supra* Introduction.

20. AFGE v. Pierce, 697 F.2d 303, 306 (D.C. Cir. 1982).

21. *Id.* at 304.

22. *Id.* at 306.

23. *See* Carter, *supra* note 11, at 133. In effect, new law would be created by the President seeking and obtaining committee approval.

24. Joint resolutions of approval are generally accepted as a constitutional alternative to the legislative veto. *See* Breyer, *supra* note 15, at 789; Watson, *Congress Steps Out: A Look at Congressional Control of the Executive*, 63 Cal. L. Rev. 983, 1084–87 (1985). For examples of proposed substitutions of approval resolutions for legislative vetoes, see Levitas and Brand, *Congressional Review of Executive and Agency Actions after Chadha: "The Son of Legislative Veto Lives,"* 72 Geo. L. J. 801, 806 (1984); L. Fisher, *Constitutional Conflicts Between Congress and the President* 178–83 (1985). Unlike simple and concurrent resolutions, joint resolutions are presented to the President. The first use committee mechanism likewise satisfies presentment because the statutory restriction could be lifted only at the President's initiative. *See infra* text accompanying notes 61–65.

25. *Chadha*, 462 U.S. at 948–51.

26. *Id.* at 958.

27. *Id.* at 958–59.

28. *AFGE*, 697 F.2d at 306.

29. *Chadha*, 462 U.S. at 951.

30. *See generally* cases discussed in L. Henkin, *Foreign Affairs and the Constitution* 89–123 (1972); *see also* W. Reveley, III, *War Powers of the President and Congress* 206–12 (1981); L. Fisher, *President and Congress* 200–204 (1972).

31. *See e.g.*, Strauss, *The Place of Agencies in Government: Separation of Powers and the Fourth Branch*, 84 Col. L. Rev. 573, 625–40 (1984) (hereinafter cited as Strauss, *Place of Agencies*).

32. "1. When the President acts pursuant to an express or implied authorization of Congress, his authority is at its maximum, for it includes all that he possesses in his own right plus all that Congress can delegate. In these circumstances, and in these only, may he be said (for what it may be worth) to personify the federal sovereignty. If his act is held unconstitutional under these circumstances, it usually means that the Federal Government as an undivided whole lacks power. A seizure executed by the President pursuant to an Act of Congress would be supported by the strongest of presumptions and the widest latitude of judicial interpretation, and the burden of persuasion would rest heavily upon any who might attack it.

2. When the President acts in absence of either a congressional grant or denial of authority, he can only rely upon his own independent powers, but there is a zone of

twilight in which he and Congress may have concurrent authority, or in which its distribution is uncertain. Therefore, congressional inertia, indifference or quiescence may sometimes, at least as a practical matter, enable, if not invite, measures on independent presidential responsibility. In this area, any actual test of power is likely to depend on the imperatives of events and contemporary imponderables rather than on abstract theories of law.

3. When the President takes measures incompatible with the expressed or implied will of Congress, his power is at its lowest ebb, for then he can rely only upon his own constitutional powers minus any constitutional powers of Congress over the matter. Courts can sustain exclusive presidential control in such a case only by disabling the Congress from acting upon the subject. Presidential claim to power at once so conclusive and preclusive must be scrutinized with caution, for what is at stake is the equilibrium established by our constitutional system.'' Youngstown Sheet and Tube Co. v. Sawyer, 343 U.S. 579, 635–38 (1952) (Jackson, J., concurring). Only Justices Black and Douglas rejected the "twilight zone" premise in *Youngstown*.

33. That is, in "the twilight zone" of shared power, legislation, or perhaps something less than legislation, is effective to resolve the power allocation question. *See generally* Watson, *supra* note 24 at 1084–1086.

34. 453 U.S. 654 (1981).

35. *Id*. at 678–88.

36. 105 S. Ct. 3325 (1985) (article III does not bar Congress from requiring binding arbitration with limited judicial review of compensation disputes among registrants in a pesticide registration scheme).

37. *Id*. at 3336.

38. *See* Note, *The Future of the War Powers Resolution*, 36 Stan. L. Rev. 1410, 1415–16 (1984). In fact, courts have only rarely invalidated statutes which arguably invade executive powers, except when the Article II power is stated clearly in the text. Carter, *supra* note 11, at 124 n. 111 (recognizing *Myers v. United States*, 272 U.S. 52 (1926), as a possible exception). In any event, I claim that the committee would be given an Article I, not an Article II power.

39. Two other purposes for the bicameralism requirement are inapplicable to the first use context. First, the Framers feared that "special interests could be favored at the expense of public needs." *Chadha*, 462 U.S. at 950. Exercise of legislative power by a mere committee ordinarily might elevate parochial interests and undermine the constitutional functions of a national and two-house legislative system. Second, the Framers were also concerned, although not of one mind, about the apprehensions of the smaller states. Those states feared that a commonality of interest among the larger states would work to their disadvantage. Representatives of the larger states, on the other hand, were skeptical of a legislature that could pass laws favoring a minority of the people.

These concerns are irrelevant to the FAS proposal because the decisions to approve or not to approve a first use of nuclear weapons can hardly be characterized as one which invites special or parochial interests to predominate over national interest. Even if there might be certain groups or states which have unique interests—such as states which could be likely candidates for enemy retaliation because they host nuclear weapons sites—the process for selection of committee members would not allow the kind of special interest domination that could occur in other contexts. The FAS proposal specifies that the elected leadership of the House and Senate will serve on the committee. The committee, therefore, could not be targeted for infiltration by senators and congressmen whose sole concern is the representation of local or special interests.

40. *Chadha*, 462 U.S. at 949–50.

41. *Id.* at 947.

42. Witness the clamor following delegate Butler's suggestion that the President be given power to declare war. A. Sofaer, *War, Foreign Affairs and Constitutional Power: The Origins* 31; *id.* 27, 31 (on the fears of convention delegates such as Pinckney, Gerry and Mason concerning presidential abuse of war power).

43. *The Federalist Nos. 26 and 69* (A. Hamilton) (J. Cooke ed. 1961); Sofaer, *supra* note 42, at 42–44.

44. *See* Sofaer, *supra* note 42, at 27–31.

45. *Id.* at 31.

46. *Chadha*, 462 U.S. at 951.

47. *See* Sen. Rep. No. 797, 90th Cong., 1st Sess. (1967).

48. *Chadha*, 462 U.S. at 951.

49. *Id.* at 949–50 (*quoting* J. Story, *Commentaries on the Constitution of the United States* 383–84 (3d. ed. 1858)).

50. *Id.* at 959.

51. The suggestion that the Senate alone would have the power to declare war was rejected at the Convention. Sofaer, *supra* note 42, at 31.

52. *Id.* at 52 (*quoting* Wilson, 2 Elliot, *Debates* 528.)

53. *Chadha*, 462 U.S. at 950 (*quoting* Joseph Story).

54. For example, World War II was authorized by Congress on the same day as the Pearl Harbor attack; and the Formosa Resolution was passed under expedited procedures which did not admit "full study and debate." Reveley, *supra* note 30, at 126. *See also* Tiefer, *infra* Ch. 10.

55. Lichter v. United States, 334 U.S. 742,779, 782 n.34 (1948).

56. *See* Stone, *supra* Ch. 1.

57. 50 U.S.C. § 1541(c) (1982).

58. 2 Elliot, *Debates* 528 (Iredell, *quoting* Wilson), *quoted in* Sofaer, *supra* note 42, at 52 n.198.

59. *Id.*

60. *Chadha*, 462 U.S. at 951.

61. *Chadha*, 462 U.S. at 946–48.

62. *Id.* at 952.

63. The fact that the committee authorization would run directly to the President, rather than to an agency, is significant. In *AFGE*, the D.C. Circuit found that committee approval mechanism did implicate the presentment requirement, but there the committee authorization ran directly to an agency, not to the President himself. 697 F.2d at 307. A committee was empowered, without any presidential involvement, to release a congressionally imposed restriction on funds for reorganization of the agency, thus offending presentment. By contrast, in the proposed first use context, the President would, of course, have the final say on whether the release of the congressionally imposed prohibition would actually be realized, i.e., in a nuclear strike ordered by the President.

64. Nixon v. General Services Administration, 433 U.S. 425, 443 (1977).

65. *Id.*, *citing* United States v. Nixon, 418 U.S. 683, 711–12 (1974).

66. *Craig*, *supra* note 14, at 8.

67. This issue is beyond the scope of this discussion. *See supra* Part II of this book.

68. *See* Strauss, *supra* note 9, at 791–92. The following analysis assumes that first use is not a unilateral presidential prerogative. *See supra* Part II of this book.

69. *Chadha*, 462 U.S. at 969 (White, J., dissenting).

70. *See In re Application of the President's Commission on Organized Crime, Subpoena of Lorenzo*, No. 85–5232, slip opinion (11th Cir. May 29, 1985).

71. *Id.*

72. *See generally* W. Gwynn, *The Meaning of the Separation of Powers* (1962).

73. The closest thing to an explicit statement of separation of powers in the Constitution is the allocation of powers among the three branches in the three articles. *See U.S. Const.* art. I, § 1, cl. 1; *id.* at art. II, § 1, cl. 1; *id.* at art. III, § 1, cl. 1.

74. *See* Banks, *Efficiency in Government: Separation of Powers Reconsidered*, 35 Syr. L. Rev. 715, 723–30 (1984). Unfortunately, the Supreme Court has sometimes obfuscated separation's meaning by downplaying the importance of one version of separation to better support an outcome which relies upon another version. *Id. See* Myers v. United States, 272 U.S. 52 (1926); United States v. Brown, 381 U.S. 437 (1965). *Chadha* is a good example: the Framers' concern with efficiency was distorted to a low profile in order to stress the protections from tyranny which would come from literal adherence to presentment and bicameralism.

75. *See Youngstown*, 343 U.S. at 637 (Jackson, J., concurring).

76. Indeed, if the check could only take the form of a statute, a mere one-third of either chamber can thwart the legislative will and leave the President unchecked. *See* Watson, *supra* note 24, at 1084–1086.

77. *See generally* Banks, *supra* note 74.

78. *Id.* at 720–23.

79. *Id.* at 723–30.

80. *See* Strauss, *supra* note 9, at 812, 815.

10

The FAS Proposal: Valid Check or Unconstitutional Veto?

Charles Tiefer

Between changing one person's citizenship status and blowing the world up, there is a substantial practical difference. This chapter concerns whether there is a constitutional one. An American decision to make the first use of nuclear weapons in a crisis—for example, to respond to a Soviet conventional invasion of Iran, South Korea or West Germany with a tactical nuclear strike—might be tantamount, in some circumstances, to blowing the world up. The constitutional questions regarding Congress' role in a first use decision remain largely unexplored. Currently, since neither the President nor Congress has specified formal procedures for an American decision for nuclear first use, presumably in a crisis the President will make that decision, and any role for Congress is uncertain.

If Congress wishes to establish something in place of solo decision making by the President, it must face the question of what it might enact in advance, for a crisis requiring a first use decision may not allow time to set up an arrangement. The Federation of American Scientists (FAS) proposal for a congressional leadership committee relies on advance congressional leadership assent, rather than congressional veto afterwards, because of the irreversibility of the decision, and the possibility, during a crisis, that a role for the leadership may be the only practical approach.

Apart from the war powers questions, treated elsewhere in this collection,[1]

The views expressed herein are solely the personal views of the author and not those of the House of Representatives or any congressional entity or person. As Assistant Senate Legal Counsel in 1979–84, the author had the principal role in drafting a brief of the Senate in *Chadha*, and both briefed and argued a number of other legislative veto cases.

this proposal raises the distinct question of the validity of the proposed *mechanism* for such a congressional role. Legislation or declarations of war do not raise a question of the constitutionality of the mechanism itself, for the Constitution provides for them. Requiring congressional leadership assent—a congressional action not amounting to enactment of legislation—raises that question of mechanism. Like the mechanisms for disapproval or termination by concurrent resolution in the Arms Export Control Act and the War Powers Resolution,[2] it is subject to question under the Supreme Court's decision in *Immigration and Naturalization Service v. Chadha*,[3] which struck down a legislative veto provision as unconstitutional.

This chapter concludes that in spite of *Chadha*, the Constitution allows mechanisms in foreign affairs like the concurrent resolutions for terminating combat interventions or arms sales and like the proposed mechanism requiring assent to a first use decision. Part I addresses the principal problem: the executive branch's broad view of *Chadha* which deems unconstitutional all such mechanisms. This broad view fails to recognize that *Chadha* concluded, as the heart of its analysis, that Congress could not use a legislative veto resolution to take back authority it had delegated in the domestic sphere. The Court rested its conclusion that a veto resolution was "legislative"—requiring enactment subject to presidential veto like a law—on the availability of the standards required by the nondelegation doctrine, and of judicial review, as dual checks on the executive.

However, the Supreme Court has recognized that the nondelegation doctrine, and the model for congressional-executive relations it established in the domestic sphere, simply do not apply in the foreign sphere. That is a realm of shared inherent power, not delegated power. The political question and standing doctrines clearly make judicial review far less available for presidential actions in foreign affairs than in domestic affairs. For these reasons, the Supreme Court's approach in *Chadha* should not deny a congressional role in a first use decision, for such a decision clearly does not fit into the *Chadha* model of restraint of the executive by the nondelegation doctrine and by judicial review.

Part II addresses whether history supports a mechanism such as the proposed one. The statutory history since Pearl Harbor supports the constitutionality of a congressional role. While the nation has chosen repeatedly to give the President broad war powers without limiting standards or judicial review, it has done so by using the check of a role for Congress. In World War II, the Korean and Vietnam wars, lesser military deployments, and the generic legislation of the 1970s, Congress consistently reserved the check of provisions for congressional termination of authority. A first use nuclear situation, even more than these past conventional wars, presents the reason which justified that check: its potential for invocation in a situation of otherwise unconstrained, and possibly ill-advised, use of awesome powers.

I. *CHADHA* EMPLOYS THE CLASSIC DELEGATION MODEL WHICH APPLIES TO THE DOMESTIC BUT NOT FOREIGN SPHERES

A. A Broad View of *Chadha*

Since *Chadha*, the executive branch has taken a public position, shared by various commentators, that generalizes the decision's holding to strike down all requirements for congressional assent in any sphere, domestic or foreign.[4] That broad view should be set forth before looking at the alternative.

The starting point is the *Chadha* case itself. Jagdish Rai Chadha was an East Indian from Kenya, who was subject to deportation because he had overstayed his student visa. In 1974, an immigration officer suspended Chadha's deportation, pursuant to Immigration and Nationality Act ("INA") provisions which allowed either the House or the Senate to disapprove or "veto" such suspensions.[5] In 1975, the House of Representatives passed a resolution vetoing the suspension of Chadha's deportation, believing that his circumstances did not warrant it.[6] Accordingly, in 1976, the INS ordered Chadha to be deported.[7]

Chadha filed in the Ninth Circuit an appeal from the deportation order, challenging the statutory provision for the congressional veto as unconstitutional. The executive branch joined Chadha in his challenge, and the House and the Senate appeared in the case to provide the official defense of the challenged provision. In 1980 the Court of Appeals invalidated the provision.[8] After argument in 1981 and the unusual step of reargument in 1982, the Supreme Court affirmed in 1983.

The facts of Chadha's case itself do not compel broad generalization of the case, as Chadha's own predicament, and the INA provision, were unique. Congress has never enacted any other legislative veto outside the INA directed at individual persons. All the rest concern actions such as regulations, impoundments, or arms sales; the House of Representatives never passes resolutions reducing the status of individuals, except under that unique INA provision.[9] Such a measure changing the status of individuals so violated tradition, in its resemblance to a bill of attainder, that the Supreme Court recognized a serious open question whether Congress could enact such a measure even in the form of a statute passed by both houses and signed by the President, let alone by legislative veto resolution.

Thus, it is the opinion's reasoning, rather than its facts, on which is based the broad view generalizing the result to invalidate all provisions for congressional roles. Chief Justice Burger, speaking for the Court, started his opinion with the facts and procedural preliminaries, respectively in Parts I and II, and a description of the legislative process in Part III. The Chief Justice declared that the Framers prescribed "a single, finely wrought and exhaustively consid-

ered, procedure''[10] for exercise of legislative power: enactment of a measure by
both houses, followed by presentment to the President for signature or veto. The
resolution vetoing Chadha's suspension of deportation, like every legislative
veto, had not gone through this procedure; only the INA itself had done so. This
part of the majority opinion was considered by all to be ''unexceptionable'',[11]
and it precedes the heart of the opinion in Part IV, concerning why the veto
resolution at issue was ''an exercise of legislative power'' in the Court's sense
of requiring enactment like a statute.

Justice White's dissenting opinion argued, along the lines of the House and
Senate defense of the INA's constitutionality, that the INA, like other modern
statutes, balanced a broad delegation of authority to the executive branch—here,
authority to suspend deportations—with the constraint of the legislative veto. Justice White relied on the nondelegation doctrine, the basic notion of constraints on
delegation: that usually, when Congress delegates power to the executive, the delegation must include standards. For example, when Congress delegates power to
set rates, it has to provide a standard, however vague, such as rates that will ''provide a fair return'' or ''reasonable'' rates. These standards provide an outer limit
against wholly arbitrary executive action and offer some basis for judicial review.
In Justice White's view, the veto served, not as a second act of legislation—not
''an exercise of legislative power'' like a statute—but just as the realization of the
INA's own limit on the delegation.[12]

In Part IV, the Court rejected this view, deeming the veto resolution itself
akin to an act of legislation. The resolution was an action that ''was essentially
legislative,'' for ''[t]he one-House veto operated in these cases to overrule the
Attorney General . . . once the Attorney General, in the exercise of legislatively
delegated authority, had determined the alien should remain. . . . ''[13] ''Since it
is clear that the action by the House . . . was an exercise of legislative power,
that action was subject to the standards prescribed in Art.I,''[14] namely, ''passage
by a majority of both houses and presentment to the President.''[15]

Chief Justice Burger described the House's immigration-related veto resolution
as an ''exercise of legislative power'' because it ''had the purpose and effect of
altering the legal rights, duties, and relations of persons, including the Attorney
General, Executive Branch officials and Chadha, all outside the Legislative
branch.''[16] The broad view of the decision frees this description from its context,
and generalizes it universally. That view considers any veto resolution which
alters ''legal rights,'' by constraining authority of any ''Executive Branch officials,'' as an ''exercise of legislative power'' and thus unconstitutional. That
view deems legislative vetoes regarding foreign affairs actions to be just as
unconstitutional as those regarding domestic ones, for whether a resolution vetoes
a foreign or a domestic action, its challengers say that it has ''the purpose and
effect of altering'' the ''legal rights''—the authority—of the President.

Both a concurring and a dissenting opinion appeared deeply concerned that
this broad view did fit the Court's decision. Justice Powell began his concurring
opinion by saying that ''[t]he Court's decision, based on the Presentment Clauses

... apparently will invalidate every use of the legislative veto. The breadth of this holding gives one pause."[17] He noted that "the legislative veto has been included in a wide variety of statutes, ranging from bills for executive reorganization to the War Powers Resolution."[18] Justice White began his dissent by stating that "[t]oday the Court . . . sounds the death knell for nearly 200 other statutory provisions in which Congress has reserved a 'legislative veto,' " on "such varied matters as war powers and agency rule making."[19] Justice White discussed the various legislative veto statutes in some detail, including, as will be further addressed below, the national emergency and war powers laws.[20]

In sum, aspects of the Court's reasoning, and the reactions of the concurring and dissenting Justices, seemed to some to support a broad view rejecting all congressional assent requirements, including those in foreign affairs matters.

B. The Delegation Model Employed in *Chadha*

On closer analysis, the Court's opinion leaves much less basis for generalization to the foreign affairs sphere (and particularly the nuclear first use sphere). In fact, numerous scholarly commentators quickly expressed an opposing view that *Chadha* did *not* invalidate the concurrent resolution provision of the War Powers Resolution.[21] On its facts, the *Chadha* case dealt with a unique legislative veto provision for reducing the status of named individuals. Moreover, while the concurring and dissenting opinions of *Chadha* asserted that the decision had broad implications, the majority opinion did not. The Supreme Court chose to write an opinion with *no* expression whatsoever as to its impact other than on the statute under consideration.[22] In contrast to the concurring and dissenting opinions, which discuss other legislative veto provisions, the Court's opinion focused meticulously on applying its tests only to section 244(c)(2) of the INA.[23] Thus, those who would generalize the opinion beyond the INA have to show why; neither the case's facts, nor any dicta of the Court discussing other statutes, did their work for them.

Turning, then, from what the Court did not say, to what it did, the Court casts its opinion in the language, reasoning, models and precedents of delegation. "Congress made a deliberate choice to *delegate* to the Executive Branch . . . the authority to allow deportable aliens to remain in this country. . . . "[24] "[T]his choice to *delegate* authority is precisely the kind of decision that can be implemented only in accordance with the procedures set out in Art. I."[25] "Congress must abide by its *delegation* of authority until that *delegation* is legislatively altered or revoked."[26] "Disagreement with the Attorney General's decision . . . no less than Congress' original choice to *delegate* to the Attorney General the authority to make that decision, involves determinations of policy that Congress can implement in only one way. . . . "[27] This focus accords with the Chief Justice's consistent views in other cases. He and the Court have accorded the model of delegation and the nondelegation doctrine, which had previously receded from attention,[28] renewed examination in recent years,[29] although the stress on it in *Chadha* was particularly great.

The Court noted the congressional defense that the INA had not set limiting standards; "Congress protests that affirming the Court of Appeals in these cases will sanction 'lawmaking by the Attorney General. . . . ' "[30] Acknowledging that such lawmaking would be forbidden, the Court itself quoted two prominent decisions on separation of powers: " 'In the framework of our Constitution, the President's power to see that the laws are faithfully executed refutes the idea that he is to be a lawmaker.' *Youngstown Sheet & Tube Co. v. Sawyer*, 343 U.S. 579, 587 (1952). See *Buckley v. Valeo*, 424 U.S., at 123."[31] Accordingly, the opinion recognized that it faced a "question of delegation doctrine."[32]

Chief Justice Burger answered with a response from the same doctrine: that the INA left no room for a legislative veto because the nondelegation doctrine was alive and well in the INA scheme. In the INA, the executive's "administrative activity cannot reach beyond the limits of the statute that created it. . . . The courts, when a case or controversy arises, can always 'ascertain whether the will of Congress has been obeyed,' . . . and can enforce adherence to statutory standards."[33] Addressing the specific "*kind of Executive action*" at issue in the case—different, as discussed below, from other kinds of action—the Court explained that "Executive action under legislatively delegated authority that might resemble 'legislative' action in some respects is not subject to the approval of both houses of Congress and the President for the reason that the Constitution does not so require. *That kind of Executive action* is *always* subject to *check by the terms of the legislation that authorized it; and* if that authority is exceeded it is open to *judicial review*. . . . "[34]

Conversely, the Court held that the nondelegation doctrine's logic forbade an INA legislative veto. In obedience to the nondelegation doctrine, the INA constrained executive action within "limits," "statutory standards," "specified circumstances," and a "check by the terms of the legislation" all bounded by "determinations of policy" by Congress.[35] Accordingly, a veto resolution acted to change previously enacted constraints—to change those "limits," "statutory standards," and so forth—without being enacted like a law. "[A] veto by one House of Congress under § 244(c)(2) cannot be justified as an attempt at amending the standards set out . . . or as a repeat of § 244. . . . Amendment and repeal of statutes, no less than enactment, must conform with Art. I."[36]

C. *Chadha* and Delegation in the Sphere of Foreign Affairs

1. *Curtiss-Wright and the Domestic/Foreign Distinction.* Thus, *Chadha* forbids a post-enactment congressional role for the "kind of Executive action" which is "always subject to check by the terms of the legislation which authorized it . . . [and by] judicial review."[37] However, the Supreme Court's nondelegation doctrine also leaves room for *other* kinds of executive power *not* subject to those checks: executive power in spheres where it is either inherent (but shared), or derived from statutes not subject to the nondelegation doctrine, or both. During the nondelegation doctrine's heyday,[38] the Court tested the doctrine in the foreign af-

fairs sphere in *United States v. Curtiss-Wright Export Corp.*[39] *Curtiss-Wright* was a decision of towering importance in its field. By its expansive view of presidential power, *Curtiss-Wright* and its progeny provided the constitutional justification for presidential exercise of vast power during and after World War II, when the United States followed presidential leadership from isolation to a world role, and then from Korea to Vietnam.[40]

However, that expansive view was merely the dicta setting the stage for the case. The issue presented squarely by the case and its holding was whether to uphold a statute as constitutional despite the breadth of its delegation. Congress had responded to a war between Bolivia and Paraguay by delegating to the President broad discretionary power to embargo arms sales to the belligerents, and making violation of such an embargo punishable as a crime. The President invoked that power, embargoed further arms sales, and subsequently initiated prosecutions against violators of the embargo. Defendants in one such prosecution challenged the statute delegating the power to embargo as too broad to survive the nondelegation doctrine.

The Court upheld the challenged act of Congress with a decisive distinction regarding delegation between the foreign and domestic spheres:

[We] first consider the *differences* between the powers of the Federal government *in respect of foreign or external affairs and* those in respect of *domestic or internal affairs.* That there are differences between them, and that these differences *are fundamental*, may not be doubted.[41]

The Court assumed "that the challenged delegation, if it were confined to internal affairs, would be invalid" for its lack of standards. However, the Court asked, "May it nevertheless be sustained on the ground that its exclusive aim is to afford a remedy for a hurtful condition within foreign territory?"[42]

To answer this, *Curtiss-Wright* detailed the history of broad statutory delegations in foreign affairs.[43] It concluded that "[p]ractically every volume of the United States Statutes contains one or more acts or joint resolutions of Congress authorizing action by the President in respect of subjects affecting foreign relations . . . [while] provid[ing] a standard far more general than that which has always been considered requisite with regard to domestic affairs."[44] The Court raised a number of practical arguments, going back to the Framers, for an entirely different model of authority in foreign affairs than the domestic delegation model. President Washington had said, and the Court quoted, that "[the] nature of foreign negotiations requires caution, and their success must often depend on secrecy."[45] Considerations of intelligence security thus applied in foreign affairs, "and especially is this true in time of war."[46] Accordingly, the Court recognized "the unwisdom of requiring Congress in this field of governmental power to lay down narrowly definite standards by which the President is to be governed."[47]

As *Curtiss-Wright* distinguished the foreign affairs sphere from the domestic delegation model, so later another key Supreme Court decision distinguished the war powers sphere from the domestic delegation model. *Lichter v. United States*[48] dealt with a challenge to the World War II statutes which delegated almost unlimited authority to recover ("renegotiate") undefined "excessive" war profits. The Court upheld the provisions against a challenge based on the nondelegation doctrine. It deemed the provisions to be "well within the constitutional war powers" insofar as "we have a *fighting* constitution" which "must be read with the realistic purposes of the entire instrument fully in mind" during "the early stages of total global warfare. . . . "[49] As discussed below, while Congress had enacted those World War II statutes with broad delegations, it had included a different form of restraint: a congressional role through provisions for congressional resolutions to terminate the granted authority.

Curtiss-Wright's and *Lichter's* fundamental teachings regarding the different nature of foreign affairs and war powers, particularly as distinguished from the model of confined domestic delegations, remain effective today. For example, in 1981 the Supreme Court upheld in *Dames & Moore v. Regan*[50] President Carter's settlement of the Iranian hostage crises, notwithstanding a lack of specific congressional delegation of authority for that settlement. The Court read broadly the implications of prior statutes and a history of congressional acquiescence in prior settlements, holding that the case involved "responses to international crises the nature of which Congress can hardly have been expected to anticipate in any detail. . . . Congress cannot anticipate and legislate with regard to every possible action the President may find it necessary to take or every possible situation in which he might act."[51] The current Justice Department not only recognizes, but emphasizes, this difference between the delegation model in the domestic sphere and the different situation in the foreign sphere.[52]

2. *The Unavailability of Delegation Checks in the Foreign Sphere*. To be sure, in the foreign sphere, as in the domestic sphere, "governmental power must be exercised in subordination to the applicable provisions of the Constitution."[53] The question is what the Constitution prescribes. *Chadha* employs, in its section assessing whether an INA veto resolution requires enactment as an "exercise of legislative power," the domestic delegation model. In the domestic sphere, the nondelegation doctrine controls the "kind of Executive action [which] is always subject to check by the terms of the legislation that authorized it; and . . . [by] judicial review. . . . "[54] In this sphere, *Chadha* deems a subsequent congressional role to be legislating, for which the Constitution requires bicameral approval and presentment.

However, in foreign affairs, there is a different "kind of Executive action," to which the nondelegation doctrine employed in *Chadha* does *not* apply, and does not insure "check by the terms of the legislation" and "judicial review." Those checks are largely or wholly absent. The political question and standing doctrines, and the considerations on which they rely, clearly make judicial review less available for presidential actions in foreign affairs than in domestic affairs.[55] Following *Curtiss-Wright* and its progeny down to *Dames & Moore*, the presidents have used vast powers in the foreign affairs sphere without specified standards (though not, as discussed below in Part II, without a congressional role). Over the years, they have employed powers to negotiate foreign claims, embargo foreign trade, and freeze foreign assets, as in regard to China and Iran; to use covert operation capabilities, as in regard to Guatemala and Nicaragua; to send American advisers, as in El Salvador; and to dispatch air, sea, and land forces for maneuvers, quarantines, or occupations, as in regard to Cuba, the Dominion Republic, and the *Mayaguez* incident. Ultimately, various presidents have exercised on widely varying occasions the discretion to initiate or to continue limited or full-scale combat operations: in Korea, Vietnam, Cambodia, Laos, Grenada, and Lebanon. Judicial review of these actions has been the exception rather than the rule, as shown by a number of recent cases denying such review of the Reagan Administration's actions in Central America.[56]

In some circumstances, specific legislated checks on presidential action may be applied, such as the Clark Amendment[57] formerly prohibiting involvement in Angola, or the Boland Amendment[58] that limited action against Nicaragua. Sometimes, the President receives authorizations with time limits, such as the 1983 resolution authorizing Lebanon intervention with an eighteen-month limit.[59] Yet in many contexts such specific checks or time limits will not be possible or would have to be couched in terms with little constraining effect, for the reasons identified in *Curtiss-Wright* and *Dames & Moore*, among others. Unpredictable foreign circumstances, secrecy and intelligence limitations, the potential for short-lived diplomatic opportunity, unscrupulous and dangerous opponents, and like considerations may preclude such specific limitations in foreign affairs matters generally.

The nuclear first use context may present the quintessential case of authority that does not follow the delegation model. Once the nation chooses to retain the option of first use, it is hard to imagine meaningful anticipatory codification of the occasions for it. Would there be bright lines without impairing relations with allies who had hitherto expected to be shielded by the nuclear umbrella? Would there be a meaningless balancing formula requiring that the President "weigh" the risk of intolerable harm to American interests overseas without such use against the possibility and effect of a nuclear counterstrike against the United States? Quite clearly, *Chadha's* linchpin—its reliance on the classic *domestic* model of statutory standards and judicial review as checks on exercise of power—does not speak to the ultimate situation of use of nuclear weapons.

There is a parallel but different way to view the distinction. *Chadha* allowed no congressional role in decisions after the INA's enactment because the INA defined the standards for executive action—as it had to, pursuant to the nondelegation doctrine. The Court viewed the subsequent congressional role (the veto resolution) as amending or repealing these previously defined standards. "Amendment and repeal of statutes, no less than enactment, must conform with Art. I. . . . Congress must abide by its delegation of authority until that delegation is legislatively altered or revoked."[60] However, regarding foreign affairs and war powers, and particularly the first use decision, delegation theory from *Curtiss-Wright* to *Dames & Moore* means that the President's sources of authority and funding[61] lack defined standards. They are either inherent (though shared with the Congress) or the result of extremely broad legislation. In the foreign affairs sphere, as *Dames & Moore* puts it, "Congress cannot anticipate and legislate with regard to every possible action the President may find it necessary to take or every possible situation in which he might act."[62] Thus, a mechanism providing for a congressional role does not amend or repeal a previous standard or limit, because there was none. Rather, it establishes a political check, in place of the domestic-style standards and judicial review which do not apply.

3. *The Model of Responsive Interaction in the Foreign Sphere.* A third perspective on this fundamental distinction follows from looking at just how powers are shared in the foreign affairs sphere. In the domestic area, the model of delegation means that the President either has, or does not have, power from a congressional delegation. For example, in *Youngstown Sheet & Tube Co. v. Sawyer*,[63] the President seized the nation's steel mills to avert a labor stoppage during the Korean War. The Supreme Court could discern immediately that Congress had not delegated to the President authority for that seizure from the clear statutory language and legislative history.

In contrast, in the foreign sphere, and particularly that of war powers, a more complex and subtle model of authorization applies than the domestic delegation model. Authorization consists of the balance between the claimed inherent presidential powers and any congressional powers of limitation, looking at the various shades of acquiescence and challenge by each branch in the respective claims and limits. For example, the Supreme Court devoted the bulk of *Youngstown*, like *Dames & Moore*, to the slippery balancing of claims of executive power against the Framers' intent and the congressional acquiescence (or lack thereof).

Many steps in foreign affairs and wartime occur on a level of responsive interaction and cue-following by the executive and Congress, not strict delegation.

For example, the War Powers Resolution mandates that "[t]he President in every possible instance shall consult with Congress before introducing United States Armed Forces into hostilities. . . . "[64] This was no isolated requirement; it developed from the Senate's National Commitments Resolution of 1969,[65] the fruit of lengthy consideration of the lessons of the Vietnam War starting with the charged hearings before Senator Fulbright's committee in 1966. Similarly, the National Emergencies Act mandates that "[t]he President, in every possible instance, shall consult with the Congress before exercising any of the authorities granted by this chapter and shall consult regularly with the Congress so long as such authorities are exercised."[66]

The Cooper-Church Amendment of 1979 illustrates a typical sequence of responsive interaction. President Nixon had triggered a major congressional debate by his incursion into Cambodia, and that debate forced the President to draw back from the incursion but not to disavow continued bombing. Ultimately, the enacted provision stated that ''[i]n line with the expressed intention of the President of the United States, none of the funds authorized . . . may be used to finance the introduction of United States combat troops into Cambodia. . . . ''[67]

A provision such as the FAS proposal for nuclear first use represents a continuation of the tradition of responsive interaction. It would operate by the President summoning the congressional leaders in a crisis, and deciding with them whether a conventional war overseas warranted escalation to nuclear weapons. It has two noteworthy aspects as a mechanism: that it works in advance, rather than afterwards, and that it works through congressional leadership, rather than resolutions of the whole body—both respects being different from the congressional roles in previous war power statutes discussed in Part II of this essay.

Both aspects respond to the unique nature of a first use crisis. Assent in advance before use, rather than veto resolutions afterwards, follows from the irreversible nature of nuclear weapons uses. In terms of the impact overseas of American use of powers, economic emergency measures can be cancelled, attacks on foreign territory halted, and troops withdrawn, far more readily than the effect of a nuclear first use could be reversed. Moreover, besides the consequences to those overseas from ''first use,'' there is, of course, the potential consequence here: the risk and effect of nuclear retaliation. Whether or not the decision in a particular crisis were to accept that risk, it is simply not useful to talk of a congressional role in deciding whether to accept that risk *after* the use of the weapons occurs. The only meaningful role is advance assent.

The more difficult question concerns whether the requirement would be assent by the houses of Congress or by congressional leadership. Clearly, if time were available, a decision by the houses of Congress, akin to their adopting a declaration of war, would have the legitimacy of using machinery more like that established by the Framers. On the other hand, if time were not available in a nuclear first use crisis, a check by the congressional leadership contains at least essential minima of democratic legitimacy. The congressional leadership has an independent constitutional base from the President, to which it is accountable. That leadership is elected by the Congress, and thus, indirectly, elected by the voting population. The leadership possesses the perspective of a separate branch, with long experience and institutional wisdom. When Congress cannot participate as a body, its leadership can. If Congress adopts a statute saying that a first use decision only allows time for leadership participation, that considered judgement defines the practical and workable in a unique situation.

4. *Judicial Treatment of Legislative Vetoes in the Foreign Sphere.* The foregoing considerations draw considerable support from the D.C. Circuit's legislative veto decisions distinguishing the war and foreign affairs sphere from the domestic. Those decisions anticipated the results and reasoning of *Chadha*, but where the majority opinion in *Chadha* remains completely silent about its application to other spheres, the D.C. Circuit addresses the matter, at least to a limited extent. The D.C. Circuit, in *Consumer Energy Council of America v.*

Federal Energy Regulatory Commission,[68] struck down in 1982 a legislative veto regarding natural gas price regulation. Its opinion was written by Judge Malcolm Wilkey, formerly Assistant Attorney General for the Office of Legal Counsel, who is a leading judicial expert on the system of checks and balances with a judicial philosophy strongly supportive of the executive.[69] Judge Wilkey's lengthy and scholarly opinion correctly foreshadowed the approach of the *Chadha* court.

Yet the opinion expressly refused to subject foreign affairs and national defense legislation to the same analysis as domestic statutes. Citing the War Powers Resolution, it stated:

Congress has often combined its delegation of foreign affairs authority to the Executive with provision for disapproval of actions by concurrent resolution. . . . As with the veto in reorganization statutes, the constitutionality of these provisions has not been resolved. . . . *[T]he foreign affairs veto presents unique problems* since in that context there is the additional question whether Congress or the President or both have the inherent power to act.[70]

Similarly, in *American Federation of Government Employees v. Pierce*,[71] the D.C. Circuit struck down a provision requiring committee approval of agency reorganizations.[72] In an opinion regarding rehearing en banc, Judges Wald and Mikva noted critically that the *Pierce* panel decision "lumps together for automatic rejection under the rubric of 'legislative vetoes' several different kinds of statutory provisions, each entailing a distinct accommodation between the executive and legislative branches."[73] Judges Wald and Mikva cited back to Judge Wilkey's opinion in *Consumer Energy* which distinguished the foreign affairs and national defense vetoes from domestic ones. Based on that citation, they warned that "statutes cannot simply be invalidated under the reasoning of our prior opinions without detailed examination of how such arrangements operate and what they are designed to accomplish."[74]

To be sure, neither *Consumer Energy* nor the rehearing statement in *Pierce* stated positively that it would uphold legislative vetoes in the foreign affairs sphere. Positive holdings to that effect (or, for that matter, negative ones) would have been dicta, so each opinion noted only that foreign affairs statutes posed "unique" problems or "distinct accommodations." Yet the *Consumer Energy* opinion, tracked by the *Pierce* statement, followed a view of the enactment process quite like *Chadha's*, while distinguishing the foreign affairs sphere. If the concurring and dissenting opinions in *Chadha* took a broad view of the impact of the majority's logic, these opinions of the D.C. Circuit took a narrow view of the impact of the same logic.

In all likelihood, a narrow view of the impact of the new Supreme Court decisions on separation of powers is the prudent one. Major Supreme Court decisions on separation of powers have often appeared to point to decisive victories for one branch, while, in time, a pendulum-like swing develops in the other direction as the Court sees old tensions in a new light. In 1927, the Court took a sweeping view of presidential removal power over officers with quasi-judicial duties; in 1935, it took a different view.[75] In 1937, *Curtiss-Wright* exalted "the very delicate, plenary and exclusive power of the President as the sole organ of the Federal government in the field of international relations."[76] In 1952, after the ascendance of presidential power in World War II and Korea, the Court swung the other way, warning in *The Steel Seizure Case* that "men have discovered no techniques for long preserving free government except that the Executive be under the law and that the law be made by parliamentary deliberation."[77] A Court willing unanimously in 1974 to bottle up the demon of Watergate by holding the President's privilege against criminal subpoenas merely "presumptive," in 1984 viewed the presidential privilege against civil suits as "absolute."[78] For now, *Chadha* was too domestically oriented in its reasoning, and too reliant on classic models that the Court itself has distinguished in the foreign sphere, to allow an early or easy generalization of that opinion to invalidate mechanisms for a congressional role in foreign affairs.

II. HISTORY SUPPORTS THE CONSTITUTIONALITY OF MECHANISMS FOR A CONGRESSIONAL ROLE IN FOREIGN AFFAIRS AND WAR POWERS

The delegation theory stated above leaves room for at least one substantial response. *Curtiss-Wright* indicated that the checks on delegation available in the domestic sphere may not be available in the foreign one, but it did not state that it required some other form of congressional check. The other factors alluded to above distinguish the foreign from the domestic sphere, but they do not inherently necessitate a congressional check in the foreign sphere. It may be argued that in the foreign sphere, there should be no check at all; that if the absence of domestic-type standards leaves a void, that void should be filled by expansive presidential power.[79] In the realm of nuclear first use, that view would mean that Congress must leave the decision to the President since the appropriate occasions for use cannot be codified in advance.

To some extent, this is a question of war powers, which must be left to those addressing that issue.[80] This chapter does not deal with the dispute over whether there should be checks on presidential war powers. It only discusses whether, *if* there is to be a check—*if* Congress decides nuclear first use should not be left to the decision making of the President—that check may include a mechanism of congressional assent. The chapter only concludes that if there is to be a check, *Chadha* does not disallow such a mechanism.

However, as Oliver Wendell Holmes said, a page of history is sometimes worth a volume of logic, and there is a historical answer perhaps more satisfying than the foregoing. Although the separation of powers is a constitutional question, the Supreme Court often respects the illumination from a history of previous congressional legislation.[81] Accordingly, the history of war powers legislation

156   First Use of Nuclear Weapons

furnishes an important source of insight on the question here, particularly since
Pearl Harbor and the Cold War thrust a world role on the federal government.
If it is asked whether, historically, the response to *Curtiss-Wright's* sanctioning
of broad delegation was for the President to receive broad power without the
check of a congressional role, the answer is no.

Justice White described the World War II history:

Congress and the President applied the legislative veto procedure to resolve the delegation
problem for national security and foreign affairs. World War II occasioned the need to
transfer greater authority to the President in these areas. The legislative veto offered the
means by which Congress could confer additional authority while preserving its own
constitutional role. During World War II, Congress enacted over 30 statutes conferring
powers on the Executive with legislative veto provisions. President Roosevelt accepted
the veto as the necessary price for obtaining exceptional authority.[82]

Typically, World War II legislation broadly delegated authority to the President,
with a provision for terminating that authority by a concurrent resolution of Congress (a resolution of the House and Senate not presented to the President). At the
war's start, the first War Powers Act enacted within a fortnight after Pearl Harbor,
on December 18, 1941, immediately rushed sweeping domestic powers into the
President's hands. It provided that the powers "shall remain in force . . . during
the continuance of the present war and for six months after the termination of the
war, or until such earlier time as the Congress by concurrent resolution or the
President may designate."[83] As noted by the leading commentator tracing the history of the legislative veto in foreign affairs, "[t]he Emergency Price Control Act
of January 30, 1942, the Stabilization Act of October 2, 1942, and the War Labor
Disputes Act of June 25, 1943, employed nearly identical references to the termination clause."[84] Presidents Roosevelt and Truman used their broad powers
without abusing them, and the termination clauses were never invoked.

This same mechanism operated during the Korean War. Unlike World War
II, Congress did not declare war in Korea, but as in World War II, after the
commencement of hostilities the President soon needed broad statutory authority
to conduct an extended conflict. Again, Congress gave that broad authority,
while constraining it with a congressional role:

The Korean War had its priority measures comparable to the World War II law. The
Defense Production Act of 1950 (PL 774) established a system of priorities and allocations
for materials and facilities, authorization for requisitioning, and price stabilization. This
act set the stage for subsequent Korean War legislation employing the concurrent resolution
termination clause.[85]

can actions short of war in the same era elicited a similar congressional response. The 1950s and 1960s were the era of the "area support resolution," vague affirmations by Congress for support of, and something like authorization for,
presidential action in such areas as Taiwan, the Middle East, and Cuba. Congress

adopted the Middle East resolution of 1957, a prelude to America's brief 1957 intervention in Lebanon, only after "[Secretary of State] Dulles conceded that [President] Eisenhower would be willing to allow congressional termination discretion."[86] Thus, the congressional resolution supporting presidential action included provision for termination of authorization by resolution of the two houses.[87]

These area resolutions provided the precedent for Vietnam. In 1964, President Johnson used the Tonkin Gulf incident as the occasion to request authority from Congress for direct military action (not an advisory role) in Vietnam. The State Department furnished a draft of what became the Tonkin Gulf Resolution. When Senator Richard Russell of Georgia, the leading Senate spokesman of his time on national security issues, found that the draft had not included any subsequent role for Congress, he protested. "[I]t was agreed that that resolution of August, 1964 would contain on its face a provision that the Congress, acting alone by concurrent resolution, could rescind it."[88] Accordingly, the final version included a provision for rescinding of the authority "by concurrent resolution of the Congress."[89]

As opposition to the war developed, in 1970 Congress repealed the Tonkin Gulf Resolution, though it did so by statute rather than by invocation of that concurrent resolution termination clause.[90] By then, a major dispute over war powers had developed, as first President Johnson claimed power to conduct the Vietnam war, and then President Nixon claimed power to extend military operations to Cambodia and Laos without the Tonkin Gulf Resolution.[91]

In 1973 Congress responded in the end by enacting binding restrictions in appropriations that terminated American involvement,[92] and eventually by generic war powers legislation. Senator Fulbright led the way, in the Senate's National Commitments Resolution of 1969,[93] but the conclusion occurred in 1974, in the War Powers Resolution. As Justice White explained:

During the 1970's the legislative veto was important in resolving a series of major constitutional disputes between the President and Congress over claims of the President to broad impoundment, war, and national emergency powers. The key provision of the War Powers Resolution, 50 U.S.C. § 1544(c), authorizes the termination by concurrent resolution of the use of armed forces in hostilities.[94]

Enactment of the War Powers Resolution traced the reasoning predicted above from the nondelegation doctrine. At first, the Senate tried in drafting the War Powers Resolution to prescribe specific standards, as in domestic legislation. The Senate proposed a version of the War Powers Resolution prescribing a detailed description of the circumstances under which the President could commit armed forces.[95] It was as if, for the issue here, the FAS were to propose a codification of the circumstances under which the President could or could not make nuclear first use. The House version did not attempt such a codification, seeing no way to prescribe standards in the war context; instead, it relied on the concurrent resolution disapproval mechanism.[96]

In the conference committee, "[a]s anticipated by all participants, this difference proved to be the most difficult to overcome."[97] The Administration criticized the Senate approach, and particularly the section detailing the circumstances for using force, describing that section as " 'among the most objectionable' and 'ill-advised' because it was not possible to anticipate 'every future exigency in which the Nation's safety and vital interests would compel the use of the Armed Forces.' "[98] On the other hand, the Administration deemed the concurrent resolution provision unconstitutional. Possibly a key step in breaking the logjam came when Professor Paul A. Freund provided a memorandum on constitutional law, endorsed by the House side and deemed "excellent" by Senator Eagleton, commending the concurrent resolution device as "the most appropriate medium" for the assertion of congressional war powers.[99]

Professor Freund expressly distinguished this sphere from others, arguing persuasively that "on the substantive premises of the bill, the provision respecting a concurrent resolution is a valid and appropriate measure, and does not raise constitutional issues of the kind mooted in connection with other categories of legislation."[100] Accordingly, the conferees accepted the House approach of the concurrent resolution mechanism, and relegated the Senate's attempted standards to a section stating "purpose and policy."[101]

As Justice White further explained, the War Powers Resolution was:

followed by others resolving similar problems: the National Emergencies Act . . . resolving the longstanding problems with unchecked Executive emergency power; the International Security Assistance and Arms Export Control Act . . . resolving the problem of foreign arms sales; and the Nuclear Non-Proliferation Act of 1978 . . . resolving the problem of exports of nuclear technology.[102]

Of course, the historical significance of these various enactments may be debated. Congress did not invoke the provisions for termination of authority by concurrent resolution in World War II, Korea, or the 1957 Mideast resolution, and it repealed the Tonkin Gulf Resolution (without immediate impact) by statute, not resolution. As to the 1970s generic laws, while other provisions of the War Powers Resolution became important during the Lebanon intervention of 1983, the provision for termination of involvement by concurrent resolution was never invoked. Of the various resolution mechanisms, the one of principal import has been the provision for disapproval of arms sales in the Arms Export Control Act. This provision has become the vehicle for major national debates on foreign policy, particularly regarding arms sales to the Middle East.[103]

Yet a purely negative perspective slights the significance of consistent historical inclusion of such provisions, and Congress' further decision, in the post-Vietnam era, to rely heavily on them for structuring the critical balance between the branches in foreign and war powers affairs. After all, presumably everyone hopes that any mechanism for congressional assent to nuclear first use would also never have to be used. Such precautionary provisions for congressional roles are like deterrent capabilities or disaster plans; absence of use is a source of relief, not proof that the precaution was unnecessary or insignificant. It is the potential for their invocation in situations of possibly ill-advised use of awesome powers, not anticipation of routine employment, which justifies them. Through these provisions, Congress expressed a continuing and consistent commitment that supreme war and foreign affairs powers, not readily subjected to standards like domestic legislation, should nevertheless be subjected to a political check.

III. CONCLUSION

Whether Congress should, as a matter of policy, constrain presidential first use of nuclear arms—and whether such constraint satisfies the constitutional law of war powers—has not been addressed. The sole concern here has been whether a mechanism for such constraint relying on congressional assent must fall under *Chadha*.

Like the provisions for congressional disapproval in the War Powers Resolution and the Arms Export Control Act, such a mechanism is constitutional. It addresses otherwise unchecked presidential authority in the foreign affairs and war powers sphere, a sphere apart from the domestic affairs sphere covered by *Chadha's* use of the delegation model and its language, reasoning and precedents. The Supreme Court has not barred such a mechanism. Whether to create one is for the public to decide.

NOTES

1. *See supra* Part II of this book.
2. Respectively, Pub. L. No. 94–329, 90 Stat. 729 (1976), 22 U.S.C. § 2776(b) (1982); Pub. L. No. 93–148, 87 Stat. 555 (1974), 50 U.S.C. § 1540 (1982).
3. 462 U.S. 919 (1983).
4. Kenneth W. Dam, Deputy Secretary of State, set forth the executive branch's position in testimony in 1983. "The fourth provision [of the War Powers Resolution], which asserted a right of Congress by concurrent resolution to order the President to remove troops engaged in hostilities, is clearly unconstitutional under the Supreme Court's holding in *Chadha*. . . . [T]he legislative vetoes contained in several sections of the Arms Export Control Act are not valid. . . . Various sections of the Atomic Energy Act, for example, [that] have provided for a legislative veto of Presidential determinations to permit nuclear exports to foreign countries . . . [are] invalid . . . [as] calling for a veto by concurrent resolution." *The U.S. Supreme Court Decision Concerning the Legislative Veto: Hearings Before the House Comm. on Foreign Affairs*, 98th Cong., 1st Sess. 68–70 (1983) (hereinafter cited as *Chadha Hearings*). For commentators concurring in this broad view, see, *e.g.*, Bolton & Abrams, *The Judicial and Congressional Response to the Invalidation of the Legislative Veto*, 1 J. L. & Pol. 299, 306 (1984) ("No variant of the legislative veto survives the constitutional holding in *Chadha* and its progeny.").
5. Section 244(c)(2) of the INA, 8 U.S.C. § 1254(c)(2) (1982).
6. H. Res. 926, 94th Cong., 1st Sess., 121 Cong. Rec. 40800 (1975).
7. *Chadha*, 462 U.S. at 928.

8. 634 F.2d 408 (9th Cir. 1980).

9. This description puts aside such clearly separate and valid matters as impeachment, contempt, disciplinary and internal housekeeping resolutions.

10. *Chadha*, 462 U.S. at 951.

11. Justice White's dissenting opinion comments, "I do not dispute the Court's truismatic exposition of these Clauses [requiring bicameral approval and presentment]. There is no question that a bill does not become a law until it is approved by both the House and the Senate, and presented to the President. . . . All of this, Part III of the Court's opinion, is entirely unexceptionable." *Id*. at 979–80 (White, J., dissenting).

12. Justice White summed up this view of the legislative veto:

It is the means by which Congress secures the accountability of executive and independent agencies. Without the legislative veto, Congress is faced with a Hobson's choice: either to refrain from delegating the necessary authority, leaving itself with a hopeless task of writing laws with the requisite specificity . . . or in the alternative, to abdicate its lawmaking function to the Executive Branch and independent agencies.

Id. at 462 U.S. at 968 (White J., dissenting).

13. *Id*. at 952–53 (footnote omitted). The opinion refers to the "Attorney General's" decision because the immigration officer who suspended Chadha's deportation acted with authority delegated by the Attorney General.

14. *Id*. at 956–57.

15. *Id*. at 958 (footnote omitted).

16. *Id*. at 952.

17. *Id*. at 959 (Powell, J., concurring).

18. *Id*. at 960 n.1 (Powell, J., concurring).

19. *Id*. at 967 (White J., dissenting).

20. *Id*. at 970–71 (White, J., dissenting). *See also id*. at 1003–05 (appendix to opinion of White, J., dissenting) (listing legislative veto provisions in the area of foreign affairs and national security).

21. For examples of the commentary supporting the constitutionality of the War Powers Resolution's concurrent resolution mechanism notwithstanding *Chadha*, see, *e.g.*, *The Supreme Court Decision in INS v. Chadha: Hearings Before the Subcomm. on Administrative Law and Governmental Relations of the House Comm. on the Judiciary*, 98th Cong., 1st Sess. 175, 186–87 (1983) (testimony of former Rep. Robert C. Eckhardt); *Chadha Hearings, supra* note 4 at 155 (Prof. Eugene Gressman); Zablocki, *War Powers Resolution: Its Past Record and Future Promise*, 17 Loy. L.A.L. Rev. 579, 590 (1984) (article by former chairman of House Foreign Affairs Committee); Berdes & Huber, *Making the War Powers Resolution Work: The View from the Trench*, 17 Loy. L.A.L. Rev. 671, 680 (1984); Carter, *The Constitutionality of the War Powers Resolution*, 70 Va. L. Rev. 101, 129–32 (1984); Note, *The Future of the War Powers Resolution*, 36 Stan. L. Rev. 1407, 1432–36 (1984). For a general discussion of *Chadha*, see Levitas & Brand, *The Post Legislative Veto Response: A Call to Congressional Arms*, 12 Hofstra L. Rev. 593 (1984).

22. Regarding other legislative veto provisions, the Court notes only in its preliminary opening "that congressional veto provisions are appearing with increasing frequency in statutes," 462 U.S. at 919, and quotes some figures on their frequency, but does not mention any particular ones, and *a fortiori*, does not mention the War Powers Resolution, the National Emergencies Act or the Arms Export Control Act.

23. "[W]e must nevertheless establish that . . . § 244(c)(2) is of the kind to which the procedural requirements of Art. I, §7, apply. . . . Examination of . . . § 244(c)(2) reveals that it was essentially legislative. . . . We hold that the congressional veto in §244(c)(2) . . . is unconstitutional." *Id.* at 952, 959. The Court's restraint in this regard contrasts strikingly with the speculation by the concurrence and dissent as to the reach of the opinion.

The Court had another opportunity in two other decisions regarding legislative vetoes to state the reach of *Chadha*. However, in each case, it affirmed summarily the lower court decisions striking down the statutes, without opinion. Process Gas Consumers Group v. Consumer Energy Council of America, 463 U.S. 1216 (1983); United States Senate v. FTC, 463 U.S. 1216 (1983). Since the legislative vetoes in these cases concerned two sets of domestic regulations, these bare affirmances provide little assistance in resolving the question of whether to generalize *Chadha* beyond the domestic sphere. As discussed below, the opinions of the lower court (the D.C. Circuit) in those cases had expressly distinguished the war powers sphere from the analysis.

24. 462 U.S. at 954 (emphasis supplied).

25. *Id.* (emphasis supplied).

26. 462 U.S. at 955 (emphasis supplied).

27. 462 U.S. at 954 (emphasis supplied).

28. FPC v. New England Power Co., 415 U.S. 345, 352–53 (1976) (Marshall, J., concurring and dissenting). The doctrine's desuetude received mixed reviews. *See, e.g.*, J. Ely, *Democracy and Distrust* 131–34 (1980); Stewart, *The Reformation of American Administrative Law*, 88 Harv. L. Rev. 1669 (1975); sources cited in Industrial Union Dep't v. American Petroleum Inst., 448 U.S. 607, 687 nn. 6 & 7 (1980) (Rehnquist, J., dissenting).

29. *See* American Textile Mfg. Inst., Inc. v. Donovan, 452 U.S. 490, 541 n.75 (1981); *id.* at 543 (Rehnquist, J. & Burger, C. J., dissenting); Industrial Union Dept. v. American Petroleum Inst., 448 U.S. 607 (1980); *id.* at 671 (Rehnquist, J., dissenting). For commentaries on the high significance given the delegation model in *Chadha*, see Abel, *INS v. Chadha: The Future Demise of Legislative Delegation and the Need for a Constitutional Amendment*, 11 J. of Legis. 317 (1985); Comment, *Scope of Rule Making After Chadha: A Case for the Delegation Doctrine?*, 33 Emory L.J. 953 (1984).

30. 462 U.S. at 953 n.16, *quoting* "Brief for Petitioner [the United States House of Representatives] in No. 80–2170, p. 40."

31. 424 U.S. at 919 n.16.

32. *Id.*

33. 462 U.S. at 953 n.16 (citations omitted). The Court cites as authority not only its own nondelegation doctrine decisions, but the leading expositions by Professor Jaffe and by the late Judge Leventhal, the foremost judicial authority on administrative law. *Id.*

34. *Id.* (emphasis supplied).

35. *Id.* at 954 & n.16.

36. *Id.* at 954. The Court followed its long analysis, based on the nondelegation doctrine, that the INA resolution was akin to legislation, 462 U.S. at 952–55, with a shorter consideration of the narrow and explicit constitutional provisions for congressional action other than by legislation (impeachment, confirmation of appointees, and ratification of treaties). 462 U.S. at 955–56. However, the Court made clear that this second line of reasoning served a separate function from the first. After both lines of reasoning, the Court added:

Since it is clear that the action by the House under § 244(c)(2) was *not within any of the express constitutional exceptions* authorizing one House to act alone, *and* equally clear that it was *an exercise of legislative power*, that action was subject to the standards prescribed in Art. I.

462 U.S. at 956–57 (emphasis supplied). Thus, the Court saw its discussion of what "was an exercise of legislative power" as one distinct line. That discussion, employing the nondelegation doctrine, defines the reach of the key holding. The discussion of the "express constitutional exceptions" serves another distinct function; it establishes, for such "legislative" matters, whether they survive as within the express constitutional exceptions from bicameralism and presentment.

37. *Id.* at 953 n.16.

38. A.L.A. Schecter Poultry Corp. v. United States, 295 U.S. 538 (1935); Panama Refining Co. v. Ryan, 293 U.S. 388 (1935).

39. 299 U.S. 304 (1936).

40. *See, e.g.*, Chemerinsky, *Controlling Inherent Presidential Power: Providing a Framework for Judicial Review*, 56 S. Cal. L. Rev. 863, 877 n. 78, *quoting* L. Fisher, *President and Congress* 207 (1972) ("The tradition of 'foreign policy [being] set aside as a presidential preserve . . . owes much to the *Curtiss-Wright* decision. . . .' ").

41. *Curtiss-Wright*, 299 U.S. at 315 (emphasis supplied).

42. *Id.* at 315.

43. The opinion also suggests that the executive might have extra-constitutional power overseas on national sovereignty grounds, dictum since disavowed by the Court. Reid v. Covert, 354 U.S. 1, 5–6 (1957).

44. 299 U.S. at 324.

45. *Id.* at 320.

46. *Id.*

47. *Id.* at 321–22. "[C]ongressional legislation which is to be made effective through negotiation and inquiry within the international field must often accord to the President a degree of discretion and freedom from statutory restriction which would not be admissible were domestic affairs alone involved." *Id.* at 320.

48. 334 U.S. 742 (1948), cited in Stone, *supra* Ch. 1, at note 24.

49. 334 U.S. at 782–83.

50. 453 U.S. 654 (1981). For a scholarly analysis of the decision and its aftermath, see Marks & Grabow, *The President's Foreign Economic Powers After Dames & Moore v. Regan: Legislation by Acquiescence*, 68 Cornell L. Rev. 68 (1982).

51. 453 U.S. at 669, 678.

52. Edward C. Schmults, Deputy Attorney General, emphasized this distinction when suggesting congressional responses to *Chadha* at a hearing on foreign affairs in 1983:

I would like to articulate for the committee what I believe to be a fundamental difference between the policy implications *Chadha* may be expected to have in the domestic area as contrasted with congressional oversight of our foreign relations and trade.

In the domestic area, [Congress believed] . . . that too many major policy decisions . . . have been delegated.

In the nondomestic areas of foreign affairs . . . involving the delicate interplay between the exercise of Congress['s] legislative power and the exercise by the President of his inherent constitutional powers . . . great care must be taken . . . to insure that the tools necessary for the President to conduct our foreign relation are not denied. In this area, much more than in the domestic area, the need for flexibility in meeting the exigencies of any particular situation should remain paramount.

Chadha *Hearings, supra* note 4, at 50–51 (testimony).

53. *Curtiss-Wright*, 299 U.S. at 320.

54. *Chadha*, 462 U.S. at 953 n.16.

55. Regarding judicial review, see Goldwater v. Carter, 444 U.S. 996 (1979); Baker v. Carr, 369 U.S. 186, 217 (1962); Chicago & S. Air Lines, Inc. v. Waterman S.S. Corp., 333 U.S. 103 (1948); Crockett v. Reagan, 558 F. Supp. 893 (D.D.C. 1982), *aff'd per curiam*, 720 F.2d 1355 (D.C. Cir. 1983), *cert. denied.* 104 S. Ct. 3433 (1984).

56. Recent decisions denying judicial review on one jurisdictional ground or another include *Crockett v. Reagan*, 558 F. Supp. 893 (D.D.C. 1982) (role of American military in El Salvador), *aff'd per curiam*, 720 F.2d 1355 (D.C. Cir. 1983), *cert. denied*, 104 S. Ct. 3533 (1984); *Conyers v. Reagan*, 578 F. Supp. 324 (D.D.C. 1984) (invasion of Grenada); *Sanchez-Espinosa v. Reagan*, 568 F.Supp. 596 (D.D.C. 1983) (covert action in Nicaragua). *But see* de Arellano v. Weinberger, 745 F.2d 1500 (D.C. Cir. 1984) (en banc) (holding justiciable a takings challenge regarding alleged seizure of private land in Honduras for a military base).

57. *See* T. M. Franck & E. Wiesband, *Foreign Policy by Congress* (1979).

58. Section 793 of the 1983 Department of Defense Appropriations Act, Pub. L. No. 97–377, 96 Stat. 1865 (1982).

59. Multinational Force in Lebanon Resolution, Pub. L. No. 98–119, 97 Stat. 805 (1983), *reprinted* at 50 U.S.C.A. § 1541.

60. *Chadha*, 462 U.S. at 954, 955.

61. The same reasoning applies whether the President proceeds with explicit authorization or under inherent power (a difference with significance regarding war powers which goes beyond the scope of this chapter). Even when the President proceeds under inherent power, he must rely on funds appropriated by Congress. In the domestic sphere, such appropriations could contain explicit limits and standards, like legislation satisfying the nondelegation doctrine. In the foreign sphere, it is true that sometimes appropriations include such limits, such as the appropriation limitations which terminated American involvement in the Vietnam conflict in 1973. However, in general, the reasons alluded to in *Curtiss-Wright* and *Dames & Moore*, and previously discussed, for why broad authorizations or delegations occur, also preclude use of numerous limits or constraints in defense appropriations.

62. *Dames & Moore*, 453 U.S. at 678.

63. 343 U.S. 579 (1952).

64. Section 3, 50 U.S.C. § 1542 (1982).

65. The National Commitments Resolution is noted *infra* note 93.

66. 50 U.S.C. § 1703(a) (1982).

67. The provision is quoted in House Comm. on Foreign Affairs, 97th Cong., 1st Sess., *The War Powers Resolution* 33 n.10 (Comm. Print 1982) (hereinafter cited as *War Powers Resolution Report*), which explained how the wording "had been negotiated among the Senate, House, and Nixon administration. . . ."

68. 673 F.2d 425 (D.C. Cir. 1982), *summarily affirmed*, 463 U.S. 1216 (1983).

69. *See, e.g.*, Nixon v. Sirica, 487 F.2d 700 (D.C. Cir. 1973) (en banc) (Wilkey, J., dissenting) (maintaining President Nixon's absolute immunity from Watergate grand jury subpoena).

70. *Id.*, 673 F. 2d at 459 (footnotes omitted and emphasis supplied). Judge Wilkey, as a strong executive supporter, might well conclude in many circumstances that "inherent" executive power excluded congressional limits, perhaps especially if they were

imposed by a legislative veto. However, even following that reasoning, he recognized that the analysis of "inherent" power follows a fundamentally different track than "delegated" power, and his own sophisticated and scholarly treatment of the latter was not one he deemed directly applicable to the former.

71. 697 F.2d 303 (D.C. Cir. 1982).

72. After the *Consumer Energy* decision, the D.C. Circuit, en banc, had adopted unanimously the *Consumer Energy* approach in *Consumers Union, Inc. v. FTC*, 691 F.2d 575 (D.C. Cir. 1982), *summarily affirmed*, 103 S. Ct. 3556 (1983).

73. 697 F.2d 308 (opinion in support of rehearing en banc). The court of appeals as a whole denied rehearing en banc.

74. *Id., citing "Cf. Consumer Energy*, 673 F.2d at 457–60 (recognizing possible exceptions, including presidential plans for executive branch reorganization, to the court's holding)."

75. *Compare* Myers v. United States, 272 U.S. 52, 135 (1926)(which held that the President could remove officers with purely executive functions, and added in dicta that he could remove quasi-judicial officers) *with* Humphrey's Executor v. United States, 295 U.S. 602, 626 (1935) (upholding provisions barring presidential removal of FTC commissioners combining quasi-judicial, quasi-legislative, and executive functions, and stating regarding the contrary dicta in *Myers* that "these [*Myers*] expressions are disapproved"); *see* Weiner v. United States, 357 U.S. 349, 352 (1958) (discussing the *Myers—Humphrey's Executor* shift).

76. United States v. Curtiss-Wright Export Corp., 299 U.S. 304, 320 (1936).

77. Youngstown Sheet & Tube Co. v. Sawyer, 343 U.S. 579, 655 (1952) (Jackson, J., concurring).

78. *Compare* United States v. Nixon, 418 U.S. 683 (1974) *with* Nixon v. Fitzgerald, 457 U.S. 731 (1984).

79. Those who would so argue might say that informal mechanisms—consultation, hearings, hortatory resolutions—together with the occasional opportunity for a binding check such as appropriation limitations or time constraints on authorizations—furnish a sufficient check.

80. *See supra* Part II of this book.

81. *Curtiss-Wright*, 299 U.S. at 322–28; *Dames & Moore*, 453 U.S. at 679–82. *See also* Haig v. Agee, 453 U.S. 280, 293–300 (1981); United States v. Midwest Oil Co., 237 U.S. 459 (1915).

82. *Chadha*, 462 U.S. at 969 (White, J., dissenting) (footnotes omitted).

83. 55 Stat. 31.

84. Buckwalter, *The Congressional Concurrent Resolution: A Search for Foreign Policy Influence*, 14 Midwest J. Poli. Sci. 434, 443 (1970).

85. *Id.* at 445. During this same period, such clauses were used in other foreign affairs legislation besides this war use. *Id.* (citing aid legislation such as Marshall Plan and Truman Doctrine, and aid statutes with provisions for concurrent resolution disapproval of military assistance agreements).

86. *Id.* at 449 (footnote omitted).

87. Resolution to Promote Peace and Stability in the Middle East, Pub. L. No. 85–87, § 6, 71 Stat. 5, 6 (1957).

88. Buckwalter, *supra* note 84, at 450 (*quoting* hearings).

89. Section 3 of H.R.J. Res. 1145, 88th Cong., 2d Sess., Pub. L. No. 88–408, 78 Stat. 384, 385 (1964).

90. Section 12 of Pub. L. No. 91–672, 84 Stat. 2053, 2055 (1971). Statutory rather than concurrent resolution termination could occur because President Nixon did not threaten to veto the termination measure, as he took the view that he needed no such authorization to wage war.

91. *See The War Powers Resolution Report*, *supra* note 67, at 26–30, 70–71, 106–10 (describing presidential justifications for, and congressional reactions to, 1970 Cambodia and 1971 Laos incursions, and 1973 Cambodia bombing).

92. This period is described in Franck & Wiesband, *supra* note 57.

93. The final form of the resolution acknowledges the role of legislative resolutions in war powers, stating that

it is the sense of the Senate that a national commitment by the United States results only from affirmative action taken by the executive and legislative branches of the United States Government by means of a treaty, statute, or *concurrent resolution* of both houses of Congress specifically providing for such commitment.

S. Res. 85, 91st Cong., 1st Sess., enacted June 25, 1969 (emphasis supplied). *See National Commitments*, S. Rep. No. 129, 91st Cong., 1st Sess. (1967).

94. *Chadha*, 462 U.S. at 970–71 (White, J., dissenting).

95. "Section 3 of S. 440 described in some detail the authorities of the President in using the U.S. Armed Forces in emergency situations." *War Powers Resolution Report*, *supra* note 67, at 142.

96. *Id.*

97. *Id.*

98. *Id.* at 143.

99. *Id.* at 144.

100. 119 Cong. Rec. 21,224–25 (1973) (*reprinting* letter of June 12, 1973, from Paul A. Freund to Rep. Pierre S. du Pont).

101. *War Powers Resolution Report*, *supra* note 67, at 146–47. The War Powers Resolution had provided expedited provisions for concurrent resolutions to terminate commitments of armed forces. 50 U.S.C. § 1546 (1982). Since Congress might use a joint resolution after *Chadha*, rather than a concurrent resolution, it also provided in 1983 for expedited provisions for joint resolutions to terminate such commitments. 50 U.S.C. § 1546a (1982).

102. *Id.* at 971 (citations omitted).

103. *See* Franck & Wiesband, *supra* note 57.

IV

PROBLEMS OF IMPLEMENTATION OF CONGRESSIONAL CONTROL

11

Congressional Authorization of Nuclear First Use: Problems of Implementation

Edwin M. Smith

The Constitution apart, practical implementation problems raise serious doubt as to the ability of the congressional nuclear planning committee proposed by the Federation of American Scientists (FAS) to assert effective authority over the use of nuclear weapons after the initiation of actual hostilities in Western Europe. First, any congressional committee entrusted with a veto over first use will confront enormous difficulties in acquiring independent and objective information upon which to base its veto decision. Part I of this paper shows that without the President's cooperation, the committee would be unable to acquire sufficient timely information to avoid either a rubber-stamp approval of the President's first use decision or a veto devoid of substantial evidentiary support.

Second, should the planning committee determine to exercise its veto after the President had concluded that first use was necessary, he may well ignore that veto. Part II shows that application of cognitive and motivational psychology and of the dynamics of small decision making groups to historical instances of executive crisis decision making leaves doubt that the President would comply with a congressional veto.

These practical problems, however, could be ameliorated by a change in the form of congressional participation. Part III of the paper describes two possible changes.

I. THE PROBLEM OF INFORMATION

Three basic information-related obstacles stand in the path of the effective exercise of the committee's veto power. First, a wartime military establishment will acquire intelligence that will differ both qualitatively and quantitatively from that acquired in peacetime. Even if the committee is continuously briefed during peacetime in preparation for its role, the changes in intelligence acquisition occasioned by the wartime context may render such preparation useless.

Second, the intelligence analysis which would form the basis of a presidential first use decision would involve inherent ambiguities. These ambiguities would make it impossible for the nuclear planning committee to challenge a presidential authorization based on information which, while ambiguous, may indicate enemy preparation to engage in a nuclear first strike.

Finally, the nuclear planning committee, in any attempt to exercise a veto, must rely on the information provided to it by the executive branch advocates of first use. Unless the executive is completely cooperative, the committee may have great difficulty developing a factual foundation for any conclusion other than the rubber-stamp approval of presidential first use.

A. Information Acquisition: The Dense Fog of War

Information acquisition is likely to prove highly problematical in the context of a European war. During such war, at least three significant changes will occur in the information collection regime. First, to the extent that the conflict has not already involved nuclear exchange, those systems dedicated to warning of nuclear attack will be operating on the highest possible level of alert, as will the strategic forces dependent on that warning. The entire strategic warning and command system will be acutely sensitive to the slightest indications of increasing danger of nuclear attack, providing overwhelming amounts of new data to centralized decision makers deeply concerned with the danger of such an attack.[1]

Second, a vast array of new information sources will be employed in the theaters of conventional conflict in order to collect the enormous amounts of tactical and operational intelligence that will allow combat units to engage and defeat enemy forces.[2] The new data will be extremely time-sensitive and will be managed in the highly decentralized manner characteristic of conventional military hierarchies.[3]

Finally, the reliability of many information assessments will be greatly degraded. Warsaw Pact forces will actively attempt to frustrate NATO intelligence-gathering activities.[4] Efforts to maintain NATO intelligence capabilities despite this interference will place great stress on data gathering routines.

The differences between the peacetime and wartime intelligence regimes have great significance. The nuclear planning committee could be prepared for its role through constant peacetime briefings. However, the altered character of the wartime information regime could well make such preparation useless. The nuclear planning committee would be overwhelmed by the number of new sources of data. The committee would be ill-equipped to evaluate assessments drawn from vast collections of time-sensitive tactical and operational intelligence.

B. Information Analysis: The Ambiguity of Intelligence

Even if information gathering were an uncomplicated process, analysis of the data would be no simple matter. Analysis of collected information allows the production of "net intelligence assessments" of the goals, capabilities, and strategies of other nations in order to construct interaction profiles suggesting the manner in which that nation may respond in particular contexts.[5] Analysts in different agencies, encountering extreme difficulty in distinguishing the "signal" of important intelligence from the "noise" of mountains of routinely collected information, may dismiss important facts.[6] Bureaucratic boundaries may cause analysts to miss important patterns in data existing in different organizations. Parochial conflicts over particular intelligence-gathering programs and methods may frustrate the coordinated collection of essential data.[7] Analysts in successive levels of bureaucracy may fail to communicate important ambiguities in that information, causing "uncertainty absorption" which may lead decision makers to place more reliance on the information than is warranted.[8]

The wartime expansion of raw data necessary to be analyzed can only exacerbate the problems of effective assessment. While the peacetime assessment process is highly centralized, the wartime performance of much of the assessment function will devolve to those tactical combat units immediately concerned, since higher commands will only be able to assess that intelligence essential to the function of controlling larger units. The vast amounts of intelligence gathered at the tactical level may not even be transmitted to high-level headquarters. Such a devolution is consistent with historical patterns of hierarchically organized conventional military forces.[9]

Evaluation of information regarding an opponent's intentions involves additional inherent difficulties. Assessments of enemy intentions may prove to be unreliable because adversaries may have multiple goals or goals which evolve with the situation.[10] The uncertainty regarding an opponent's intentions may even reflect that opponent's real ambivalence.[11]

An example demonstrates the intelligence problem faced by the nuclear planning committee as well as one of the crucial problems of the FAS proposal. The FAS proposal indicates that a President authorizing a preemptive nuclear strike in response to an imminent nuclear attack on United States forces would not require committee approval.[12] But the proposal offers no indication how the nuclear planning committee could distinguish between situations requiring prior committee approval and those allowing independent presidential retaliation. The committee could not effectively challenge assessments indicating that a preemptive first use was necessary. Analysts faced with potential evidence of Soviet preparation for a preemptive attack against NATO's tactical or theater nuclear capability would have to judge both Soviet intentions and capabilities based on inherently ambiguous data. They would also have to infer whether any such strike would be nuclear or conventional.[13] Any presidential preemptive first use decision would be based not only on centrally analyzed strategic intelligence, but also on high-level military command analyses constructed from any tactical battlefield assessments. The nuclear planning committee could not be prepared in advance to evaluate such battlefield assessments because much of the underlying raw data could be entirely unavailable and the available intelligence could well be ambiguous.

Critical distinctions between a valid presidential preemptive strike and a nuclear first use requiring committee approval may therefore not be possible in a wartime context. The presence of ambiguities in intelligence data would force the nuclear planning committee to rely primarily on political grounds in exercising a veto. Arguments contesting the practical necessity of a nuclear strike would be extremely difficult for the committee to make. The threat of subsequent inquiry proceedings would not deter any presidential preemptive action, since the ambiguity of the contemporaneous intelligence would cast doubt on any factual contentions that the nuclear planning committee could offer, while committee opposition could be subsequently characterized as opportunistic politics during a national emergency.

C. Information Dependency: The Executive Monopoly

A nuclear planning committee would face additional problems flowing from the presidential monopoly over intelligence. A President coming before the nuclear planning committee would by definition assert the necessity of first use. Complete control of the essential information would lie in the hands of the executive. The President would support any request for approval of first use of nuclear weapons with as forceful a case as can be imagined. The nuclear planning committee could only have access to contradictory information if the President chose to provide it. A President convinced of the necessity of immediate first use could fail to provide the committee with the data necessary to support a veto.

On the other hand, the committee may not find it easy to oppose the President in the context of such an international crisis without some factual support. A veto without some factual basis would have little practical credibility, increasing the tendency of a committed executive to ignore it. The committee cannot escape tremendous pressures to support the President's choice. However, an approval which granted the President the benefit of the doubt would eliminate the threat of later inquiry. The absence of any alternative information may make independent congressional decision making impossible, reducing planning committee response to either factual insupportability or bare formality.

II. EXECUTIVE DECISION MAKING: STICKING TO THE NUKES

Several recent works based on studies of the foreign policy process reveal a range of obstacles to well-reasoned executive decision making in crisis situations.

Crisis decision makers may be highly resistant to any challenges to their decisions in order to minimize the stress occasioned by the making of those decisions and may exhibit the tendency to preserve cohesion at the expense of full inquiry into alternative policies. Even if executive decision makers did not fall prey to these obstacles, they may well conclude that subsequent personal sanctions may be a small price to pay to insure the best interests of the nation. If any controversy remains as to the constitutionality of the enactment of the FAS proposal, the President might accept the judgment of those advocating first use, leaving constitutional issues and potential sanctions to be determined later.

A. Psychological Sources of Executive Decision Making Failure

The psychological obstacles of irrational consistency and defensive avoidance, the problem of small group dynamics, and the interrelated difficulties posed by bureaucratic politics and organizational process all seriously limit executive crisis management.

Irrational consistency and defensive avoidance can lead to inadequate analysis and inappropriate action based on inaccurate images preserved in the decision makers' minds by the rejection of challenging evidence. Decision makers base their conclusions on contemporary data and previously formed "images" of reality.[14] Irrational consistency results when decision makers selectively process new information in order to preserve the integrity of those previously developed images of reality.[15] Information handling of this sort can generate erroneous conclusions about reality and about opposing crisis decision makers.[16]

Similarly, the stress caused by the uncertainty of crisis decisions can generate efforts by decision makers to reduce that stress.[17] When the range of available alternatives offers little respite from that uncertainty, decision makers may seek to reduce stress by adopting strategies of defensive avoidance, attempting to deny responsibility for the decision or to exaggerate greatly the attractiveness of existing alternatives.[18] Both irrational consistency and defensive avoidance can lead to failures of the rational analytic process essential to crisis management.[19]

Small group dynamics can generate conformity pressures and "groupthink," phenomena which inhibit full exchange of ideas and opinions. Under certain circumstances, direct pressures may be asserted against members of decision groups to force them into consistency with the views of the group.[20] In addition, more subtle pressures for conformity may arise from "groupthink," a pattern of behavior in highly cohesive decision groups causing the suppression of challenging opinions and data and the overestimation of the probabilities of successful execution of collectively chosen policies.[21]

To reach a decision to resort to nuclear weapons in the European scenario, an executive decision making group, possibly acting from a groupthink-generated conviction of its own efficacy, morality and invulnerability, would have to conclude that first use was essential to the national interest. Such a group would not quietly comply with a veto exercised by a nuclear planning committee made up of relatively uninformed and amateurish outsiders whose conclusions will necessarily be unacceptable. Unfortunately, the viability of the FAS proposal turns on just such an expectation.

B. Ignoring the Committee: The Rational Approach

Psychology aside, a President may conclude that the national interest requires a conscious and intentional refusal to comply with a committee veto. Although the President would then stand in breach of any legislative enactment implementing the FAS proposal, the motivations for such a breach can be easily described.

A President committed to first use would have concluded that interests vital to the survival of the nation would otherwise be lost. Under such circumstances, congressional frustration of an executive first use decision would appear to threaten the continued existence of the nation. The nuclear planning committee may argue that compliance with its veto is required by the President's oath to preserve and defend the Constitution. However, the President would believe effective defense of NATO to be compelled by that same oath. Those convinced of the inevitability of escalation from first use to full-scale strategic nuclear war must conclude that the President's position is in error. However, American policy regarding nuclear weapons in Europe assumes the possibility of limited battlefield use.[22] Consequently, a President could well hold a strong conviction that his oath of office *required* a first use of nuclear weapons.[23]

Under wartime circumstances, the executive may choose to disregard any threats of sanctions and ignore the nuclear planning committee's veto in order to save the nation. Successful first use of nuclear weapons limited to European soil would allow the President to be seen as the savior of the American nation. Even if the President contemplated the risk of subsequent impeachment proceedings, he might conclude the prospect of damage to his political career to be a small cost to pay for the preservation of the nation. After all, if the President is right the nation will be saved; if he is wrong and full-scale strategic war follows, no one will be around to impeach him.

The FAS proposal imposes upon the secretary of state the statutory responsibility for certifying the nuclear planning committee's judgment rather than that of the executive decision making group in which he had participated.[24] The secretary's loyalty to the President may well be stronger than any commitment to enforce the committee's veto,[25] particularly where controversy exists as to the constitutionality of the implementing legislation. Once the dynamics of group-think are considered, the doubtfulness of reliance on cabinet officers to implement the veto becomes evident.

III. RECOMMENDATIONS FOR ALTERNATIVES

Revision of the FAS proposal may avoid some of the practical problems raised thus far. Some difficulties vanish where the President is only required to consult with the nuclear planning committee. However, mere consultation could not prevent unilateral presidential first use. A second alternative might prove more effective. In addition to establishing the proposed planning committee, the proposal could amend the National Security Act to add two members of the committee as non-voting observers of the National Security Council ("NSC").

A. Required Consultation

Rather than requiring the establishment of a nuclear planning committee empowered to exercise a veto power over presidential first use, a revised FAS proposal could require only that the President consult with the committee. While a bare consultation requirement clearly weakens the role of the committee, it offers at least three advantages.

First, the consultation proposal maintains some opportunity for legislative participation and comment on a first use decision. This would preserve the opportunity for the committee to raise relevant political and ethical considerations. Second, the modified proposal could reduce the executive perception of the legislature as a hostile political competitor in foreign policy. Finally, a consultation requirement reduces the problem of information sources for the committee, since the committee no longer faces the same duty to second guess the executive decision. Residual information needs may be fulfilled by a regular peacetime briefing.

Unfortunately, the modified proposal also incorporates very serious disadvantages that, on balance, outweigh the advantages. The committee would have no viable institutional means for challenging the practical presidential monopoly of' power over the decision to resort to nuclear weapons. In addition, the consultation proposal provides little motivation for a President to attend to legislative concerns with more than formal response. Furthermore, a consultation requirement fails to reach the stated constitutional goal of "no single first use decision maker," since only power-sharing could make first use the joint decision that advocates of the FAS proposal contended would be required under the Constitution.

B. Congressional Observers in the NSC

A more promising revision might involve a novel approach to participation in the first use decision making process. Under this alternative, the nuclear planning committee could be established with the veto power contemplated in the original FAS proposal. However, to facilitate exercise of that veto, two designated members of the nuclear planning committee would be added to the statutory membership of the NSC[26] as observers with the right to attend meetings of the NSC or of any subgroup responsible for reaching the final executive decision to resort to the first use of nuclear weapons.[27] This NSC modification approach offers substantial advantages of several different kinds for effective implementation of the FAS proposal.

The first advantage involves access to information. The NSC conducts the formalized coordination and policy planning functions of the presidency in national security affairs.[28] Should the President rely on the NSC in making a first use decision, that organization will receive essential intelligence information reflecting the broad range of potential risks and advantages involved. Congressional observers of the NSC decision process will have direct and simultaneous access to both the NSC's intelligence and its analysis. When those observers return to participate in the congressional committee, their presence should greatly ease the information problem confronting the committee in responding to a presidential first use proposal. By providing clarification of the NSC's considerations as well as criticism of the NSC's presumptions, these observers could perform an invaluable function.

Second, congressional observers may diminish the risk of groupthink tainting the NSC decision making process by decreasing the critical tendency of other NSC participants to perceive themselves as part of an homogeneous, tight-knit group. Even if the NSC manifests symptoms of groupthink the committee observers may expose the weakness of the decision to the committee and to the President during their review of the first use decision.

Third, the particular legislative perspective could be introduced into the first use decision process at an earlier point. The FAS proposal implies that Congress offers a different view on questions of war and peace from that of the executive branch. The constitutional structure also reflects that belief.[29] Congressional observers might bring the NSC to an earlier recognition of the larger political and normative trade-offs of a first use decision. Even without the exercise of a veto, their participation could create the very benefits that the constitutional structuring of a formal legislative role in the war making decision was initially intended to generate.

Further, participation of congressional observers could improve cooperation of the two branches. The current FAS proposal could seriously increase adversarial and competitive interaction between the branches at precisely the time when cooperative interaction may be most essential to national survival. Congressional NSC observers may reduce the necessity for a primarily justificatory and defensive executive presentation of the first use proposal before the nuclear planning committee.

Finally, observer participation in NSC meetings after the exercise of a committee veto would greatly increase the likelihood that the secretary of state would comply with any statutory obligation to implement the veto. The presence of the observers would pointedly remind the secretary of his obligations. Any refusal to cooperate with the observers would constitute a clear signal of the executive intent to ignore the veto.

Unfortunately, this proposed modification appears to have several disadvantages as well. One legal issue would need clarification. The Constitution forbids any member of Congress from being appointed to any office under the authority of the United States created during that member's term in office, and it prohibits any person holding an office under the United States from being a member of Congress during the continuation of that office.[30] Further, only the President has the power to appoint officers of the United States.[31] A question could be raised as to the applicability of these clauses to participation by nuclear planning committee members in the NSC.

There is some indication that the purpose of the former provision was to prevent the President from exerting undue influence over members of Congress through the distribution of appointive executive positions.[32] Both provisions depend upon the definition of "officers of the United States." The participation of committee observers in the NSC need not involve appointment to or exercise of any executive office. In fact, the very legislative information-gathering function served by the observers has been approved by the Supreme Court.[33] A constitutional clause intended to prevent executive dominance should not prevent an effective legislative mechanism for imposing congressional constraints on executive war making decisions.

Opponents of this proposal might argue that it reduces the ability of a President to adopt freely the most appropriate type of advisory body. Scholars concerned with the NSC have noted that its structure and function have changed with the varied decision making styles of the occupants of the White House.[34] Unless skillfully drafted, a legislative requirement of observer participation may inadvertently impose rigidity upon the NSC structure.

The presence of congressional observers may also motivate executive resort to alternate covert decision channels prior to any discussions at which observers would be present. Advocates of first use may resort to outside bargaining sessions to reach a consensus for presentation in the NSC in the presence of congressional observers. Similarly, small informal subgroups of the NSC may begin to meet outside of the presence of the observers. Resort to either of these tactics could frustrate the effectiveness of the proposal. However, reliance by executive decision makers on either approach would be likely only if there were an intent to suppress serious residual questions where the executive branch was already irrevocably committed to first use. Under such circumstances, no approach to legislative participation would be viable.

Finally, congressional observer participation in the NSC could increase security risks. The proposal would involve adding new participants to a highly sensitive decision process. Without confidence in the ability of the congressional observers to protect the sensitive information to which they had access, the security of the decision process could be jeopardized. In fact, unless congressional observers participated regularly in the NSC process, their mere attendance at NSC meetings could serve notice that the United States was considering the first use. Provision for security analogous to those surrounding congressional intelligence committees would be required.

IV. CONCLUSION

The proposal offered by the FAS faces severe problems of implementation when considered in the context of a European conflict with Warsaw Pact forces. Although many of these difficulties may be less significant in other contexts, advocates of the proposal point to the European scenario as the paradigm case for its operation. A number of practical problems with intelligence and decision making combine to cast serious doubt on the viability of the original proposal. Modification of the proposal may ameliorate some of the difficulties, but others may prove intractable.

NOTES

1. R. Bretts, *Surprise Attack: Lessons for Defense Planning* 58 (1982).
2. W. Kennedy, "The World's Intelligence Organizations," *in* W. Kennedy, *Intelligence Warfare* 48 (1983) (hereinafter cited as *Intelligence Warfare*).
3. *See* P. Bracken, *The Command and Control of Nuclear Forces* 57 (1983).
4. The Soviet military forces will undertake "radioelectronic combat" in order to disrupt the communications necessary for effective command and control of enemy forces. They also use deception techniques to confuse observation, in addition to making direct attacks on intelligence-gathering personnel and equipment. *See id.*, at 108; Friedman, "Intelligence and the Electronic Battlefield," *In Intelligence Warfare, supra* note 2, at 85–86, 89–91; Department of the Army, *Soviet Army Operations* 5–80 to 5–82 (April 1978).
5. Bracken, *supra* note 3, at 100–105.
6. Kennedy, "What Is Intelligence," *In Intelligence Warfare, supra* note 2, at 12–14; G. Allison, *Essence of Decision: Explaining the Cuban Missile Crisis* 120 (1971).
7. *See* G. Allison, *supra* note 6, at 118–23.
8. A. George, *Presidential Decisionmaking in Foreign Policy: The Effective Use of Information and Advice* 86 (1980).
9. Bracken, *supra* note 3, at 113–14.
10. Nations are not unitary rational entities, but complex entities made up of many large organizations having a multiplicity of intentions and motivations. Kincade, "The Range of Options," *in* H. Roderick, *Avoiding Inadvertent War: Crisis Management* 150–51 (1983). *See generally* Allison, *supra* note 6. Consequently, government actions provide inconsistent signals reflective of many differing intentions, making their interpretation very difficult. Kincade, *supra* at 151.
11. An adversary may not have a well-developed intent; the failure to collect clear information may result from the fact that there is no clear information. R. Betts, *supra* note 1, at 96.
12. Stone, *supra* Ch. 2. The possible resort of Soviet forces to chemical weapons to

attack United States nuclear forces on the European battlefield also poses a particularly difficult problem. The Soviets maintain an extensive array of chemical weapons which could be delivered by dual capable systems. *See* Department of Defense, *Soviet Military Power* 71–72 (1985 ed.). Such an attack would cause millions of civilian casualties. *See* Meselson and Robinson, *Chemical Warfare and Chemical Disarmament*, Sci. Am., at 44–45 (April 1980). However, preparation for a preemptive attack on Soviet long-range dual capable systems in order to avoid the chemical attack could appear to be an attack aimed primarily at Soviet nuclear weapons systems. Although this apparent nuclear preemption would probably involve United States long-range dual capable systems operating in a conventional mode, the Soviets may perceive the United States attack as one involving nuclear weapons. Ultimately, the President may find it most logical to engage in actual nuclear preemption rather than risk Soviet nuclear preemption resulting from misperception.

13. Many of the weapons available for such strike would be "dual-capable" systems which could deliver either nuclear or conventional munitions. *See* G. Allison, A. Carnesale, & J. Nye, *Hawks, Doves, and Owls: An Agenda for Avoiding Nuclear War* 110 (1985).

The U.S. has indicated that it may respond to chemical attack with nuclear retaliation. Department of Defense, *Annual Report to The Congress for Fiscal Year 1986* 282. The FAS proposal is not clear whether nuclear preemption of a chemical attack would require nuclear planning committee approval, even though a chemical attack on United States forces in NATO countries could have a massively devastating effect on soldiers and civilians alike. Obviously, grave risks are posed by any resort to weapons of mass destruction.

14. R. Jervis, *Perception and Misperception in International Politics* 145–46 (1976); R. Lebow, *Between Peace and War: The Nature of International Crisis* 104 (1981).

15. Jervis, *supra* note 14, at 143, 172–81; Lebow, *supra* note 14, at 105.

16. Lebow, *supra* note 14, at 199–200.

17. I. Janis & L. Mann, *Decision Making: A Psychological Analysis of Conflict, Choice, and Commitment* 46 (1977); Lebow, *supra* note 14, at 107–08.

18. One consequence is the propensity for decision makers to resort to "bolstering." Janis & Mann, *supra* note 17, at 58; Lebow, *supra* note 14, at 110. Bolstering includes a series of psychological tactics which may result in the failure to recognize dangers inherent in the least objectionable decision option. Janis & Mann, *supra* note 17, at 87, 91–95; Lebow, *supra* note 14, at 87, 110; George, *supra* note 8, at 38–39.

19. Lebow, *supra* note 14, at 111–15.

20. George, *supra* note 8, at 81–92.

21. The definitive work on this phenomenon is I. Janis, *Groupthink: Psychological Studies of Policy Decisions and Fiascoes* (1982 ed.). *See also* George, *supra* note 8, at 93–96; Lebow *supra* note 14, at 152, 293–95.

22. *See* L. Freedman, *The Evolution of Nuclear Strategy* 383 (1981). In fact, some Europeans fear that the superpowers might seek to limit a nuclear war to Europe alone, increasing their risk while reducing the danger to the major protagonists. Voight, "Nuclear Weapons in Europe: A German Social Democrat's Perspective," *in* J. Pierre, *Nuclear Weapons in Europe* 98, 102 (1984).

23. If Presidents consistently resisted the constitutionality of the FAS proposal, as all Presidents have with the War Powers Resolution, see Note, *A Defense of the War Powers Resolution*, 93 Yale L. J. 1330, 1332 (1984), then the resolution of the controversy may

be left to the political process, since the courts may avoid peacetime resolution of the controversy under the "political question" doctrine, see *Baker v. Carr* 369 U.S. 186 (1962), making the President's wartime view of the veto's constitutionality of equal practical significance to that of Congress.

24. Stone, *supra* Ch. 1.

25. The secretary of state is a statutory member of the National Security Council. Other members include the President, the Vice President, and the secretary of defense. National Security Act of 1947 as amended, Sec. 101(a), 50 U.S.C. § 402(a) (1982).

26. *Id.*

27. For example, in an early version of the FAS proposal, the President Pro Tempore of the Senate and the Speaker of the House could be the appointed members. Alternatively, the nuclear planning committee could select those members thought to be most appropriate.

28. A. Jordan and W. Taylor, *American National Security: Policy and Process* 89 (1984 ed.).

29. The Framers of the Constitution understood that the decision to go to war would be of great importance to citizens who would be required to make enormous sacrifices for the benefit of the state. *See* 2 *The Records of the Federal Convention* 318–19 (M. Farrand, rev. ed. 1937); J. Javits, *Who Makes War* 10–15 (1973); L. Henkin, *Foreign Affairs and the Constitution* 80–81 (1972). Granting power to Congress to formally declare war insured that the decision would be the result of deliberation by a sober legislative process. *See* T. Eagleton, *War and Presidential Power* 9 (1974); A. Schlesinger, *The Imperial Presidency* 405 (1973).

30. U.S. Const. art. I, § 6.

31. U.S. Const. art. II, § 2, cl. 2.

32. *The Federalist No. 77*, at 458–59 (A. Hamilton) (C. Rossiter ed. 1961).

33. *See* Buckley v. Valeo, 424 U.S. 1, 137–138 (1975).

34. *E.g.*, Endicott, "The National Security Council," *in* J. Reichert & S. Sturm, *American Defense Policy* 521, 525 (1982 ed.). On President Kennedy's use of an NSC subgroup during the Cuban Missile Crisis, see George, *supra* note 8, at 211–13.

12

A Congressional Committee on National Security: The Perspective from the Hill

William G. Miller

Since World War II, Congress has not played a meaningful role in making major national security policy decisions regarding the use of nuclear weapons, introduction of our forces into possible or actual hostilities, and other actions which might place the nation at risk. In the period before the United States entered World War II, without consulting Congress Franklin D. Roosevelt ordered the Navy to sink Nazi submarines. Since then, the invasion of Cuba and the dispatch of military forces to Grenada and the Marines to Beirut, to name but a few examples, were ordered without serious consultation with Congress. On the contrary, such decisions have been made by the President and his White House advisers alone. The National Security Council ("NSC") has been the place where most, if not all, presidential national security deliberations take place and decisions are made,[1] though crucial national security decisions may be made in other White House settings or with the advice of ad hoc groups, such as President Lyndon B. Johnson's "Tuesday Lunch Group."

Congress throughout the post–World War II period has been disposed to give the President the discretionary powers necessary to act effectively and quickly when the United States is in grave danger. But the experience of Vietnam and a number of other presidential actions that have put the United States to some degree at risk have resulted in restrictive legislation such as the War Powers Resolution,[2] the Hughes-Ryan Amendment[3] and the Intelligence Oversight Act.[4] It is fair to say that at the present time, the majority view is that the President should have the discretionary authority to forestall attack. Further, there is still overwhelming support for delegating to the President the authority to move expeditiously in times of crisis or emergency. But there also is a strongly held view in the Congress and elsewhere that the President should not be given the sole authority to put the nation at risk unless there first has been full consultation and a formal action by the Congress.

If this view is correct, then Congress must take the steps necessary to shape such authority and to achieve constitutional balance. But for almost forty years, the Congress has not had a legislative counterpart to the NSC. Congress can and should act to create a committee to serve as an effective and constitutionally appropriate legislative partner with the President and his chief advisers. A congressional national security committee would have two functions: first, and most important, it would consult with the President and his chief advisers on the crucial national security issues that come before the President and his inner circle for policy consideration and decision. Second, and closely related to the first, it would function as the formal agent of the legislature as a whole on vital national security matters.

This chapter will explore the advisability of a congressional national security committee composed of the House and Senate leadership, to serve as a counterpart to the President, his chief advisers, and the NSC.

I. KEY NATIONAL SECURITY ACTIVITIES ARE NOW OUTSIDE CONGRESSIONAL PURVIEW

As an institutional matter, the most important decisions made by the President in the NSC or in other high level White House decision making groups are presently not subject to the purview of the Congress. Congress does not receive notification or copies of NSC decisions. It has not had formal access to NSC proceedings or records or to other presidential national security orders or decisions except in connection with a few investigations, the most notable being the Watergate inquiry, the investigations by the Church Committee in 1975–76 into allegations of illegality and improper behavior by the intelligence agencies of the United States, and a study of Iranian policy in 1980. In practice, there has been no effective means of consultation between the Congress and the President and the NSC or other key White House policy-making groups, even though the decisions made there concern war and peace and the very existence of the nation.

A. The NSC Is the Most Important National Security Decision Making Body

The use of the NSC since it was established in 1947 by one of the provisions of the National Security Act[5] has varied according to the style and preferences of the President in office, but the NSC has grown steadily over the years in power and influence. The NSC is the key coordinating body for the President in carrying out national security decisions. In all significant respects, it is the nerve center for all national security activities. It is not only the place where most, if not all, national security decisions are made, but also the institutional locus of discussions of policy alternatives with or for the President.

The gravity of the decisions that are made in the NSC cannot be minimized. Most important are decisions about policy concerning the strategic issues, including first use of nuclear weapons. Down the scale are decisions about a whole range of conventional force issues such as the dispatch of United States forces on rescue missions or the supply of urgently needed equipment. Many, indeed most, of the decisions made in the NSC and in other high level groups of key advisers are not of great urgency. They are by any definition long range. But some of the decisions are in response to immediate crises, such as the seven-day Cuban missile crisis or instability in Lebanon. Of the greatest concern are those decisions which by their nature place the nation at risk, creating a situation of potential danger where one did not exist before.

The NSC adviser in the past several administrations has been almost as important as the secretaries of state or defense. In the case of Kissinger and Brzezinski, the NSC adviser has on occasion been the most important aide to the President. The NSC staff has a correspondingly dominant role in the bureaucracy.

B. The NSC and Its Records Are Generally Unavailable to Congress

Despite the NSC's importance, the records of its decisions have not regularly been made available to the Congress. In fact, White House lawyers in successive administrations of both parties have maintained that all presidential records, including NSC papers, are the property of the President, and that neither the Congress nor the public has any right to those papers. Although examples of every type of NSC document from every administration have found their way into the files of the relevant congressional committees, neither any committee of the Congress nor the Congress as a whole has had access to NSC decisions or papers or other presidential decision documents as a matter of right or practice on a comprehensive, systematic or timely basis.

The only exception is the product of The Intelligence Oversight Act,[6] requiring the President to report in writing all decisions or findings on covert action and to keep the two intelligence oversight committees of the Congress "fully and currently informed" of all intelligence activities. Covert actions and other intelligence activities are the most sensitive and fragile functions engaged in by the United States government. They involve the security of the nation, often in the most essential ways. They affect its real power, its international reputation, and the efficacy of its foreign and defense policies. Since 1976, the intelligence committees of both Houses have, in fact, with very few exceptions been fully informed, pursuant to this statute, of all intelligence activities that might affect the essential security of the United States.

Based on the past ten years' experience, the House and Senate intelligence committees have worked out effective, useful relationships with the executive branch, including the NSC, on oversight of the full range of intelligence activities. These relationships provide the most compelling evidence that NSC records of the most important decisions affecting the national security of the country could safely and efficiently be shared with a congressional national security committee.

C. The Isolation of Congress from NSC Decisions Violates Congressional Intent

The intent of Congress expressed in the Declaration of Policy section of the National Security Act[7] is "to provide a comprehensive program for the future security of the United States; to provide for the establishment of integrated policies and procedures for the departments, agencies and functions of the government relating to the national security. . . . " The Act expressly provides that "the function of the Council shall be to advise the President with respect to the integration of domestic, foreign and military policies relating to the national security *so as to enable the military services and the other departments and agencies of the Government to cooperate more effectively in matters involving the national security.*"[8]

Congress did not intend to exclude itself from national security matters. On the contrary, its purpose, as the legislative history of the National Security Act of 1947 makes abundantly clear,[9] was to enable the government as a whole to function more effectively in the area of foreign policy and defense. The Armed Services Committees of both houses of Congress held hearings on the bill and worked with the executive branch on the final language of the Act. Since Congress created the NSC to enable the executive to function more effectively in national security matters, it can also create a committee to be available for consultation on key national security decisions, to be informed of the NSC's activities, and to have access to presidential national security decisions, studies and deliberations.

II. ARGUMENTS FOR EXCLUDING CONGRESS ARE LOGICALLY AND HISTORICALLY FLAWED

The executive branch and proponents of unilateral presidential authority have offered a host of arguments for excluding Congress from national security decision making. First, they argue that executive privilege bars congressional access to the necessary information. Second, they argue that Congress is institutionally incapable of maintaining the security necessary to assure secrecy. Third, they argue that even with secure access to essential national security information, Congress cannot, for reasons of speed and availability, act with the expedition required for national security decision making. They also point to Congress' alleged inexpertise as a fourth reason why it cannot effectively participate in national security decision making.

Even if they were correct, these arguments for excluding Congress would at best be reasons to amend, rather than ignore, the constitutional scheme of shared decision making. But they are, in any event, belied by logic and history.

A. Executive Privilege and the Need for Information Security

One argument that has been often made in isolating Congress from decision making is that such decision making is protected by "executive privilege," which bars disclosure even to Congress of NSC advice and the nature of give and take in NSC proceedings. Few would object to the idea that the President needs a "sounding board," and that he should be able to test his thoughts in a confidential way with close confidants. The NSC and its ad hoc and informal variants have been sheltered in the past by arguments of this kind. But it is clear that the NSC is not a quiet corner for private musings. On the contrary, it is the place where the most important national security decisions are made. The work of the NSC, and certainly NSC decisions, do not by any definition fall into the category of private confidences.

Are there, however, national security secrets that because of their sensitivity cannot be shared with the Congress? A somewhat similar question arose during the formative period of the Senate Select Committee on Intelligence.[10] The most contentious legislative issue between the executive branch and the Church Committee in the years 1975–76 was whether the Congress had the right to intelligence information, and if so, to what degree and under what conditions. This issue was discussed almost daily with the Ford and Carter administrations. Both Presidents Carter and Ford were directly involved, as were the vice-presidents, four directors of the Central Intelligence Agency, three attorneys general and legions of lesser officials and lawyers.

The Senate Select Committee based its claim to any and all information concerning the intelligence activities of the United States on its need to have the information in order to carry out its legislative duties in these areas. Since the information generated by the intelligence agencies was paid for by funds appropriated by the Congress, Congress has a right to such information and the right, indeed the duty, to monitor the activities of the intelligence agencies to determine whether public funds were being properly spent in accord with legislative intent.

The Senate view became law in 1978. The language of the congressional oversight provision of the National Security Act of 1947[11] provides that the intelligence committees of the Congress shall be "fully and currently informed of all intelligence activities which are the responsibility of, are engaged in by, or are carried out for or on behalf of, any department, agency, or entity of the United States, including any significant anticipated activity. . . . "

This right of access on the part of the intelligence oversight committees is based on the language contained in the Atomic Energy Act of 1946[12] which accorded to the Joint Committee on Atomic Energy a right to any and all information pertaining to nuclear energy and related issues. Section 202 of that

Act states that it shall be the duty of the relevant departments and agencies to keep the Joint Committee "fully and currently informed."[13] The provision of information in the degree the Committee desired and when the Committee desired it was satisfactory, according to the testimony of members who served throughout that Committee's existence.

This precedent of access to information by the Joint Committee on Atomic Energy was crucial at the time the intelligence oversight committees were being established. The precedent and the powerful support of key Senators who had served on the Joint Committee made the effort to obtain similar authority for the intelligence oversight committees a much easier task. The record of access, of security, and of cooperation with the executive branch on the part of the Joint Committee on Atomic Energy was viewed by most parties as an appropriate and effective model.

Since it could therefore not be credibly argued that national security secrets could not be given Congress because they had never before been provided, the next fallback was security. The argument was that Congress was an open institution which could not maintain the security necessary to keep secrets. The clear implication was that the Congress could not be trusted to keep secrets because of the temptations of partisan politics, a natural desire to use the publicity value of sensational and exotic exposes, and because sound security practices required a kind of institutional discipline that was alien to Congress.

The difficulty with the argument was that it could be turned with equal force against the higher reaches of the White House, executive branch departments and agencies, and the NSC itself. For example, in 1976 it was shown that many more leaks had come from the White House and the executive branch than from Congress. Both the Director of the CIA and the President attested, to their regret, that the White House and the departments and agencies, including the CIA, had more serious security breaches than the Congress. Indeed, they praised the Senate Intelligence Committee for its tight security.

Both the Church Committee and successor oversight committee worked closely with the White House, the FBI and the intelligence agencies to develop sound security practices and procedures. For example, a requirement for staff employment is a security clearance. In addition to investigation done by the committee itself, the FBI conducts a security investigation similar to investigations done for prospective employees in the intelligence agencies or NSC staff. A full field check is done by all other intelligence agencies as well. Only after these steps have been taken will the committee consider hiring a staff member. The offices, safes, secure telephones, file systems and conference rooms all meet security standards established by security experts in the FBI, CIA and other intelligence agencies. There are regular inspections of these facilities and procedures to be ure the security is of the highest possible standard. A large proportion of the taff of the Intelligence Committee has served in the intelligence agencies and elated departments and agencies and is familiar with the requirements of necssary security. Finally, the security staff of the Committee are experienced security officers with considerable relevant service in the line intelligence agencies.

There were, however, other more difficult security issues that faced the Church Committee than clearances or physical security. They centered on "the need to know" so-called "sources and methods" and on deep-rooted institutional loyalties. From the point of view of the intelligence agencies, very few operatives or analysts had a need to know anything beyond their areas of responsibility. Only a few policy makers at the top needed comprehensive knowledge or complete access to all available information. Indeed, even within particular areas, there is a hierarchy of knowledge, or in the terminology of the intelligence community, a series of increasingly restricted "compartments." The most sensitive compartments are reserved for the smallest possible group of policy makers because of the fragility of the sources of information, or, in some cases, the political risks involved.

From the viewpoint of Congress, on the other hand, its need to know is conceptually the opposite. For legislative policy making it is important to know as much as possible from as many sources and viewpoints as possible. If information is to be "compartmented," it is because it is not relevant to the policy making function. For example, in most cases, the names of agents who acquire information or of the exact technical means by which some information has been obtained are not relevant to policy considerations.

Yet over a period of years a reasonable formula of compartmentation has been developed adequate to both the needs of the intelligence agencies to protect their sources and methods and the comprehensive needs of a policy making and oversight body. In essence, the oversight committee is willing to limit access to fragile sources and methods to a small group of members and staff on a rotating basis, while reserving the right to all information wherever it deems it necessary. In no case has the committee waived the requirement that a few of its members and staff always be fully and currently informed.

Nevertheless, are there any kinds of national security information that cannot, as a constitutional matter, be shared by both the executive and legislative branches? As one example, White House Counsel Lloyd N. Cutler and I, as Staff Director to the Senate Intelligence Committee, drew up a series of hypothetical cases in an attempt to clarify what information, if any, must be reserved to the President alone. While no actual historical examples of such information were identified, one hypothetical example was conceded by both sides as a valid possibility: the so-called "mole in Ruritania" example. Assume that an information source has suddenly become known to the President alone. This source holds the key to the survival of the United States, and, because of a complicated series of circumstances, if the President informs anyone else of the source, that act itself would destroy both the source and the United States. In this extremely improbable case, it was agreed the President had a constitutional duty not to tell anyone, including Congress. But if the circle of knowledge could safely be extended by one or two beyond the President, Congress could no longer be excluded. There was no logical or legal basis for presuming more loyalty or security in a White House aide than in a committee chairman. Constitutionally, certainly, once the circle is widened beyond the President himself, the legislature has as much right to the information as the executive branch.

B. The Need for Expeditious Action

Another argument against congressional participation is that the time-urgency of national security decision making prevents consultation with Congress. This urgency allegedly makes the congressional deliberative process impossible; indeed the attendant delay could endanger the security of the nation.

Although this argument is plausible, it is not supported by the historical record. Even in sudden emergencies like the seizure of the *Mayaguez*, the shooting down of KAL 007, or the rescue of Americans in Grenada, there was sufficient time available for extensive consultation with Congress before decisions were made. In fact, the *Mayaguez* rescue might have been accomplished without loss of life if there had been more deliberation using the better information which later became available. In the case of Grenada, the political crisis on that small island had been brewing for several years, the Carter administration had consulted with Congress, and consultation by the Reagan administration would clearly have been desirable. In the KAL 007 incident, it was several days before the facts were available even to the executive.

It is clear, however, that the President could within his constitutional authority act without consultation if he reasonably believed that any delay would seriously endanger the security of the United States or certainly result in the death of Americans. The constitutionality of his actions would in these cases be measured by the results. But few, if any, issues that come before the President in the NSC or its informal variants for consideration, deliberation, or decision are of this immediacy. The case usually cited as an example of an urgent matter—the Cuban Missile Crisis—in fact extended over seven days, and the roots of the crisis went back months and years before the event.

The problem of congressional availability for time-urgent decisions was addressed in the Vietnam period. Senator Mike Mansfield first decided that, as a technical matter, Congress would never be out of session. When not formally in session it would be in recess, subject to recall of the chair. In addition, he established an informal duty roster of the leadership. Further, he ordered the Secretary of the Senate to maintain a list of telephone numbers for each member so that they could be contacted at any time and brought back to Washington within twenty-four hours, no matter where they were. As a practical matter, moreover, the leadership, by the nature of its role, is "always around" and would be available for consultation as readily as Cabinet officers or members of the NSC.

Another example illustrates the availability of Congress for crisis consultation. The Senate Intelligence Committee's first chairman, Daniel K. Inouye, made sure that he could be contacted by telephone, even when in Hawaii, within minutes. His successors have followed his example.

It is clear, therefore, that the Congress can organize itself to meet, discuss, advise, or decide on urgent issues. It is not much more difficult to assemble congressional leadership than it is the membership of the NSC. Secure telephones, teleprinters, available aircraft and other forms of transport all serve to make it possible for a responsible congressional committee to assemble quickly and confer on urgent national security issues.

Finally, Congress has the means, through its own rule making process, to clear the decks at any time and set aside all other business to attend to urgent matters. Although changes in the rules are generally very difficult to make and usually are the result of long debate and deliberation, specific changes can relatively easily be incorporated into legislation.[14] A good case in point is Section 8 of Senate Resolution 400,[15] which created the Senate Intelligence Committee. It provides for votes within stated time frames on vital intelligence matters, such as the disclosure of classified material. The War Powers Resolution,[16] which was passed by the Congress over President Nixon's veto, restricts the time allowed for debate and also prescribes time frames for votes.[17]

The simplest way to assure expedited procedure in national security decision making is to incorporate the desired procedure in the enabling resolution creating a congressional national security committee. Clearly, if the leadership of both parties is involved in pressing a particular issue to debate or vote, the Congress will have little difficulty in adapting its agenda to meet a crisis.

C. Congressional Inexperience

Composing any national security committee or committees of the majority and minority leaders, the chairman and ranking minority member of the Armed Services, Foreign Relations and Intelligence Committees, is also an answer to the "inexperience" argument. Rarely, if ever, has an administration come into office with cabinet officers and other high appointed officials who have as much direct experience with foreign policy and defense issues and first hand acquaintance with the world's leaders as the senior members of the House and the Senate. Indeed, the Senate has been the training ground for presidential leadership in foreign policy and defense. The leadership is selected not only because of their seniority and the power that comes with seniority, but also because they are "greybeards" or "wisemen" with long experience, familiarity with recurring issues, and direct acquaintance with the world's leadership, as well as with the complexities of domestic politics. These historical attributes of the congressional leadership give credence to the idea of a national security committee or committees in the Congress with the ability to work usefully with the President and the NSC on the vital issues of national security.

III. CONGRESS SHOULD CREATE A LEADERSHIP COMMITTEE FOR NATIONAL SECURITY CONSULTATION

The experience of congressional committees such as the Joint Atomic Energy Committee and the intelligence oversight committees of both houses proves that a national security committee composed of the congressional leadership could address national security issues effectively, expeditiously, and with appropriate confidentiality and security. It makes practical sense and it is constitutionally appropriate to have the political leadership of both executive and legislative branches work together on a continuing basis on vital matters of national security.

A. Creating the Committee

There are many ways Congress could create a legislative counterpart to the NSC and its ad hoc informal variants. It could do so by statute, but this route would entail lengthy hearings and long delay. By far the simplest way initially would be for the leadership of both houses to convene an ad hoc bipartisan committee composed of the majority and minority leaders, and the Chairman and ranking minority members of Armed Services, Foreign Relations and the Intelligence Committees to serve as a consultative body, available to meet with the President and the NSC and any other key executive branch national security decision making group that might emerge. An ad hoc informal leadership group could be created immediately without formal legislative action.

When the leadership thought the time right, it would be appropriate, and in the long run more effective, for both houses to pass identical resolutions to empower this national security leadership group with the legislative authorities the committee would need, by using the constitutional power of the Congress to organize itself as it sees fit.

B. The Power and Jurisdiction of a National Security Committee

If a national security committee or committees composed of the leadership were created, it should have the legislative powers accorded to any standing committee, including the following: the committee would require access to any and all reports, studies and papers produced by the NSC or any department or agency or any other group of the United States government related to national security decisions. Such information should be available "fully and currently" and as may be required prior to anticipated activities, with every reasonable precaution being taken to assure the protection of national security secrets and the confidentiality of deliberative processes.

A congressional national security committee would not take away jurisdiction or erode the authority of the other standing committees. On the contrary, if the committee came into existence, it would bring Congress for the first time into an area of crucial national importance that had been outside congressional purview. A congressional national security committee would serve in part as the coordinator, integrator and "traffic cop" for the Congress in national security matters. Because the membership of the national security committee would include the chairmen and ranking minority members of the key standing committees, the power of the disparate committees that fall under the rubric of national security, like Armed Services and Foreign Relations, would in fact be strengthened.

C. Consultation, Not Oversight

Closely related to the jurisdictional issue is the very practical question of how much time and attention could reasonably be expected from a relatively small committee composed of the "natural" congressional leadership in national security, since it is obvious that the leaders are already burdened with other duties. The many duties of the congressional leadership are somewhat analogous to those of the President and his chief cabinet officials and other national security advisers. Just as the President and the heads of departments and agencies must delegate the details of carrying out policies, so must the congressional leadership rely on the standing committees to carry out the tasks of overseeing the actions of the executive branch, and monitoring how the policies and monies authorized by Congress are being directed and spent.

It is clear that a national security committee composed of the congressional leadership could not function in the manner of the standing committees. Such a committee could not devote the time and attention necessary for effective oversight. But the congressional leadership is by habit and experience conditioned to direct issues that come to their attention requiring oversight, monitoring or investigation to the relevant standing committees.

The standing committees of the Congress require large staffs to assist the members of the Armed Services, Foreign Relations and Intelligence Committees to prepare hearings, and to review the complex operations, budgets and plans of the huge departments and agencies under their jurisdiction. A leadership national security committee would require only a small staff experienced with both legislative and executive branch national security activities and operations. This small experienced staff would work closely with the National Security Adviser and his staff and with the staffs of the relevant standing committees to enable effective close consultation to occur when crucial issues of national security emerge.

The purpose of a committee composed of the congressional leadership is to be available to meet with the President and his chief advisers on the really crucial matters that affect the United States, matters of defense and war and peace. The committee would not have to meet with the President and his chief advisers more than two or three times a year to consider long range policies and decisions. It would, of course, be available immediately for consultation on sudden emergent crises.

Consultation, of course, means many things. There is an all too familiar kind of "consultation" which informs Congress at a point when the decision or action has already been taken. This kind of consultation is, at best, a kind of record keeping.

There is a second type of consultation which could be likened to taking the temperature. Selected, usually sympathetic Senators or Congressmen are informed in a private way about the direction of administration policies. The purpose of "consultation" in these instances is to get advice on the likely reaction of Congress to policies or decisions that they had no part in determining.

Finally, there is full consultation, which means fully discussing an issue with a microcosm of the Congress and seeking advice and reactions before a policy is decided. In most cases this means a committee. A good example of prior notification that often ripens into full consultation is the notice of covert action programs by the CIA which is given to the intelligence committees of both houses of Congress. There have been a number of occasions when covert action programs have been modified or terminated as a result of this form of prior notification. Section 3 of the War Powers Resolution also calls for consultation with Congress "in every possible instance before introducing United States Armed Forces into hostilities or into situations where imminent involvement in the hostilities is clearly indicated by the circumstances."[18] This requirement has not worked, partly owing to the provision's failure to specify with whom the President should consult. Designation of a national security committee could fill this void.

Congress could also compel consultation before an action may be taken. It could do this by language incorporated in the statute authorizing the activities of an executive branch entity. Good examples of this legislative path are, as indicated earlier, the consultative provisions written into the Atomic Energy Act of 1946[19] and the Intelligence Oversight Act,[20] which require full consultation concerning all activities within those committees' jurisdictions, including prior notification of significant anticipated activities.

In the case of statutorily required consultation regarding any intelligence activities, prior notification is *not* linked to a requirement for approval by Congress of the anticipated action. What was intended was a procedure that would result in full, meaningful consultation before decisions were made, but not in a congressional veto, through delay or inaction, of vital national security action. The same would be true of consultation with a congressional national security committee.

IV. CONCLUSION

The national importance of the issues considered and the decisions presently made by the President, his chief advisers, and the NSC, without the involvement of Congress—decisions that could put the nation at risk when it was not before, ranging from going to nuclear war on a scale that could result in global conflagration, to the disposition of United States forces and the expenditure of vast sums of money in furtherance of foreign policy or defense goals—are of such gravity that there are overwhelming reasons to create a congressional counterpart to the NSC. Among the most important of those reasons is the need for constitutional balance to enable the full diversity of American opinion to be expressed through the Congress on any decision as serious as war or peace. A national security committee composed of the congressional leadership could bring this balance and work effectively with the President and the NSC.

NOTES

1. R. Pious, *The American Presidency* 362–71 (1979).
2. 50 U.S.C. § 1541(a) (1982).
3. 22 U.S.C. § 2422 (1982).
4. Pub. L. 96–450, 94 Stat. 1975 (1980) (adding Title V—Accountability for Intelligence Activities—to the National Security Act of 1947, 50 U.S.C. §§ 401–05 (1980)) (hereinafter cited as *Intelligence Oversight Act*).
5. 50 U.S.C. §§ 401–402 (1982).
6. *See supra* note 4.
7. 50 U.S.C. § 401 (1982).
8. *Id.* § 402 (emphasis added).
9. *See* 1947 U.S. Code Cong. Service 1483.
10. The Senate Select Committee was established in 1976 to provide centralized oversight of the intelligence communities. S. Res. 400, 94th Cong., 2d Sess., 122 Cong. Rec. 14,673 (1976).
11. 50 U.S.C. §§ 401, 413 (1982).
12. Atomic Energy Act of 1946, Ch. 724, 600 Stat. 755, 772–73 (1946).
13. Atomic Energy Act of 1954, Ch. 1073, 68 Stat. 919, 956 (amending Atomic Energy Act of 1946).
14. There are also other ways to get action on vital matters that suddenly emerge. For example, under the rules of the Senate a request by two Senators is all that is needed to require the presiding officer to close the doors of the Senate chamber to consider confidential issues in closed session.
15. S. Res. 400, 94th Cong., 2d Sess., 122 Cong. Rec. 14,673 (1976).
16. 50 U.S.C. § 1541 (1982).
17. *Id.* at §§ 1543–44 (1982).
18. H.J. Res. 542, Pub. L. 93–148, 87 Stat. 555 (1973) (codified at 50 U.S.C. § 1542 (1982)).
19. Ch. 724, 60 Stat. 755 (1946).
20. *See* note 4.

13

The Justiciability of the FAS Proposal

Arthur L. Berney

One of the oldest and most central "tenets of American constitutionalism" holds that the best guarantor of liberty is "deliberately fragmented centers of countervailing power."[1] The Federation of American Scientists (FAS) proposal calling for Congress to pass legislation limiting the President's authority to order a first use is an appeal to such countervailing power. If the President felt bound by such legislation that would be the end of the matter. But what if the President considered the legislation an unconstitutional infringement of his powers and refused to abide by the law's terms? No one doubts that in such circumstances the political resolution of the dispute between the executive and legislative branches of government is appropriate and even desirable. But in the prolonged absence of such political resolution, may the judiciary decide the dispute? In a word, is the President's unilateral determination regarding the scope of his war powers *justiciable*?

This chapter attempts to answer this question. After reviewing the sharply divided scholarly opinion on the question in Part I, the chapter surveys the cases in Part II. This survey shows that, contrary to first impressions, the courts have not denied the justiciability of clear and certain—essentially ministerial—statutory limits on the President's war power. Whether the FAS proposal is or can be cast in such a form, however, is a different question, which Part III reluctantly answers "no." Nevertheless, the conclusion supplies the broader answer that neither the possibility of presidential defiance nor the probability of judicial

The author would like to acknowledge the able research and editorial help of Madelyn Leopold and Nila Pusin. In the interests of space, a portion of this essay treating the war powers issue was omitted. Its conclusions were in accord with those of Professor Ides, *supra* Ch. 6: Congress has the constitutional power to enact a first use restriction.

abstention should deter "the people," through their elected representatives, from any effort to reduce the risks of nuclear war, including the FAS proposal.

I. SCHOLARLY OPINION

On the discussion of whether "courts could contribute much to the accommodation" of a President-Congress conflict, few have contributed more than Professor Alexander Bickel.[2] In a speech concerning the legality of the Vietnam War and the propriety of suits to enjoin it, he presented his view that where "prudence" dictates abstention, the courts abstain and are well advised to do so.[3] Even though he thought the President had exceeded his constitutional authority in Indochina, Bickel unequivocally stated that the courts, as a matter of policy, should not rule upon challenges to that authority:

> I think the Court has been wise to exercise its discretion so as to avoid passing on the constitutionality of the war. . . . If the Court were to hold the war unconstitutional, the effect . . . would be to make it less likely than otherwise that Congress will assume its responsibility, now and in the future. . . .
>
> But there is another aspect of the problem. The Court cannot declare war unconstitutional and then do nothing about it. . . . The Court cannot well forbid—as it has been asked to do—the sending of some soldiers to Vietnam, but allow those already there to remain indefinitely. . . . The Court, rather, would inevitably be drawn into directing and supervising the conclusion of the war, just as it has directed and supervised the desegregation of the public schools in the South. . . .
>
> I assume the President would accept the judgment that our entry into this war—his predecessor's entry—was unconstitutional, and he would obey it. But he would have to know what to obey, and the Court would have to tell him. . . . The Justices could do it, as a technical matter. They would simply retain jurisdiction, the President would report to them from time to time, and they would issue directives. There is nothing impossible about this, but it is wrong.[4]

Professor Ratner, relying on the part of the *Baker v. Carr* test that declares that "prominent [among the elements of a nonjusticiable political question] is . . . the impossibility of deciding without an initial policy determination of a kind clearly for nonjudicial discretion,"[5] concludes in accord with Bickel that military "disengagement [would] involve the courts in formulation of military and foreign policy that far transcends the judicial dispute resolving function."[6]

If the matter were left there, it would be easy to understand and distinguish the cases upon which Professor Velvel based his very different conclusion that the courts have treated disputes involving war powers as justiciable.[7] None of the cases cited by Velvel, however, involved an effort to end a war, or undermined its pursuit in any significant respect. Almost all involved claims that the particular exercise of the war power wrongly deprived someone of a property interest.[8] Therefore, with one or two exceptions to be discussed later,[9] these cases did not prominently entail military or foreign policy issues. Instead the courts saw these cases as concerning pecuniary interests[10] or the discrete, personal, established kinds of harm that the courts are typically geared to protect against.

The distinction then between those separation of powers cases the courts have been willing and those they have been unwilling to hear lies in the different views courts traditionally take toward established, concrete *legal* wrongs as compared to inchoate *political* wrongs. This explains why the Court would hear a claim that one has been denied his right to trial by jury through improper executive action,[11] or a claim that one's ship was improperly seized,[12] but would turn a deaf ear to the plea that the President may not coerce a person to fight, and possibly kill or be killed, in an undeclared war.[13] There is no clause in the Bill of Rights that declares "no man may be required against his will to bear arms." And the owner of ship cargo can show in detail what has been taken from him, while the harm the war opponent suffers by contrast is prospective and uncertain.[14] Moreover, it is a harm that he suffers in common with all others who would prefer not to fight in a war they oppose and for which their representatives did not vote.[15] Similarly, the "right" not to be cremated in a nuclear holocaust belongs to all creation—but precisely because it is shared with all, it presumably is not capable of judicial protection.[16] One cannot, therefore, quarrel with the commentators who, for the reasons set forth above, thought the legality of the Vietnam War was a political question and as such beyond the legitimate authority of the judicial branch,[17] nor with those who would assert that the courts should not interfere in a conflict between the President and the Congress over first use policy. Discretionary and prudential choices, to use Professor Bickel's terms, by definition are subject to differences of opinion.

However, a few commentators, notably Professor Choper, have taken the argument a step further and have asserted categorically that courts should stay out of separation of powers conflicts.[18] Professor Choper's thesis, by his own admission, is not borne out by the cases.[19] Although one might dispute how substantial a role the Court should play in preserving the lines of division and interaction among the three branches of government, it is difficult to sustain the contention that it be "almost none." The error Professor Choper may have committed is the one Professor Velvel identifies when he notes that "[t]here is a clear distinction between the question whether a court can decide which branch of government is entrusted with responsibility for a particular political decision such as whether to fight a war, and the question whether the courts are to participate in making the political decision itself."[20]

Professor Wechsler, evincing a healthy appreciation of the court's institutional place in our society, avoids resolving a compound and subtle question about the elusive and shifting line of authority between the two political branches, by answering instead a different, simpler question. If there is a "textually demonstrable constitutional commitment of [an] issue to a coordinate political department,"[21] then the Court has no choice but to abide by its decision[22] and may legitimately do so by abstaining from reviewing it.[23] If, however, in disputed circumstances it is not clear to which of two departments a matter is assigned, the Court cannot resolve that dispute by abstaining.

In short, wisdom in *Baker v. Carr* dwells less in the compendium of considerations combined in the Baker's "half dozen" test than in other language of Justice Brennan's opinion:

. . . There are sweeping statements to the effect that all questions touching foreign relations are political questions. Not only does resolution of such issues frequently turn on standards that defy judicial application, or even involve the exercise or discretion demonstrably committed to the executive or legislature; but many such questions uniquely demand single voiced statement of the Government's views. Yet it is error to suppose that every case or controversy which touches foreign relations lies beyond judicial cognizance. Our cases in this field seem invariably to show a discriminating analysis of the particular question posed, in terms of the history of its management by the political branches, of its susceptibility to judicial handling in the light of its nature and posture in the specific case, and of the possible consequences of judicial action.[24]

II. GUIDANCE FROM THE CASES

Concerning the "political question" doctrine Professor Henkin wrote in 1972:

Despite common impressions and numerous citations, there are in fact few cases, and apparently no foreign affairs case, in which the Supreme Court ordained or approved . . . judicial abstention from constitutional review. . . . In the foreign affairs cases commonly cited the courts did not refrain from judging political actions by constitutional standards; they judged them but found them constitutionally not wanting.[25]

There have been no subsequent Supreme Court holdings that require amendment of this observation.[26]

A. The Vietnam War Cases

Most analogous to a hypothetical case brought to enforce a congressional constraint on the President's first use option are the series of cases brought to challenge the Vietnam War.[27] The question presented was whether the President could legitimately pursue the war without congressional assent or, later on, in the face of congressional limitations. In the first use situation the question is whether the President could escalate a war to nuclear weapons without congressional assent or in violation of congressional restrictions on such use. Although it is widely apprehended that the federal courts held the Vietnam War challenges to be nonjusticiable,[28] the truth is that they were far from unanimous in that judgement.

Luftig v. McNamara,[29] the earliest of the reported cases, set the tone of the initial unequivocal judicial reaction. The *per curiam* opinion of the prestigious Court of Appeals for the District of Columbia stated:

It is difficult to think of an area less suited for judicial action than that into which Appellant would have us intrude. The fundamental division of authority and power established by the Constitution precludes judges from overseeing the conduct of foreign policy or the use and disposition of military power; these matters are plainly the exclusive province of Congress and the Executive.[30]

Later opinions were more discursive, but only slightly less resolute.[31] Focusing more on presidential than congressional powers, the court in *Atlee v. Laird*[32] rested its determination of nonjusticiability on a combination of factors, most pertinent of which was the "no judicially manageable standard" aspect of the political question test:

Denominating our military activities a "war" could lead to consequences in our foreign relations completely beyond the ken . . . of this Court to evaluate. . . .

Additionally, we can conceive of no set of judicially manageable standards to apply to reach a factual determination whether we are at war. . . .

As already stated, it would be impossible to gather and evaluate properly the information necessary for deciding whether Congress meant to authorize the military activities in Vietnam. . . .[33]

The early war cases were not surprising. As long as the courts assumed, as they had a right to do at this stage of the war, that Congress was in agreement with the presidential implementation of the war policy, they had no basis for taking the cases because there was no dispute between the political branches. The only question a claimant could put was whether Congress was constitutionally required to declare war formally.

The reading is borne out by the opinions written after protest against the war gained respectability and Congress began struggling to curtail our involvement in Indochina. In *Berk v. Laird*[34] the court, relying on the Gulf of Tonkin Resolution and congressional appropriations, found that the President was acting within the legitimate scope of his authority. The court held that the political question did not bar a resolution on the merits.[35] In a companion case, the Second Circuit reaffirmed its view that the question presented was justiciable, but that the actions of Congress, including the furnishing of manpower and materials, were sufficient to authorize or ratify military activity in Vietnam.[36] The Second Circuit "stuck to its guns" even after Congress repealed the Tonkin Resolution.[37] Next, in a very interesting decision[38] which took seriously the *fait accompli* argument against authorization by appropriation[39] and the nondelegability of war powers argument,[40] for the first time a district court earnestly entertained the possibility of a declaratory judgment against the government.

Near the culmination of this line of cases a federal judge actually issued an injunction, with leave for an appeal, against the bombing of Cambodia.[41] The court construed a series of congressional enactments as prohibiting the continued bombing of Cambodia. Applying the simple principles of agency law, the court said it is the usual rule that the principal (Congress) may limit the duration of any authorization it gives to the agent (the Executive).[42] The Second Circuit reversed,[43] reverting, in large measure, to the political question doctrine it had earlier abandoned. Finding no "judicially manageable standards" upon which to assess the President's claim that the bombing was a "tactical decision" within the discretion of the President, the court ordered the dismissal of the case.[44]

Although it seems to raise doubt that courts will step into such cases even where the congressional lead is clear and certain, there are some very good reasons for discounting this case. Foremost among them is the fact that the court did not concede that Congress had explicitly ordered the cessation of the bombing. In fact, the court, applying the plain meaning rule, said Congress had authorized military action up until the cutoff date of August 15, 1973, which was seven days after the date the case was being heard.[45] Thus, the case does not fully repudiate the concept that Congress has the last word on the use of force, as long as it clearly enunciates that word.

As previously noted, the Supreme Court had maintained sphinx-like silence on the justiciability of the Vietnam war cases.[46] Only Justices Douglas and Stewart broke this stony silence in their dissent from the Court's persistent refusal to grant review. Both justices believed that, at a minimum, the justiciability issue should have been fully addressed.[47] In *Massachusetts v. Laird*[48] Justice Douglas went further and indicated that he considered such cases justiciable. Answering the Solicitor General's argument that the power to declare war includes "a power to determine, free of judicial interference, the form which its authorization of hostilities will take," Justice Douglas said:

This may be correct. But, as we stated in Powell v. McCormack, 395 U.S. 486, the question of a textually demonstrable commitment and what is the scope of such commitment are questions [this Court] must resolve for the first time in this case. Id. at 521. . . . It may well be that it is for Congress, and Congress alone, to determine the form of its authorization, but if that is the case we should make the determination only after full briefs on the merits and oral argument.[49]

The outlines of the contemporary debate within the Supreme Court in the war cases, though shrouded by the Court's *certiorari* review practices, may be perceived in the opinions written in *Goldwater v. Carter*.[50] In that case, which involved a challenge by members of Congress to the President's unilateral abrogation of the defense treaty with Taiwan, there emerged a division within the Court basically along the lines adumbrated above in our discussion of the war cases. Four members of the Court, in an opinion written by Justice Rehnquist, concurred in a judgment of dismissal based on nonjusticiability. Justice Rehnquist wrote:

I am of the view that the basic question presented by the petitioners in this case is "political" and therefore nonjusticiable because it involves the authority of the President in the conduct of our country's foreign relations and the extent to which the Senate or the Congress is authorized to negate the action of the President.[51]

Diametrically opposed, Justice Brennan wrote in dissent:

In stating that this case presents a nonjusticiable "political question," Mr. Justice RHENQUIST, in my view, profoundly misapprehends the political-question principle as it applies to matters of foreign relations. Properly understood, the political-question doctrine restrains courts from reviewing an exercise of foreign policy judgment by the coordinate political branch to which authority to make that judgment has been "constitutional[ly] commit[ted]." But the doctrine does not pertain when a court is faced with the antecedent question whether a particular branch has been constitutionally designated as the repository of political decisionmaking powers.[52]

Justice Powell attempted to find a middle position. He concluded that the matter was not ripe for judicial review because Congress had not yet taken action asserting its constitutional authority. In his view:

The Judicial Branch should not decide issues affecting the allocation of power between the President and Congress until the political branches reach a constitutional impasse. Otherwise, we would encourage small groups or even individual Members of Congress to seek judicial resolution before the normal political process has the opportunity of resolving the conflict.[53]

Explicit in Justice Powell's position, and implicit in all the other opinions save that of Justice Brennan,[54] is the conclusion this chapter presses: once Congress asserts its powers, either to limit or to displace the President's exercise of his powers, in contexts in which both branches have legitimate claims of authority, the Court's duty is to resolve the dispute in cases in which it has jurisdiction.

B. Judicial "Bobbing and Weaving" in the Reagan Era

It is difficult to predict what degree of precision courts will demand of congressional standards or limits before they are willing to weigh in against executive recalcitrance. It is possible that what we have described as judicial willingness to respect clear congressional direction, as and if it is forthcoming, is not that at all, but instead only the courts' inclination to go along with the political outcome whatever it happens to be. The power of judicial review cannot be truly ascertained until a court says "no" to someone. What can be said, with certainty, is that the courts will not say "no" unless they are left no room to avoid an answer. Two recent cases indicate that the courts, given any room to interpret, will use it to continue to "bob and weave."

In *Crockett v. Reagan*,[55] some members of Congress brought an action against President Reagan to enjoin continued military assistance to the government of El Salvador. The central charge was that the dispatch of fifty-six members of our armed forces in El Salvador was in derogation of Congress' power to declare war, as implemented by the War Powers Resolution ("WPR").

The WPR requires that absent a declaration of war, a report be made to the Congress within 48 hours of any time when United States Armed Forces have been introduced into hostilities or into situations where imminent involvement in hostilities is clearly indicated by the circumstances [footnote omitted], and that 60 days after a report is submitted . . . , the President shall terminate any use of . . . [f]orces unless Congress declares war, enacts a specific authorization for such use, or extends the 60-day notice period. . . .[56]

The district court held the cause of action nonjusticiable on two grounds. First, the court found that the "factfinding that would be necessary to determine whether U.S. forces have been introduced into hostilities or imminent hostilities," and if so, "at exactly what point in time" that occurred, is beyond the ken of a court and thus "renders the case in its current posture nonjusticiable."[57] Second, the court found that the sixty-day period begins to run from the time a report was filed or the time when Congress required the filing of a report.[58] In the absence of a report or a congressional request for one, it would be impossible to fathom the intent of Congress.[59] Therefore, a court would not be operating under the direction of Congress, but in effect would be imposing its view of what the executive should do, in violation of justiciability principles.

The court appears correct when it opines that Congress never really considered what would happen under the WPR if no report were filed and Congress called for none. This point approached the question, which may have been on the court's mind throughout, as to why the plaintiffs had not first sought a "mandatory withdrawal" resolution under the WPR or at least a bill calling for a report.[60] The answer may be that the plaintiffs knew that they would not find congressional majorities for such actions. If that were the case, the court was right to conclude that it did not have a relevant mandate from Congress upon which to secure judicial intervention in executive decision making.

The lesson of *Crockett* is that congressional limitations on the President's control of our armed forces have to be precise and unequivocal before courts will enforce them. Failure to heed that lesson apparently also doomed the suit brought by the group of Congress members to enjoin the recent Air Force test of its antisatellite weapon. The statute involved in *Brown v. Weinberger*,[61] although described by the plaintiffs as "a clear and nondiscretionary statutory condition precedent,"[62] was if anything more porous than the WPR. The statute provided:

Notwithstanding any other provision of law, none of the funds appropriated or made available in this or any other Act may be obligated or expended to test in space the miniature homing vehicle (MHV) anti-satellite warhead launched from an F–15 aircraft unless the President determines and certifies to Congress . . . (1) that the United States is endeavoring, in good faith, to negotiate with the Soviet Union a mutual and verifiable agreement with the strictest possible limitations on anti-satellite weapons consistent with the national security interest of the United States . . . [63]

Once the President issued Presidential Determination No. 85–19, on August 20, 1985, purporting to meet the certification requirement, the plaintiffs were forced to argue that, contrary to the certification, the President was not "endeavoring in good faith to negotiate." In the foreshadow of the upcoming summit meeting it is difficult to see how a court could go behind the certification, and it refused to do so.[64]

In summation, it is submitted that the courts will enforce legislation limiting the scope of the President's first use options, if and only if the legislation requires unambiguous, nondiscretionary duties that leave no room for interpretation, fact finding or judgment calls. To the degree possible, the legislation must cast the President's duties in near ministerial terms.

III. Justiciability of Nuclear War Policy and the FAS Proposal

The profound questions of war and peace and the related policy questions of foreign affairs and national defense are not, as such, justiciable questions. Predictably our courts would refrain from adjudicating the constitutionality of the nation's nuclear war plans, including its first use plans. The determination of where the awesome power of nuclear defense and war strategy rests, is, in a most fundamental sense, a policy question. As such it must be decided by the political branches of government in response to the political process.

The argument that the President constitutionally has the power to initiate the use of nuclear weapons, whether as an exercise of control of foreign policy or as commander in chief of military forces deployed throughout the world, ultimately rests on the existing policy of nuclear deterrence. Whether to modify or, for that matter, to repudiate that policy is itself a major policy question. Likewise, whether Congress, under its numerous war powers is empowered to wrest control of the nuclear strategic arsenal from the President, or, less drastically, claim a greater share in the control of that arsenal, is eminently another large policy matter. We cannot expect or wish the Court to interject itself on policy questions of this magnitude.

None of this, however, reaches the question of the role the courts might play should Congress take it upon itself to so act. If Congress, for example, were to devise some certain, specific means of sharing first use decision making, the courts could review the congressional action *in an appropriate case*.[65]

The only question left is perhaps the most difficult of all: what constitutes *an appropriate case*. Or to put the matter differently, can Congress devise a statute that is specific and demanding enough to avoid the pitfall of the political question doctrine and yet comprehensive enough to fulfill its framers' purpose of fore-closing certain forms of first use? A statute, for example, that simply declared that the United States shall not use nuclear devices first to repel a conventional attack is certainly comprehensive enough, but it creates no demand that could possibly lead to a case. As the cases in Part II of this essay demonstrate, courts' continuing reluctance to be drawn into separation of powers disputes will lead them to exploit any ambiguity or delegation question as a ground for refusing to hear the case on the merits. Justice Powell's opinion in *Goldwater*[66] reflects the reality that whatever else courts may say, they will avoid judicial review in the politically charged atmosphere of these cases, if they possibly can. If a judicial test is desired, the statute must create a clear testing point—where compliance or noncompliance is exposed. In other words, to use Justice Powell's term, the statute must produce an "impasse."

One part of the FAS proposal concerns a plan that may lead to an "impasse" before the fateful moment of decision arises. This part of the plan envisions the establishment of a special "Nuclear Planning Committee" with the extraordinary authority to veto proposed first uses, or less controversially, to consult with the executive department regarding such use.

Aside from the merits of the committee idea, its inclusion increases the like-lihood that courts would view the proposal as nonjusticiable, because its in-volvement would postpone a justiciable inter-branch impasse or until it was too late for review. Furthermore, if a court did review the case, a decision would very likely go off on the question whether Congress could delegate its nuclear war powers to a committee.[67] Courts would consider the latter matter either a political question or premature.[68]

This leaves as the only possible justiciable matter any reporting requirement built into the proposal. The power of Congress to investigate and inform itself is well established.[69] Congress could pass a no first use restriction, requiring that all relevant executive departments report regularly to a Congressional Ov-ersight Committee concerning any contingency plans or proposals for the first use of nuclear weapons and all relevant military intelligence. To put teeth in this requirement, the President could be required to certify that such reports are complete and accurate. The failure to fulfill the requirements of this duty could carry criminal sanctions and, in the case of bad faith by the President, would be a *prima facie* case of "high crime and misdemeanor."[70]

But this limited possibility of judicial review, assuring that information and consultancy functions are fulfilled, does not seem like much. If the flow of information ceases during a real crisis, there will hardly be time to complain to a court. Moreover, since the flow of information is totally within the control of the executive department, the congressional committee itself could never be sure whether it was receiving all the relevant information.[71] Selective information would undermine the congressional oversight or participation. A court would be one step further removed and would be in no better position to gain the information it would need in order to determine if a presidential certification provision had been faithfully met.[72]

IV. CONCLUSION

The realization of the slight and possibly meaningless part judicial review can play requires us to face honestly the pragmatic underpinning of the judicial role in our system. In the last analysis we cannot help being skeptical about our ability to devise legal means of controlling the President's power to use nuclear weapons as long as they remain at his disposal.[73] And, if the only evidence of noncompliance is violation of the limitation set down, *we may be talking about the greatest moot case ever*.

Yet, confronting this realization leads to another: that eliminating the threat of first use, or the more general threat of nuclear annihilation, cannot be up to the courts or, for that matter, up to the President. It is up to the people. The FAS proposal is basically one opposing the use of nuclear weapons to resist or repel conventional attacks on our NATO allies or similar attacks that "threaten our vital interests" abroad. In its most radical light, this proposal calls for a declaration that, beyond our own territories, there are no vital interests or foreign commitments important enough to warrant our initiation of a nuclear exchange. To claim that it is beyond the power of Congress to declare such a policy is not only constitutionally wrong; it is truly frightening. Such a claim would mean that "we the people," acting through our elected representatives, could never take it upon ourselves to reverse the commitment to the arms race that holds the world in the thrall of nuclear terror. There is no event, short of the war we all dread, that should forestall the efforts of the people to reduce the risks of nuclear war. Though no court may ever confirm it, the FAS proposal is such an effort.

NOTES

1. L. Tribe, *American Constitutional Law* 1, 2 (1978).

2. A. Bickel, *The Least Dangerous Branch* (1962); Bickel, *The Supreme Court, 1960 Term Foreword: The Passive Virtues*, 75 Harv. L. Rev. 40, 46 (1961).

3. Bickel, *Congress, the President and the Power to Wage War*, 48 Chi-Kent L. Rev. 131, 144–45 (1971).

4. *Id.*

5. Baker v. Carr, 369 U.S. 186, 217 (1962).

6. Ratner, *The Coordinated Warmaking Power—Legislative, Executive and Judicial Roles*, 44 S. Cal. Rev. 461, 482 (1971).

7. Velvel, *The War in Vietnam: Unconstitutional, Justiciable and Jurisdictionally Attackable*, 16 U. Kan. L. Rev. 449, 480–81 nn. 138 & 139 (1968) (listing 21 cases).

8. At least eighteen of these cases involved property claims. Velvel, *supra* note 7, at 480–481 n. 138.

9. *See infra* text accompanying notes 29–32.

10. Although the Court no longer focuses on pecuniary interests as such, the tendency to equate "personal stake" with pecuniary or proprietary interests remains. *See* Frothingham v. Mellon, 262 U.S. 447, 487 (1923); *cf.* Flast v. Cohen, 392 U.S. 83 (1968). *But see* Justice Harlan's dissent in *Flast*, 392 U.S. at 118–19.

11. Ex Parte Milligan, 71 U.S. (4 Wall.) 2 (1866); Reid v. Covert, 354 U.S. 1 (1956).

12. The Prize Cases, 67 U.S. (2 Black) 635 (1862); Little v. Barreme, 6 U.S. (2 Cr.) 170 (1804).

13. Massachusetts v. Laird, 400 U.S. 886 (1970); Mora v. McNamara, 387 F.2d 862 (D.C. Cir.), *cert. denied* 389 U.S. 934 (1967); Mitchell v. U.S., 369 F.2d 323 (2d Cir. 1966), *cert. denied*, 386 U.S. 972 (1967). *See also The Selective Service Draft Cases*, 245 U.S. 366 (1918); United States v. Macintosh, 320 U.S. 605 (1931).

14. Mottola V. Nixon, 464 F.2d 178, 181 (9th Cir. 1972), *reversing* 318 F. Supp. 538 (N.D. Cal. 1970). *But see* Berk v. Laird, 428 F.2d 302, 306 (2d Cir. 1970); *cf* United States v. Sisson, 294 F. Supp. 511 (D. Mass. 1968).

15. *Cf.* Frothingham v. Mellon, 262 U.S. 447, 488 (1923); United States v. Richardson, 418 U.S. 166, 179 (1974); Schlesinger v. Reservists Committee to Stop the War, 418 U.S. 208, 217 (1974).

16. *Cf.* United States v. SCRAP, 412 U.S. 669 (1973).

17. Ratner, *supra* note 6, at 480–87; Monaghan, *Presidential War-Making*, 50 B.U.L. Rev. 19, 33 (1970); Bickel, *supra* note 3, at 144–45; Bickel *supra* note 2, 75 Harv. L. Rev. at 46; *cf.* Rostow, *Great Cases Make Bad Law: The War Powers Act*, 50 Tex. L. Rev. 833, 892 (1972). *Contra*, Schwartz & McCormack, *The Justiciability of Legal Objections to the American Military Effort in Vietnam*, 46 Tex. L. Rev. 1033 (1968); Velvel, *supra* note 7, at 479–85.

18. J. Choper, *Judicial Review and the National Political Process* 263 (1980). Professor Choper makes some important qualifications of this sweeping statement. *Id.* at 271.

19. *See id.* at 272, *citing The Steel Seizure Case*, 343 U.S. 579 (1952); at 336, *citing United States v. Nixon*, 418 U.S. 683 (1974); at 342, *citing Nixon v. Administrator of General Services*, 433 U.S. 425 (1977). *Cf.* Powell v. McCormack, 395 U.S. 486 (1969).

20. Velvel, *supra* note 7, at 480. Professor Velvel's argument failed to convince the courts. *See* Velvel v. Nixon, 287 F. Supp. 846 (D. Kan. 1968), 415 F.2d 236 (10th Cir. 1969), *cert. denied*, 396 U.S. 1042 (1970.

Professor Ratner falls into the same trap as Choper when he asks "Why should the judiciary interfere with hostilities authorized by the President and not disapproved by Congress?" *Supra* note 6, at 482. The answer to this question is, as Bickel and others have suggested, that the judiciary should not interfere. If Congress approves, there is usually ample evidence of this, and a court that demonstrates it leaves the matter where it belongs—with Congress. However, it does not help to delude ourselves that the Constitution settled the answer. Silence is not necessarily assent. *See* R. Bolt, *A Man for All Seasons*, 150–52 (1960).

21. Baker v. Carr, 369 U.S. 186, 217 (1962).

22. *See* Powell v. McCormack, 395 U.S. 486, 520 (1969).

23. *See, e.g.*, Wechsler, *Toward Neutral Principles of Constitutional Law*, 73 Harv. L. Rev. 1, 7–8, 9 (1959). Wechsler's view is clearly vindicated in *Powell v. McCormack*. But much in *Baker v. Carr*, 369 U.S. 186, 217 (1962), appears to be in accord with Bickel's view, *supra* note 3. The scholarly debate goes on. *See* Henkin, *Is There a "Political Question" Doctrine?*, 85 Yale L.J. 597, 622–25 (1976).

24. Baker v. Carr, 369 U.S. 211–12 (1962).

25. L. Henkin, *Foreign Affairs and The Constitution* 213 (1972).

26. *But see* Goldwater v. Carter, 444 U.S. 996, 1002–1005 (1979) (Rehnquist, J., concurring). *See* text accompanying note 50, *infra*.

27. For an extensive list of such cases, see Holtzman v. Schlesinger, 484 F.2d 1307, 1323 n. 3 (D.C. Cir. 1973).

28. *See* Van Alstyne, *Congress, The President and the Power to Declare War: A Requiem for Vietnam*, 121 U. Pa. L. Rev. 1, 2 (1972); Carter, *The Constitutionality of the War Powers Resolution*, 70 Va. L. Rev. 124 (1984).

29. 252 F. Supp. 819 (D.D.C. 1966), *aff'd*, 373 F.2d 664 (D.C. Cir.) *cert. denied*, 387 U.S. 945 (1967). *See also* United States v. Mitchell, 246 F. Supp. 874 (D. Conn. 1963), *aff'd*, 369 F.2d 323 (2d Cir. 1966), *cert. denied*, 386 U.S. 972 (1967).

30. 373 F.2d at 665–66.

31. *See, e.g.*, Davi v. Laird, 318 F. Supp. 478 (W.D. Va. 1970). *Accord*, Mora v. McNamara, 387 F.2d 862 (D.C. Cir.), *cert. denied*, 389 U.S. 934 (1967); Velvel v. Johnson, 287 F. Supp. 846 (D. Kan. 1968), *aff'd on other grounds*, 415 F.2d 236 (10th Cir. 1969), *cert. denied*, 396 U.S. 1042 (1970); Gravel v. Laird, 347 F. Supp. 7 (D.D.C. 1972). *See also* Henkin, *supra* note 25, at 622–25.

32. 347 F. Supp. 689 (E.D. Pa.), *aff'd without opinion*, 411 U.S. 911 (1972). *See also* Luftig v. McNamara, 252 F. Supp. 819 (D.D.C. 1966), *cert. denied*, 387 U.S. 945 (1967).

33. 347 F. Supp. at 705–07.

34. 429 F.2d 302 (2d Cir. 1970).

35. On remand, the district court granted the government summary judgment on the basis that Congress had authorized hostilities in a manner sufficiently explicit to satisfy constitutional requirements. The district court held nonjusticiable the narrower issue of whether Congress had to proceed by a declaration of war. Berk v. Laird, 317 F. Supp. 715 (E.D.N.Y. 1970).

36. Orlando v. Laird, 443 F.2d 1039 (2d Cir. 1971).

37. *See* Da Costa v. Laird (II), 448 F.2d 1368 (2d Cir. 1971).

38. Mottola v. Nixon, 318 F. Supp. 538 (N.D. Cal. 1970). The Ninth Circuit reversed on the basis of lack of standing, 464 F.2d 178 (9th Cir. 1972), inasmuch as plaintiffs, reservists, had not been specifically assigned to the war zone in Cambodia. Thus, the appellate opinion did not reach the lower court's rather strong statement on justiciability: " . . . unless the President receives, upon his request or otherwise, such a [war] declaratory consent, either general or limited, as soon as reasonably possibly, any undeclared war becomes a usurpation by the President or an abdication by the Congress—or, perhaps both." 318 F. Supp. at 553.

39. *Id*. at 543. This argument is that Congress' appropriations cannot be treated as a ratification because faced with the facts in the field, it has no real choice but to continue to provide for the defense of our forces.

40. *Id*. at 545.

41. Holtzman v. Schlesinger, 361 F. Supp. 553 (E.D.N.Y. 1973), *rev'd*, 484 F.2d 1307 (2d Cir. 1973).

42. *Id*. at 563.

43. Holtzman v. Schlesinger, 484 F.2d 1307 (2d Cir. 1973).

44. *Id*. at 1310, 1312.

45. 484 F.2d at 1313. In a sense, the case was a "plea bargain." Although the executive

had insisted earlier that Congress had no right to fetter his use of force, the Secretary of State submitted an affidavit committing the government to the termination of bombing on August 15. Viewed in this light, the court had already served its purpose of encouraging an accommodation of the political branches, and the executive yielded to the explicit will of the Congress.

46. Van Alstyne, *supra* note 28, at 2 n. 3.

47. Mora v. McNamara, 389 U.S. 934 (1967) (Douglas and Stewart, J.J., dissenting from denial of *certiorari*); *see also* Mitchell v. United States, 386 U.S. 972 (1966) (Douglas, J., dissenting). Justices Harlan and Brennan also may have been troubled by the failure of the Court to address the justiciability issue. *See* Massachusetts v. Laird, 400 U.S. 886 (1970) (Harlan, J., dissenting from denial of filing bill of complaint as an original matter); Atlee v. Laird, 411 U.S. 911 (1971) (Brennan, J., voting to note probable jurisdiction).

48. 400 U.S. 886 (1970).

49. *Id.* at 892.

50. 444 U.S. 996 (1979).

51. *Id.* at 1002.

52. *Id.* at 1006–07. Justices Blackmun and White also dissented, arguing that the justiciability claim could not be resolved without plenary consideration. *Id.* at 1006.

53. *Id.* at 997.

54. Justice Brennan's opinion, resting on his judgment that the President alone has the power to recognize and withdraw recognition from foreign regimes, intimates nothing about how he would view the different question of the power of the President and the Congress regarding war and peace making. *Id.* at 1007. Even Justice Rehnquist intimates some support for the proposition in the text. *Id.* at 1003 and particularly note 1 at 1004.

55. 558 F. Supp. 893 (D.D.C. 1982), *aff'd*, 720 F.2d 1355 (D.C. Cir. 1983).

56. *Id.* at 895. *See* WPR Sections 4, 5(b), 50 U.S.C. §§ 1543, 1544(b) (1982).

57. *Crockett*, 558 F. Supp. at 898–99. The court did not hold that courts should not interfere with executive discretion. "Plaintiffs do not seek relief that would dictate foreign policy but rather to enforce existing law." *Id.* at 898. Nor did it accept the argument that courts may not hear cases "involving the apportionment of power between the executive and legislative branches." *Id.* at 898. It is plain that what bothered the court was its lack of "resources and expertise (which are accessible to Congress) to resolve the disputed questions of fact concerning the military situation in El Salvador." *Id.* at 898–99.

58. *Id.* at 901.

59. The court noted that congressional inaction could just as well signify general agreement with the President's appraisal that no report was required. *Id.* at 901.

60. The case, in this light, could have been dismissed on "ripeness" or "standing" grounds. Indeed, Judge Bork, concurring in the affirmance on appeal, preferred to rest the case on lack of standing in suits by members of Congress. *See Crockett*, 720 F.2d at 1356 (Bork, J., concurring).

61. Brown v. Weinberger, Civil No. 85–2867 (D.D.C., Sept. 12, 1985).

62. *Id.*, Plaintiffs' Brief in Support of Motion for Temporary Restraining Order 15 (Sept. 9, 1985).

63. Department of Defense Authorization Act, 1985, Pub. L. No. 98–525, § 205, 98 Stat. 2509.

64. The motion to dismiss on grounds of lack of standing and non-justiciability was

granted in an unreported decision by Judge Norma Holloway Johnson. *See supra*, note 61.

65. A court might continue to decline to play a role because of its perceived inability to cause a resistant executive to relinquish exclusive control of these ultimate weapons in this insecure world. This "prudential" consideration, however, is inappropriate. In other contexts the Court has recognized that appropriate respect for the executive includes the presumption that he will abide by the rulings of the Court. *But see* Ex Parte Merryman, 17 F. Cas. 144 (C.C.D. Md. 1861). The fact that *Merryman* stands as an isolated instance of executive recalcitrance is significant. When President Nixon faced the possibility that the Court would force revelation of information that would lead to his downfall, he declared, albeit reluctantly, that he would accede to a "definitive decision" of the Court. *See* United States v. Nixon, 418 U.S. 618 (1974).

66. 444 U.S. 996, 997 (1979) (Powell, J., concurring).

67. *See* Immigration and Naturalization Service v. Chadha, 462 U.S. 919 (1983); *see generally supra* Part III of this collection. Even assuming a court decided that Congress could so delegate its powers, it would not necessarily follow that the President would be ordered to yield any of his command discretion to such a committee. This is not a delegation question but rather a question of whether Congress in any guise can constitutionally intrude itself into the "micromanagement" of the use of military force. *See* Moore and Turner, *supra* Chs. 3 & 4, respectively. Arguably, the delegation of prosecutorial discretion recognized in *United States v. Nixon*, 418 U.S. 683 (1974), could serve as an analogy though it is clearly distinguishable.

68. *See* Goldwater v. Carter, 444 U.S. 996, 997 (1979). Closely related to the ripeness problem, the committee aspect of the plan might cause the Court to question whether the Constitution provided guidance on the delegability of the war-declaring power of Congress to a congressional committee. The President's interpretation of delegability would presumably deserve as much deference as the Congress', since his veto power was entailed. After all, a bill that simply said the President cannot use nuclear weapons first would be subject to a presidential veto. A congressional committee override of his decision to use such weapons in a particular context would not present him with an opportunity to exercise his veto authority. *But see* Banks, *supra* Ch. 9, text accompanying notes 61–63. In such circumstances, the Court might not even pass on the delegation question; it would just leave the entire matter to be resolved politically.

69. The investigatory and informatory functions are conceded to be inherent in the legislative process. Congress has wide and substantial powers in this sphere. *See* McGrain v. Dougherty, 273 U.S. 135, 175 (1927); Buckley v. Valeo, 424 U.S. 1, 137–38 (1976). The functions are backed by contempt power. 2 U.S.C. § 192 (1857).

70. U.S. Const. art. II, § 4.

71. *See* Smith, *supra* Ch. 11, Part I.

72. *Compare* Brown v. Weinberger, Civil No. 85–2867 (D.D.C., Sept. 12, 1985).

73. This is not to say that abstract constitutionality is unimportant. Even assuming that the question of presidential nuclear war powers generally, or the particular application considered here, will never be tested by a court, both the Congress and the President are, or ought to be, vitally interested in the constitutionally correct course. There is more to constitutional law than whether the Court is the right or wrong forum to review a particular issue. There is also the question whether the resolution of the issue is "right or wrong as an element in the living development of constitutional justice." Tribe, *supra* note 1 at iii.

14

The Constitutionality of the FAS Proposal: A Critical Summary

Peter Raven-Hansen

"I can go into my office and pick up the telephone and in 25 minutes 70 million people will be dead," President Richard Nixon told a group of congressmen in 1973.[1] Thus fittingly a President put the real world problem that prompted this book. The problem is that today a single American decision maker can order a first use of nuclear weapons that would escalate conventional hostilities into nuclear war. Dr. Jeremy Stone suggests in Chapter 1 that if there is time for a group decision, leaving this decision to a single man offends common sense.

Does it also offend the Constitution? If not, may Congress prohibit presidential first use without its approval? If time precludes approval by the full Congress, may a committee of its leaders grant such approval in its place, as the Federation of American Scientists (FAS) has proposed? Unless the constitutional issues are resolved in favor of the FAS proposal, the additional practical issues of implementation are moot. This summary therefore addresses the constitutionality of the FAS proposal alone.

In Part I, I conclude that presidential first use is constitutional by reason of congressional acquiescence. What Congress has given, however, it can take back. There is therefore no constitutional impediment to a statutory ban on first use. Part II concludes that the constitutional case for permitting a congressional committee to act for the full Congress to lift that ban is much closer. The strongest argument for this aspect of the FAS proposal is constitutional necessity: the committee is a political check on the President that is essential to preserve the constitutional equilibrium in the nuclear age.

I. PRESIDENTIAL FIRST USE UNDER THE CONSTITUTION

The best approach to this legal issue is gradual: to consider successive gradations of presidential nuclear war powers, depending on "their disjunction or conjunction with those of Congress.''[2] The President's constitutional authority to use nuclear weapons can be arranged on a scale ranging from the declared war, when his powers are reinforced by those of Congress, to presidential first use in violation of a congressional ban on first use.

A. Presidential Use of Nuclear Weapons in a Declared War

"When the President acts pursuant to an express or implied authorization of Congress, his authority is at its maximum, for it includes all that he possesses in his own right plus all that the Congress can delegate.''[3] One theory of the illegality of presidential first use in a declared war is that neither President nor Congress may order first use because under the Constitution or international law "the Federal Government as an undivided whole lacks power.''[4] The requirement in the FAS proposal for a declaration of war that explicitly suspends the ban on first use[5] suggests—although the FAS has not urged—a second and more modest theory of unconstitutionality: that first use is illegal unless the declaration of war expressly authorizes nuclear war.

"[W]hen we committed to Congress the power to declare war, we did not grant the power to declare Armageddon.''[6] Because any first use posits a substantial risk of a strategic nuclear exchange which would cause enormous population loss to the United States, some scholars argue that any first use offends the goal-setting preamble to the Constitution and the affirmative duties of survival inherent in due process.[7] But even proponents of what one critic has called this "Constitution of good intentions''[8] concede the preliminary and unenforceable quality of these arguments, which have yet to command any substantial scholarly following.

Arguments premised on international law fare no better. Were scholars not hopelessly divided about the content of international law of nuclear war,[9] there would still remain substantial doubt of its domestic authority in opposition to the joint authority of President and Congress.[10] Thus, Professor Louis Henkin has concluded that a congressional violation of international law is "constitutionally irrelevant.''[11]

The alternative theory of illegality at least cites case law and history for support. In 1800, Justice Chase noted that "Congress is empowered to declare a general war, or Congress may wage a limited war; limited in place, in objects, in time.''[12] Arguably the Quasi-War with France in 1798 was such a war because Congress only empowered the President to enter into naval hostilities.[13] There is thus some authority for Congress to declare a war limited to conventional weapons. But it hardly follows that any limitation should be read into a declaration of war that is unqualified on its face. Not only would such an interpretation defy the usual logic of statutory construction, by which exceptions to a general grant of power must be spelled out,[14] it is also contrary to the only historical precedent on point: President Truman's use of nuclear weapons in World War II pursuant to a general declaration of war.

But further discussion of presidential power in a declared war may be irrelevant because apparently no nation has declared war since World War II.[15] In fact, as early as 1871, legal scholars pronounced that "there are quite a number of instances where wars between the most civilized nations have commenced and carried on without a formal declaration of any kind."[16] It was also well established by then that "[h]e who is attacked, he says, and wages only a defensive war, need not make a formal declaration, as the state of war is sufficiently determined by the declaration of conduct of the enemy."[17] This first category of presidential nuclear war power is therefore today only a legal abstraction because formal declarations of war are obsolete, and because, in any event, no declaration is necessary to conduct defensive war, the only kind that we say we will conduct.

Nevertheless, this category carries lessons for further analysis. First, it emphasizes the essentially unlimited war power of the President when he acts with congressional approval. Second, unless the obsolescence of the declaration of war means the obsolescence of most of the congressional war power as well, it inescapably sets up the power of Congress to authorize war by action less formal than a declaration of war. Third, it provides historical support for finely tuned congressional authorizations of war—war limited as Congress may declare.

B. Presidential Use of Nuclear Weapons in Undeclared Hostilities Absent a Congressional First Use Ban

Formal declaration of war is not the only constitutional method for defining a state of war. "The constitution establishes the mode in which this government shall *commence* wars . . . but it has no power to prescribe the manner in which others should begin war against us."[18] By hostile conduct, an enemy can initiate hostilities that activate the President's commission as commander in chief to respond without awaiting congressional authorization.[19] In that event, does the scope of the President's commission depend upon the conventional or nuclear character of the resulting hostilities?

Certainly nothing in the constitutional text points to such a distinction. The commander in chief commission is undifferentiated. Even if a principle of proportionality is built into the President's power to repel sudden attacks, proponents of presidential nuclear war power assert, a Warsaw Pact attack with conventional weapons on our NATO allies and our armed forces in Europe would pose such a significant threat to the Western democracies collectively that the defensive first use of nuclear weapons would not constitute a constitutionally disproportionate response. In fact, the NATO Treaty defines such an attack as an attack on the United States.[20] Once war has been initiated against us, whether it conventional or nuclear in character, the President may respond with our armed forces as he sees fit. "[T]he constitutional rule must be the same whether the forces are nuclear or conventional."[21]

The contrary view espoused by Stone turns less on the distinction between nuclear and conventional forces than on a distinction between a war which is unlimited, in that it places the United States directly at risk, and hostilities which are limited, in that they pose no such immediate risk. Thus an enemy's nuclear attack, by first strike, irrevocable launch, or imminent launch against the United States, places the country at immediate risk and therefore activates the President's powers as commander in chief to conduct unlimited war using comparable force.[22] But enemy first use abroad, even against our armed forces, and conventional attack at home or abroad, do not in the nuclear era place the United States at immediate risk or therefore activate the President's unlimited war powers. To such attacks, Stone argues, the President may respond only with the minimum force necessary to stave off the attack until he can obtain authorization from Congress for general hostilities.

Were the President to order first use in these limited settings, he would so risk initiating a general nuclear exchange,[23] putting the nation at immediate and incalculable risk, that he would be usurping Congress' right to decide on a general and unlimited war. Nothing in the NATO Treaty equates an attack on our NATO allies with such a war, and nothing therein constitutionally could, given its ratification by the Senate alone.[24] In fact, the Treaty expressly invokes our "constitutional processes"[25]; it does not replace them. By these processes, only Congress, argues Stone, has the authority to authorize the use of greater force than necessary to respond to the attack or to commence an unlimited war when none has been initiated by enemy action.

History again saves us from having to resolve the question because Congress *has* probably authorized presidential first use in such circumstances. Unless Congress' power to authorize hostilities is exhausted by the obsolete declaration of war power—a reading that is hardly compelled by the constitutional text—it has the power to authorize hostilities by other means. In 1946, Congress gave the President the authority to "direct the [Atomic Energy Commission] to deliver such quantities of special nuclear material or atomic weapons to the Department of Defense *for such use as he deems necessary* in the interest of national defense."[26] One draftsman of this provision later explained that "[w]e wrote the provision because we realized that the atomic weapon so far exceeds in capacity to destroy normal weapons that we must put a solemn obligation on the President that *the President alone can designate when and where an atomic weapon is to be used.*"[27] The Department of Defense has since cited this Act in conjunction with the President's commander in chief powers as authority for his nuclear war powers.[28]

United States war plans have since contemplated the first use of nuclear weapons, especially in the European theater.[29] For example, President Carter told the United Nations General Assembly in 1977 that "we will not use nuclear weapons except in self-defense; that is, in circumstances of an actual or conventional attack on the United States, our territories or armed forces *or such an attack on our allies*."[30] More recently Secretary of Defense Weinberger advised Congress that first use was contemplated "to help deter major conventional attack against United States forces and our allies, especially in NATO.''[31] Over the same period, with knowledge of our first use policy, Congress has consistently funded the deployment of nuclear weapons for the European theater without restricting their use. Even without the initial grant of power in The Atomic Energy Act, ''congressional inertia, indifference or quiescence may sometimes, at least as a practical matter, enable, if not invite, measures on independent presidential responsibility.''[32] Congressional acquiescence in the claim of presidential first use authority appears to refute Stone's argument that it is unlawful.

One objection to this theory is that Congress has acquiesced in too much. The initial delegation alone literally gives the President the authority to use nuclear weapons as he sees fit, including arguably even in a first strike, without prior congressional approval. Whatever the constitutionality of lesser delegations by acquiescence, Congress cannot give up decisions of this magnitude. Stated more broadly, the objection is that the nuclear war power is non-delegable; ''postdated declarations of war'' are ineffective.[33] Because the delegation doctrine ''ensures to the extent consistent with orderly governmental administration that important choices of social policy are made by Congress,''[34] this objection essentially restates Stone's argument that first use poses a fundamental policy question that only the legislature may decide.

The Court, however, has never ruled the war power non-delegable, and its decisions in fact leave doubt whether any Article I, section 8 power is.[35] More to the point, the Court has expressly upheld wartime delegations so broad that they might have been invalid in time of peace,[36] emphasizing the impossibility of precise standards in the areas of foreign affairs and war powers and the need to read a ''fighting constitution . . . with the realistic purposes of the entire instrument fully in mind'' during ''the early stages of global warfare. . . .''[37] The standard of ''the interest of national defense'' is sufficiently precise in the circumstances, especially in light of its elaboration by the President into a first use policy considerably narrower than any literal reading of the initial delegation. The impossibility of precise standards for first use and the need for constitutional flexibility during a global cold war suggest that the delegation of first use authority to the President is probably constitutional.

If the first objection is that Congress has acquiesced in too much, a second is that it has acquiesced in too little, or nothing at all. The theory of acquiescence presupposes both constructive notice of the claim of power to Congress, which may be inferred from the consistency, frequency, scope and duration of such claims or practices, and meaningful opportunity for Congress to disapprove.[38] Our nuclear policy has shifted over time from massive retaliation to first use, raising doubts that Congress had notice at every point along the way of what it was acquiescing in, according to this objection. Moreover, such notice as it has had is of our willingness to use nuclear weapons first, not necessarily that the decision will be made by the President alone. To the contrary, the NATO Treaty ratification debates emphasized, as do the Treaty's provisions, that such decisions would be made by our constitutional processes.[39] Finally, Congress has never really had any meaningful opportunity to disapprove. The initial delegation in the Atomic Energy Act was made before any other nation had nuclear weapons, when the issue put to Congress was only whether the President or his military subordinates—a General Jack D. Ripper[40]—would be entrusted with the decision to use nuclear weapons.[41] Subsequent appropriations were for weapons which could be used either for first or second use.

But one can readily concede that the acquiescence theory has often been overextended without rejecting it in the first use context. The flaw in the previous objection is that it treats history one frame at a time rather than cumulatively. Thus, our nuclear policy *has* evolved over time, but it is today unmistakably first use in the paradigm NATO setting. The 1946 delegation *was* distinguishable at the time, but the Defense Department has since relied upon it for broader presidential nuclear war power without correction from Congress. Appropriations *are* inherently ambiguous, but Congress has never attempted to limit them to second use only and has never been presented by them with a fait accompli by which a refusal to vote the funds might immediately endanger American lives, unlike appropriations for the Vietnam War.[42] Finally, the Senate has actually had one opportunity to disapprove first use and voted 68–10 to reject the very prohibition on first use under discussion here, although in a form which omitted the committee proposal.[43] Whatever the force of any single circumstance in this history, cumulatively they satisfy the exacting standards for congressional acquiescence in the twilight zone of concurrent powers.

While congressional acquiescence thus arguably invalidates Stone's broader theory of the unconstitutionality of presidential first use, it also sets the stage for the analysis of the last category of presidential nuclear war power. If Congress has validated presidential first use by its silence and its appropriations, can it not invalidate it by legislating a ban on first use?

C. Presidential First Use in Violation of a Congressional Ban

The FAS proposal is a ban on first use absent the consent of a congressional leadership committee or explicit authorization in a declaration of war. If the President violates that ban, "his power is at its lowest ebb, for then he can rely only upon his own constitutional powers minus any constitutional powers of Congress over the matter."[44] Such an assertion of presidential nuclear war power can only be sustained if Congress is "disable[ed] from acting upon the subject"[45] under the Constitution.

The argument that Congress is, at least in the paradigm case of a conventional attack on NATO, takes its origin in the preconstitutional experience of the Framers. The very experience of the Continental Congress with committee control over General Washington cited by Stone was a major reason that the Framers subsequently vested military command in the President as the single commander in chief.[46] Committee command was plainly inefficient and could be fatally so in a close war because "the direction of war most peculiarly demands those qualities which distinguish the exercise of power by a single hand.'"[47] As a result, the Court said in *Fleming v. Page*[48] in 1850, the President was "authorized [as commander in chief] to direct the movements of the naval and military forces placed by law at his command, and to employ them in the manner he may deem most effectual to harass and conquer and subdue the enemy." Accordingly, proponents of presidential first use authority conclude that "what forces and weapons to employ, and in what manner in order to defeat an enemy in the event hostilities break out—are confided exclusively by the Constitution to the President."[49]

They also argue that even Congress' conceded powers under Article I, section 8 do not extend into this core command authority. The greater power to create and regulate armed forces or particular weapons systems does not include any lesser power to control their deployment during constitutionally authorized hostilities. As the Court of Claims stated in *Swaim v. United States*,[50] "Congress cannot in the disguise of 'Rules for the Government' of the Army impair the authority of the President as Commander in Chief." Nor could it obtain the same result by wielding its appropriations power or "necessary and proper" legislative powers. Both authorize legislation only in service of powers elsewhere confided in the Congress, of which command is not one.[51]

Congress *has* restricted the choice of weapons by legislation enacted pursuant to treaty obligations,[52] but that is by virtue of its express authority to define offenses against international law. Such restrictions do not reflect any general domestic lawmaking power to "micro-command" the armed forces.[53]

The counter-arguments originate in the very same case law cited by proponents of presidential first use authority. In decisions like *Fleming v. Page*, the Court states that the President as commander in chief "is authorized to direct the' movements of the naval and military forces *placed by law at his command.*"[54] Congress by law provides the means for conducting hostilities. No less than seven of the eighteen clauses of Article I, section 8 confer war powers on the Congress, most prominently the power to raise, support and regulate "armies" and "a navy." But because the Constitution nowhere defines "armies" or "navy," much less "air force," the power to create these armed forces necessarily includes the power to define them by size, firepower, weaponry or whatever—to impose what Professor Carter terms "definitional restrictions" on the forces given the President to command.[55]

Consequently, proponents of congressional first use authority argue that there is little question that Congress could decline to raise and support nuclear weapons, or fund them but prohibit their use, or even give them to our forces in the field but prohibit their use without prior congressional authorization. Indeed, congressional control over the size and quality of the arsenal has been the historical norm, rather than the exception.[56] Moreover, what forces Congress has raised, supported and defined, it can decommission or redefine. There is no constitutional ratchet that would prevent Congress from withdrawing nuclear weapons from the arsenal it gives the President to command.

Proponents of congressional first use authority illustrate their point in part by pointing to statutory controls on the procurement of chemical weapons.[57] They concede that these controls implement international law regarding the production of chemical weapons, but international law vests Congress with no lawmaking power that it does not have already. The express power to "define . . . Offenses against the Law of Nations," or general power to implement treaties, to which proponents of presidential first use authority point by way of explanation of these statutory weapons controls, cannot be used to alter the constitutional structure of war powers.[58] If Congress has the power to restrict the President's ability to command chemical weapons, it can also restrict his ability to command nuclear weapons with or without the aid of international law.

Proponents of congressional first use authority also reject any temporal limits on that authority. The fact that a particular restriction operates in "real time" during hostilities is sometimes circumstantial evidence that it improperly intrudes on the President's command.[59] But there is no constitutional impediment to the imposition of otherwise appropriate definitional restrictions by Congress on the armed forces during hostilities. If Congress can enact definitional restrictions on the armed forces before their engagement, it can do so after their engagement as well.

Thus far, this debate is familiar and not much affected by the nuclear or conventional character of hostilities. There is, however, also common ground that bears more directly on their character. Proponents of presidential first use authority concede that the President could not order a bombing raid on Beijing during the Vietnam War, to use Professor Moore's example.[60] Even if hostilities in Vietnam were constitutionally authorized, a raid on Beijing would so exceed the objectives of the authorized war and so risk "greatly enlarged war or even World War III" that it would lie beyond his command authority.[61] Proponents of congressional first use authority, for their part, concede that Congress may not under guise of controlling the arsenal decide "tactics in the context of ongoing military operations"[62]—"whether we're going to attack Pork Chop Hill," to use Mr. Turner's example.[63]

Having identified this common ground at the extremes of presidential and congressional authority, we can now ask where lies the first use of nuclear weapons during conventional hostilities in Europe? Is it more like the raid on Beijing, and therefore surely subject to congressional limitation, or like the platoon deployment on Pork Chop Hill, and therefore within the President's core command authority? Or does it lie somewhere in the hotly disputed ground between these extremes?

Posing the question this way seems to me to answer it. The significant risk that any first use will escalate the war into a strategic exchange alone analogizes it to the raid on Beijing. In fact, according to some observers, its sole purpose is to threaten such escalations as part of a NATO policy of "suicidal deterrence . . . intended to enforce deterrence by necessitating that any war [against NATO in Europe] be nuclear."[64]

Moreover, as Stone notes,[65] any first use will have primarily a political rather than military, let alone narrowly tactical, purpose: to signal NATO willingness to go nuclear rather than to obtain any immediate tactical gain on the nuclear battlefield. "If in a conventional confrontation with the Soviet Union the United States were to fire a single nuclear weapon at a bridge in Eastern Europe," Paul Bracken notes, "the physical destruction of the bridge would pall in comparison to the fact that a nuclear weapon had been used for the first time since 1945."[66] Which bridge, when and what megatonnage are questions distinct from whether to use nuclear weapons first. The former are the kinds of operational questions that for efficiency reasons the Framers assigned to the commander in chief—the kind involved in an attack on Pork Chop Hill. But the latter does not require the same kinds of operational information or tactical judgment. It is essentially a policy judgement. For all these reasons, a limitation on first use is well within the war power of Congress before or during conventional hostilities in Europe, and, indeed, might well be inherent in the President's defensive war powers had not Congress already acquiesced in first use.

But there is an additional constitutional justification for a first use ban. Under the original constitutional design, congressional control of the means of war is not just antecedent, but continuing. Congress must not only create armed forces for the President to command, but must continue to support and maintain them after their creation. Indeed, the Framers expressly limited appropriations for armies to a period of two years.[67] Members of Congress "are not at liberty to vest in the executive department permanent funds for the support of an army, if they were even incautious enough to be willing to repose in it so improper a confidence."[68] As a result, the necessity for continued congressional provision of the means to conduct hostilities was originally a built-in and inescapable limitation on presidential war making—the republic's ultimate check on the dog of war.

Today the check is obsolete. With the creation of a massive nuclear stockpile and the advent of a war that would be over in hours, no continuing congressional check is effective. Once the President decides to use nuclear weapons, he will not need to go back to Congress for the means to continue nuclear hostilities; he has the means already, and hostilities will not continue long. Accordingly, the only effective check left to Congress is antecedent: the imposition of definitional restrictions on nuclear forces. That check therefore is not just within the war powers of congress, but it may be the one meaningful nuclear war power left to Congress under the Constitution today.

Many of these same arguments against presidential first use authority are made in analyzing his power in the absence of a congressional limitation. But in the twilight zone of concurrent power, Justice Jackson noted, "any actual test of power is likely to depend on the imperatives of events and contemporary imponderables rather than on abstract theories of law."[69] And when power depends on "the imperatives of events," the President will nearly always be the winner because of his superior ability to act and to react. After Congress has expressly drawn the line and banned first use, however, the burden shifts and "abstract theories of law," by which we have chosen in large measure to be governed, may decide the question of power. Presidential claim to first use authority in the teeth of a congressional ban is "at once so conclusive and preclusive [that it] must be scrutinized with caution, for what is at stake is the equilibrium established by our constitutional system."[70] In the nuclear age, that constitutional equilibrium can best be maintained by acknowledging that Congress can assert control over the conventional or nuclear character of hostilities, even as it can control the character of a declared war by the terms of the declaration.

II. FIRST USE APPROVAL BY A CONGRESSIONAL LEADERSHIP COMMITTEE

The foregoing summary implies that if Congress can constitutionally ban first use, it can constitutionally rescind the ban. Although Stone argues that in the paradigm case of a conventional attack on NATO there would be sufficient time for the President to ask for rescission of such a ban, he acknowledges that there might not be enough time for Congress to act as a body.[71] May Congress instead act through a committee of its leadership that could convene and decide more rapidly than the full Congress?

The Supreme Court's decision in *Immigration and Naturalization Service v. Chadha*[72] suggests a negative answer. The Court held that a one-house legislative veto which "had the purpose and effect of altering the legal rights, duties and relations of persons . . . outside the legislative branch"[73] unconstitutionally offends both the presentment and bicameralism requirements for legislative action under the Constitution. Because a decision of a congressional committee to authorize first use at the President's request would alter his legal rights and duties under the pre-existing ban on first use, it, too, appears to violate the constitutional requirements for legislative action.[74] That these requirements are impractical in the circumstances of the first use decision may be constitutionally irrelevant. The Constitution compels compliance with processes "that often seem clumsy, inefficient, even unworkable. . . ."[75]

More recently, Justices Stevens and Marshall voted in *Bowsher v. Synar*[76] to strike down portions of the Gramm-Rudman-Hollings deficit reduction act because

even though it is well settled that Congress may delegate legislative power to independent agencies or to the Executive, and thereby divest itself of a portion of its lawmaking power, when it elects to exercise such power itself, it may not authorize a lesser representative of the Legislative Branch to act on its behalf.

While the majority opinion went off on another point,[77] the concurring opinion by Justices Stevens and Marshall strengthens the *Chadha* challenge to the committee component of the FAS proposal.

Three arguments are made in these essays in rebuttal to this straightforward but powerful attack on the committee proposal. First, committee approval is not in form a legislative veto and is therefore not unconstitutional *per se* after *Chadha*. Second, the constitutional requirements for the exercise of shared war and foreign affairs powers are different from those for the exercise of mere domestic powers within the familiar model of domestic delegation that informs *Chadha*. Finally, the obsolescence of the original constitutional checks on presidential war powers justifies creation of a limited new check in order to preserve the balance between the branches.

A. The Form of Committee Action

The first rebuttal argument proceeds from scholarly definitions of the legislative veto and the fact that it was such a veto that the Court struck in *Chadha*. A legislative veto is essentially a legislative nullification of an executive exercise of statutory authority previously delegated to it by Congress.[78] But the FAS proposal initially delegates nothing to the President; it prohibits first use. Committee disapproval of the President's request for first use authority is therefore neither a nullification nor a withdrawal of previously granted authority. Functionally, the FAS proposal is a prohibitory statute which authorizes the committee to repeal the prohibition at the President's request. It establishes a condition precedent, not a condition subsequent, to delegation. "Such a provision is not a legislative veto," Professor Banks concludes.[79]

It may not be, yet *Chadha* struck down not just a "veto," but a mechanism for exercise of legislative power, which, as such, was subject to the usual procedural requirements for lawmaking. "Whether actions taken by either House are, in law and fact, an exercise of legislative powers," the Court said, "depends not on their form but upon 'whether they contain matter which is properly to be regarded as legislative in its character and effect.' "[80] Committee approval of first use under the FAS proposal, like the one-house legislative veto at issue in *Chadha*, alters legal rights and duties outside the legislative branch by relieving the President of a duty not to use nuclear weapons first. In fact, the functional formulation of the FAS proposal as a prohibition which can be "rescinded" or "repealed" by the committee exposes this argument of form as a mere play on words. "Amendment and repeal of statutes, no less then enactment, must conform with Art. I," *Chadha* teaches us.[81]

B. The Context of Committee Action

Mr. Tiefer distinguishes *Chadha* by emphasizing the context rather than the form of committee action. The one-house legislative veto in *Chadha* was essentially a device to check the executive exercise of previously delegated domestic authority to suspend deportation. But, under the nondelegation doctrine of administrative law, this "kind of executive authority is always subject to check by the terms of the legislation that authorized it . . . [and by] judicial review,'' the Court noted in *Chadha*.[82] An additional check in the form of a one-house veto was therefore unnecessary. Moreover, that veto improperly sought to change the statutory standards of the original delegation without enacting new law in accord with Article I procedures. In the classic model of delegated domestic powers, there is no constitutional room for post-enactment legislative action short of new Article I legislation.

That model, however, is not readily transferable from the context of domestic affairs to the context of foreign affairs and war powers. In the latter, the statutory specification of standards for executive action is often impossible. ''Congress cannot anticipate and legislate with regard to every possible action the President may find it necessary to take or every possible situation in which he might act.''[83] Not only has the court therefore tolerated legislation which would have failed the test for domestic delegations,[84] but it has stayed its own hand by the artful deployment of standing, ripeness and political question doctrines.[85]

The resulting unavailability of legislative standards and judicial review to check executive action in the context of foreign affairs and war powers has necessitated the development of other, formal and informal political checks in what Tiefer describes as ''the model of responsive interaction.'' In this model, congressional authorization consists not of black and white delegations, so much as ''various shades of acquiescence, . . . responsive interaction, and cue-following by the executive and Congress''[86]; not of ordinary legislation, so much as sub-statutory history and understandings. Congress therefore has a long history of acquiescing in sweeping grants of presidential authority in the foreign affairs and war powers context which it makes subject to sub-statutory checks in the forms of vetoes and oversight.[87]

The nuclear war power presents ''the quintessential case of authority''[88] beyond the classic domestic delegation model. The meaningful codification of standards for first use is impossible; the futility of their judicial enforcement after the event, self-evident. In these circumstances, the creation of a sub-statutory political check, by requiring the assent of a leadership committee to first use in a conventional war, is arguably a constitutional departure from the strict delegation model and the attendant procedural requirements applied in *Chadha*. Indeed, the previous analysis of the President's nuclear war powers supports this conclusion by showing that it is largely from various shades of acquiescence, responsive interaction, cue-following and sub-statutory history and understandings that the President has drawn his present first use authority in the first place.[89]

An objection to this argument is that one should take the Court at what the Court said. Although both the dissent and the briefs in *Chadha* reminded the Court of numerous legislative vetoes in the foreign affairs and war powers context and invited it to narrow its analysis, its opinion nowhere reserves the questions posed by such vetoes. Tiefer responds that the opinion, in fact, makes no expression whatsoever concerning its impact on other statutes, and that what it said was carefully limited to the statute before the Court.[90] Yet in light of the scope which the dissent gave the majority opinion, and the Court's subsequent summary affirmances of decisions striking down different (albeit domestic) forms of legislative veto,[91] it is the narrow construction which carries the burden of proof.

On the other hand, *Chadha* would not be the first time that the Court has seemingly written in broad constitutional sweep, only to retract substantially on a second look. The Court's sweeping statement of presidential removal authority in *Myers v. United States*,[92] after all, was followed a scant decade later by its nearly as sweeping retrenchment in *Humphrey's Executor v. United States*,[93] restricting removal from the independent agencies.

A second objection may be harder to answer. Even the leading cases cited for the proposition that the constitutional test for congressional action in the domestic context differs from the test in the foreign affairs and war powers context do not say that "anything goes" in the latter. As Professor Glennon points out, they hold not that the nondelegation doctrine is inapplicable in that context, but only that it does not have equal application.[94] What is its application? What is the test for congressional action in the foreign affairs and war powers context? Unless constitutional limits can be identified and applied, Tiefer's model of responsive interaction would appear to be extra-constitutional—a characterization of foreign affairs powers suggested fifty years ago in dicta by Justice Sutherland,[95] but long since repudiated by the great weight of legal scholarship, if not in so many words by the Court itself.[96]

For Professor Carter, the relevant—and fatal—test is whether congressional action "signifies that the Congress as a whole refuses its consent to a continuation (or a beginning) of hostilities."[97] Historically, Congress could have signified that refusal by failing to vote a declaration of war or other antecedent authorization, but today the President is conceded "authority to order American forces into combat as he chose[s], except when Congress act]s] affirmatively to limit his discretion."[98] Congress may do so by concurrent resolution, and, because the negative vote of a single house would suffice to defeat a declaration of war or other authorization of hostilities, by a one-house resolution. "[N]othing less . . . can logically manifest this lack of *congressional* consent, because no one but the Congress is the Congress."[99] The FAS proposal clearly fails this test. Its limited membership cannot reliably manifest even the consent or refusal of a single house, which might overwhelmingly disagree with it, let alone the full Congress.

But is this test appropriate for nuclear war powers? Carter rejects any distinction between nuclear and conventional war powers, but his theory of war powers was formulated for the latter as part of a justification of the War Powers Resolution.[100] Like the Resolution, the theory generally substitutes for antecedent congressional authorization of presidential use of force, a subsequent opportunity for congressional disapproval of the "continuation of hostilities," thus freeing the President to deploy American armed forces quickly in the modern world.[101] By Carter's theory the President no longer needs to obtain authorization; instead, it is Congress which must act if it disapproves of his initiative.

The problem with this theory, apart from the arguable violence it does to the original constitutional design,[102] is that there will be no meaningful subsequent opportunity for congress to disapprove on "the day after." Like the other continuing and post hoc checks on the presidential war power set forth in Article I,[103] the opportunity to veto is ineffective against a use of the nuclear war power because of the nature of the weapon. The alternative of antecedent approval by the full Congress is equally impractical, however, because of the "exigencies of time," as Carter concedes.[104]

Consequently, to insist on a congressional role for the full Congress or even one house is to require the Congress either to abdicate or deny the nuclear war power to the President. Abdication defeats the constitutional goal of legislative control of the commitment to war, but denial may defeat the constitutional goal of national defense in some circumstances.

C. Constitutional Necessity for Committee Action

Posed with these bleak alternatives, Professors Ides and Banks apply a different test for congressional action in the nuclear war powers context—necessity. Only by acting through a committee can the Congress assert some legislative control over the nuclear or conventional character of war and also timely authorize nuclear war when it deems it appropriate. So viewed, the committee is not merely a convenient shortcut for congressional action, like the veto struck down in *Chadha*, but instead an essential political check on the President to preserve the constitutional equilibrium. "An otherwise legitimate objection to alterations based on convenience," Ides asserts, "should not be used to prevent a narrow modification based on stark necessity."[105]

If this test of necessity was based solely on the commodious wording of the necessary and proper clause alone, it would perhaps be easy to dismiss as constitutional "myth."[106] But it is a test that the Court itself has developed and applied, though with fitting parsimony. In *Nixon v. Administrator, General Services*,[107] the Court gave the fullest statement of the test in the context of a separation of powers challenge to a statute providing for the disposition of presidential papers.

[I]n determining whether the Act disrupts the proper balance between the coordinate branches, the proper inquiry focuses on the extent to which it prevents the Executive Branch from accomplishing its constitutionally assigned functions. United States v. Nixon, 418 U.S. [683], at 711–12. Only where the potential for disruption is present must we then determine whether the impact is justified by an *overriding need* to promote objectives within the constitutional authority of Congress. *Ibid.*

The "overriding need" to promote the constitutional objectives of the Congress may therefore justify limited disruption of the accomplishment of other constitutional objectives. Since the disruption of the presidential objectives of assuring confidentiality and candid deliberation was minimized by a narrow delegation of archival authority to another executive officer in *General Services*, and the disruption was justified by the overriding need to provide the presidential papers for future chief executives, historians and students of public policy, the Court upheld the statute on its face.

The *General Services* test only articulated what the Court had already previously applied in *United States v. Nixon (The Tapes Case)*[108] and *Humphrey's Executor v. United States*.[109] In *The Tapes Case*, necessity for evidence in a criminal prosecution overcame the President's constitutionally based evidentiary privilege, and therefore justified judicial enforcement of a subpoena against him, even though the Constitution makes no express provision for it. Necessity also justified the extraordinary delegation of concededly executive prosecutorial authority to a Special Prosecutor independent of the Chief Executive, although the court did not reach this issue in this form.[110] In *Humphrey's Executor*, the perceived necessity for independence from the President justified the creation of executive officers removable only for cause, although the result was to sanction and encourage the growth of a fourth branch of government said to lie "outside" the three created by the Constitution.[111] In both cases, necessity justified limited new checks on the President that were supplementary to the original constitutional scheme.

Proposed checks which have failed the necessity test are just as instructive. As Tiefer has argued, the legislative veto failed in *Chadha* largely because of the sufficiency of the existing checks, furnished by statutory standards and judicial review, against executive abuse of delegated domestic authority. In *Nixon v. Fitzgerald*,[112] the Court held the President immune to private causes of action for damages in part because they were "not needed to serve public interests" in view of the availability of impeachment, the electoral process and other existing political checks on presidential misconduct.[113]

Does the FAS proposal for committee approval of first use pass the necessity test as articulated by the Court? If Congress has the power to prohibit first use altogether, any device for lifting that prohibition arguably enhances, rather than disrupts executive power, by yielding the President a weapon that he is otherwise denied.[114] Moreover, because committee approval permits rather than compels presidential first use, the President retains discretion—a check—over first use after committee approval. Thus, the first prong of the *General Services* test appears satisfied.

At the same time, the committee device permits at least part of Congress to exercise control over the nuclear or conventional character of certain wars. Since the alternatives are either no congressional control at all or denial of any first use to the President, this result promotes the objectives of congressional war powers under the Constitution, even if it does not achieve them fully. That the committee consists of the elected leadership of the Congress enhances its accountability and its legitimacy as a surrogate for the full Congress,[115] and attests that it is the minimum intrusion on bicameral process consistent with its objectives. In short, the committee device is a necessity for meaningful congressional participation in first use decisions under the exigencies of time, and thus satisfies the second prong of *General Services*.[116]

The proponents of the necessity test are properly cautious in advancing it. It was rejected in *Chadha*, the only case in which it was used primarily to justify a rearrangement of checks internal to a branch in order to promote objectives of that branch.[117] It is also one thing to add a new check, and quite another to replace an existing check—full congressional approval—with a different one—committee approval. Finally, the asserted "necessity" isn't really; Congress always has the option of prohibiting first use, unrealistic as that may be.

Thus, it is fair to say that it requires a leap of constitutional faith to uphold the committee component of the FAS proposal. But that leap is hardly greater than the one many have made already in conceding the President alone the constitutional authority to initiate nuclear war. Opponents of the committee component of the FAS proposal may well be right to reject the theory of necessity of a new constitutional check, but they cannot at the same time implicitly invoke it to justify extraordinary presidential nuclear war powers without upsetting the balance between the branches.

III. CONCLUSION

Professor Berney is probably correct in concluding that the courts are not likely to take the question of the constitutionality of any statute enacting the FAS proposal in its present form.[118] But constitutional questions do not cease to matter just because the courts will not answer them. Their oaths of office charge members of Congress and the President alike with independent duties to consider the constitutionality of the arrangements of government. As Professor Berney reminds us, "[t]here is more to constitutional law then whether the Court is the right or wrong forum to review a particular issue; there is also the question whether the resolution of the issue is 'right or wrong as an element in the living development of constitutional justice.' "[119]

There remain numerous practical questions of implementation,[120] not to mention defense strategy, which are only tentatively broached in Part III. But the touchstone for the implementation questions is ultimately not whether the FAS proposal, or one of several variants proposed by Professor Smith and Mr. Miller in Part III, will work perfectly. Instead, it is whether the existing system of a single nuclear war decision maker is inevitably better.

Constitutionally right or wrong, practically better or worse, the FAS proposal confirms the truth of Louis Fisher's conclusion in *Constitutional Conflicts Between Congress and President*: "Congress may stand against the President or stand behind him, but it should not stand aside as it did year after year during the Vietnam War, looking the other way and occasionally complaining about executive usurpation."[121] Congress has stood by and ceded the President the nuclear war power by default. The FAS proposal presents it with the opportunity to reconsider, if not reclaim, that power.

NOTES

1. Remark, *quoted* by Rep. Charles G. Rose III, *cited in* press release from office of Sen. Alan Cranston (Feb. 11, 1976).

2. Youngstown Sheet & Tube Co. v. Sawyer, 343 U.S. 579, 635 (1952) (Jackson, J., concurring).

3. *Id.*

4. *Id.* at 636–37.

5. *See supra* Introduction, note 1.

6. M. Ball, "Nuclear War: The End of Law," in *Nuclear Weapons and Law* 287, 295 (A. Miller & M. Feinrider ed. 1984) (hereinafter *Nuclear Weapons and Law*)

7. *See, e.g.*, Miller, "Nuclear Weapons and Constitutional Law," in *id.* 235; Lewis, "Commentary on the Constitutional Debate," in *id.* 268–69 (noting possible fundamental right of survival tied to due process).

8. Brubaker, "The Frail Constitution of Good Intentions," in *id.* 299.

9. *See, e.g.*, E. Collier, *Nuclear Weapons Use: International Law and the United States Position* 9–14 (Cong. Res. Serv. Rep. No. 84–109 F) (1984) ("no clear consensus has yet formed on how the existing rules apply to the use of nuclear weapons").

10. *See, e.g.*, Brubaker, *supra* note 8, at 303–05; Glennon, *Raising the Pacquete Habana: Is Violation of Customary International Law by the Executive Unconstitutional?* 80 Nw. U.L. Rev. 321 (1985). Chief Justice John Marshall noted that international law is but "a guide the sovereign follows or abandons at his will. . . . It may be disregarded." Brown v. United States, 12 U.S. (8 Cr.) 110, 128 (1814).

11. L. Henkin, *Foreign Affairs and the Constitution* 410 n. 11 (1972).

12. Bas v. Tingy, 4 U.S. (4 Dall.) 37, 43 (1800). *Accord*, Talbot v. Seeman, 5 U.S. (1 Cr.) 1, 28 (1800) (Marshall, C.J.) ("congress may authorize general hostilities . . . or partial hostilities. . . . ").

13. Act of July 9, 1798, ch. 68, § 1, 1 Stat. 578. *See generally* A. Sofaer, *War, Foreign Affairs and Constitutional Power* 139–61 (1976).

14. E. Crawford, *Statutory Construction* 610–12 (1940).

15. *See* Moore, *supra* Ch. 3, text accompanying notes 6–7; Carter, *supra* Ch. 8, text accompanying note 29.

16. H. Halleck, *International Law* 354 (1871).

17. *Id.* at 356. This truism was effectively acknowledged by the Framers when they substituted "declare war" for "make war" in Article I, reserving to the President the power to repel sudden attacks. *See generally* Ides, *supra* Ch. 6, text accompanying notes 45–50; Sofaer, *supra* note 13, at 31–32.

18. W. Whiting, *War Powers Under the Constitution of the United States* 39 (1972) (*reprinting* 1871 rev. ed.).

19. *Id.* at 39–40. *See* Turner, *supra* Ch. 4, text accompanying notes 30–35.

20. North Atlantic Treaty, art. 5, Apr. 4, 1949, T.I.A.S. No. 1964 (hereinafer *NATO Treaty*).

21. *See* Carter, *supra* Ch. 8, text accompanying notes 59–60.

22. *See* Stone, *supra* Ch. 2.

23. *See, e.g.*, J. Schlesinger, *Report to Congress on Nuclear Force Posture in Europe Under P.L. 93–365* (May 1975) ("The first use of theater nuclear forces, even in very limited ways, carries grave risks of escalation. . . . ''); P. Bracken, *The Command and Control of Nuclear Weapons* 164 (1983) (first use is intended and likely to be uncontrollable pursuant to European NATO strategy of "suicidal deterrence"); Ravenal, *Counterforce and Alliance: The Ultimate Connection*, 6 Int'l Security 126 (1982) (suggesting that "damage-limiting" strikes against the Soviet nuclear arsenal must follow first use in Europe); *First Use of Nuclear Weapons: Preserving Responsible Control*, Hearings Bef. Subcomm. on Int'l Security and Sci. Affairs of the House Comm. on Int'l Rel., 94th Cong., 2d Sess. 193 (1976) (Sec'y of Defense James Schlesinger) ("First use could conceivably, let me underscore conceivably, involve what we define as strategic forces and possibly, underscore possibly, involve selective strike at the Soviet Union.'').

24. *See* Glennon, *supra* Ch. 5.

25. NATO Treaty, *supra* note 20, art. 11.

26. Pub. L. No. 79–585 (1946), *codified as* 42 U.S.C. § 2121(b)(1) (1982).

27. 120 Cong. Rec. H10,688 (July 21, 1974) (Rep. Holifield). *But see infra* note 41.

28. Letter from L. Niederlehner (Acting General Counsel to Dep't of Defense) to FAS (Sept. 25, 1975), *reprinted in* 28 F.A.S. Public Interest Report (Nov. 1975).

29. *See, e.g.*, T. Sorenson, *Kennedy* 662 (1965); Bracken, *supra* note 23, at 9 ("all American war plans called for the immediate use of atomic weapons at the outbreak of another war"). As early as the Berlin Crisis, NATO plans called for first use of nuclear weapons in some circumstances, and first use against North Korea or China was discussed during the Korean War. Collier, *supra* note 9, at 19.

30. Washington Post, October 5, 1977, at A–8.

31. U.S. Dep't of Defense, *Annual Report to Congress: Fiscal Year 1983* I–18.

32. Youngstown Sheet & Tube Co. v. Sawyer, 343 U.S. 579, 635–38 (1952) (Jackson, J., concurring). *See generally* Glennon, *United States Mutual Security Treaties: The Commitment Myth*, 24 Colum. J. Transnat'l L. 201 (1986).

33. Miller & Cox, *Congress, the Constitution, and First Use of Nuclear Weapons* 30 (1986) (citing, by analogy, the impeachment power); Van Alstyne, *Congress, the President, and the Power to Declare War: A Requiem for Vietnam*, 121 U. Pa. L. Rev. 1, 15–17 (1972).

34. Industrial Union Dept. v. American Petroleum, 448 U.S. 607, 685 (1980) (Rehnquist, J., concurring). *See generally* Glennon, *supra* Ch. 5, text accompanying notes 57–63.

35. *But cf.* National Cable Television Ass'n, Inc. v. United States, 415 U.S. 336, 340–41 (1974) (suggesting that revenue power cannot be delegated).

36. *See* Tiefer, *supra* Ch. 10, text accompanying notes 39–52 (discussing *United States v. Curtiss-Wright Export Corp.*, 299 U.S. 304 (1936); *Lichter v. United States*, 334 U.S. 742 (1948); and *Dames & Moore v.Regan*, 453 U.S. 654 (1981)); *see also* Carter v. Goldwater, 444 U.S. 996, 997 (1979) (mem.) (Powell, J., concurring); *cf.* Hirabayashi v. United States, 320 U.S. 81 (1943).

37. *Lichter*, 334 U.S. at 782–83.

38. *See, e.g.*, *Youngstown*, 343 U.S. at 611 (Frankfurter, J., concurring) (discussing *United States v. Midwest Oil Co.*, 236 U.S. 459 (1915)); *see generally* Glennon, *The Use of Custom in Resolving Separation of Powers Disputes*, 64 B.U.L. Rev. 109 (1984) (proposing the variables of consistency, numerosity, duration, density, continuity, and normalcy to test whether presidential acts rise to the level of a custom, and the variables

of notice and opportunity to make meaningful objection to test whether Congress has acquiesced in it).

39. *See generally* Glennon, *supra* Ch. 5, text accompanying notes 82–110.

40. *See Dr. Strangelove or How I Learned to Stop Worrying and Love the Bomb* (1984).

41. *See* 120 Cong. Rec. H10,688 (July 21, 1974) (Rep. Holifield) ("That particular provision was written in especially so that no trigger-happy general could take one of these atomic bombs and start dropping it anywhere in the world and start an atomic war"). *See generally* Memorandum from A. Adler to A. Locklear (ACLU Comm. on Nuclear Weapons & Civil Liberties), Re: Atomic Energy Act and Presidential Authority to Order Use of Nuclear Weapons (Dec. 1984) (reviewing legislative history).

42. Drawing inferences from appropriations for nuclear weapons also does not offend the provision of the War Powers Resolution forbidding inferences of congressional authorization from general statutory provisions, including appropriations acts. War Powers Resolution sec. 8(a)(1), 50 U.S.C. § 1547 (1982). Since the first use under discussion here assumes that United States armed forces in Europe are already under attack, the Resolution is inapplicable. *Id.* § 1541(c). Moreover, it is questionable whether the Congress that enacted the Resolution's "interpretation" provision can control future Congresses by requiring a particular form of authorization. *Compare* A. Sofaer, U.S. Dep't of State, *The War Powers Resolution and Antiterrorist Operations* 2 (1986) *with* 1A *Sutherland's Statutory Construction* §27.04, at 464 (Sands 4th ed.).

43. *See supra* Introduction, text accompanying notes 2–4.

44. *Youngstown*, 343 U.S. at 637 (Jackson, J., concurring).

45. *Id.* at 638.

46. Stone, *supra* Ch. 1, text accompanying note 3. Louis Fisher has said of the same history, "The Precedents are from the wrong period. The office of President of 1787 was created as a separate and independent branch, not as a mere agent of Congress (its status under the Continental Congress)." L. Fisher, *Constitutional Conflicts Between Congress and the President* 285–86 (1985).

47. *The Federalist No. 74* (A. Hamilton) (J. Cooke ed. 1961). *See also The Federalist No. 70*, at 471 (A. Hamilton) (J. Cooke ed. 1961).

48. 50 U.S. (9 How.) 602, 614 (1850).

49. Turner, *supra* Ch. 4, text preceding note 16.

50. 28 Ct. Cl. 173, *aff'd*, 165 U.S. 553 (1897).

51. *See supra* Ch. 7, Part V (Moore).

52. 50 U.S.C. §§ 1511–20 (1982).

53. *See supra* Ch. 7, Part II (Moore).

54. 50 U.S. (9 How.) at 614 (emphasis added). *See generally* Carter, *supra* Ch. 8, text accompanying notes 33–38.

55. *See* Carter, *supra* Ch. 8, text accompanying notes 23–26; Ides, *supra* Ch. 6, text accompanying notes 63–67.

56. *See* Ides, *supra* Ch. 6, text accompanying notes 60–61, 64–67.

57. *Id.*

58. *Compare supra* Ch. 7, Part III (Moore) *with* Ides, *supra* Ch. 6, note 67 (citing *Reid v. Covert*, 354 U.S. 1 (1957).

59. *See* Moore, *supra* Ch. 3, text preceding note 19.

60. J. Moore, *Law and the Indo-China War* 564 (1972).

61. *Id.* One criterion for permissible presidential command decisions suggested by

Professor Moore is therefore "whether the action runs a high risk of major escalation." *Id*. Similarly, he would defend congressional prohibitions on the use of internationally prohibited chemical or biological weapons in part because "the profound effects on international relations and the grave risk of escalation and unnecessary suffering suggest a strong congressional competence in such decisions." *Id*. at 566.

62. *See* Ides, *supra* Ch. 6, text preceding note 70.

63. *See supra* Ch. 7, Part III (Turner).

64. *See, e.g.*, Bracken, *supra* note 23, at 164.

65. *See* Stone, *supra* Ch. 1, text following note 15.

66. *See* Bracken, *supra* note 23, at 92.

67. U.S. Const. art. I, § 8, cl. 12.

68. *The Federalist No. 26*, at 168 (A. Hamilton) (J. Cooke ed. 1961).

69. *Youngstown*, 343 U.S. at 637 (Jackson, J., concurring).

70. *Id*. at 638.

71. Stone, *supra* Ch. 1, text following note 23.

72. 462 U.S. 919 (1983).

73. *Id*. at 954.

74. The case against the committee proposal is both stronger and weaker than *Chadha*, however. The Framers overwhelmingly rejected a proposal to give the Senate the power to make war, after hearing George Mason of Virginia argue that the Senate was "not so constructed as to be entitled to it." Sofaer, *supra* note 13, at 31. Whether Mason was referring to the Senate's deliberative process or its political composition, this history gives special emphasis to the requirement of bicameralism for congressional authorization of war. On the other hand, there is substantial doubt that the Framers intended the presentment requirement to apply to declarations of war. *See* Henkin, *supra* note 11, at 32–33, 295 n5 (noting division among scholars).

75. *Chadha*, 462 U.S. at 944.

76. 106 S. Ct. 3181, 3205 (1986) (footnote omitted).

77. The majority found the act unconstitutional because it permitted Congress, by its agent, to execute the law, *Id*. at 3192.

78. *See* Banks, *supra* Ch. 9, text accompanying notes 14–18.

79. *Id*. text accompanying note 23.

80. *Chadha*, 462 U.S. at 952 (*quoting* S. Rep. No. 1335, 54th Cong., 2d Sess. 8 (1897).

81. *Id*. at 954.

82. *Id*. at 953 n. 16 (citations omitted).

83. Dames & Moore v. Regan, 453 U.S. 654, 669, 678 (1981). *See* Tiefer, *supra* Ch. 10, text accompanying notes 37–62.

84. *See* cases cited *supra* notes 36 and 37. *See also* United States v. Curtiss-Wright Export Corp., 299 U.S. 304, 321–22 (1936) (acknowledging "the unwisdom of requiring Congress in this field of governmental power to lay down narrowly definite standards by which the President is to be governed").

85. *See* cases cited in Tiefer, *supra* Ch. 10, at note 55; Berney, *supra* Ch. 13, text accompanying notes 27–64.

86. Tiefer, *supra* Ch. 10, text accompanying notes 63–67.

87. *Id*. text accompanying notes 64–67, 82–103.

88. *Id*. at text following note 59.

89. *See* summary, *supra* text accompanying notes 27–32, 40–43.

90. Tiefer, *supra* Ch. 10, text accompanying notes 22–23.

91. Consumers Union, Inc. v. FTC, 103 S.Ct. 3556 (1983) (two-house veto; *see also* American Federation of Government Employees v. Pierce, 697 F.2d 575 (D.C. Cir. 1982) (committee approval).

92. 272 U.S. 52 (1926).

93. 295 U.S. 602 (1935). *See generally* Tiefer, *supra* Ch. 10, text accompanying notes 75–78.

94. Glennon, *supra* Ch. 5, text accompanying note 54.

95. United States v. Curtiss-Wright Export Corp., 299 U.S. 304 (1936).

96. *See* Glennon, *supra* Ch. 5, text following note 51.

97. Carter, *supra* Ch. 8, text preceding note 63.

98. *Id.* text accompanying notes 57–58.

99. *Id.* text preceding note 63. Thus, Professor Carter argues that the war power is not delegable from the full Congress (or a house) to a committee.

100. *See generally* Carter, *The Constitutionality of the War Powers Resolution*, 70 Va. L. Rev. 101 (1984).

101. *See* Carter, *Commentary—The Constitution and the Prevention of Nuclear Holocaust: A Reaction to Professor Banks*, 13 J. of Legis. 206, 213 (1986).

102. Every good trial lawyer can attest to the significance of the allocation of the burden of going forward; with respect to war powers, the allocation may be of constitutional significance. Certainly casting the burden on Congress to disapprove facilitates war more than leaving the burden to obtain authorization where the Framers placed it: on the President. The Carter theory is also peculiarly one-sided. By it, on one hand, the asserted implied authorization for the President to order forces into combat as he chooses is derived from an uneven history of presidential initiatives and congressional silences, punctuated only occasionally by actual legislative authorizations by the full Congress, while, on the other hand, congressional disapprovals may be found only in one-house vetoes or concurrent resolutions.

103. *See supra* Summary, text following note 68.

104. Carter, *supra* Ch. 8, text accompanying note 72.

105. Ides, *supra* Ch. 6, text preceding note 82.

106. *See supra* Ch. 7, Part V (Moore); *cf.* Carter, *supra* Ch. 8, text following note 61 ("... the urgent necessity for political solutions to the nuclear conundrum does not alter the meaning of the structural provisions establishing the system of balanced and separated powers").

107. 433 U.S. 425, 443 (1977) (emphasis added).

108. 418 U.S. 683 (1974).

109. 295 U.S. 602 (1935).

110. The issue of the constitutionality of this new check on the President was avoided by the executive's self-imposition of regulations establishing the Special Prosecutor. *Id.* at 695–96. Congress subsequently created an independent prosecutor by legislation which has been upheld against constitutional attack from the executive in the lower courts. *See* Banzhaf v. Smith, 588 F. Supp. 1498, 1505–06 (D.D.C.) (upholding constitutionality of ethics in Government Act of 1978, 28 U.S.C. §§591 *et seq.*), *rev'd on other grounds*, 737 F.2d 116 (D.C.Cir. 1984). *But see* Nathan v. Smith, 737 F.2d 1069, 1077 (D.C.Cir. 1984) (Bork, J., concurring) (Act "raises serious constitutional questions relating to the separation of powers").

111. 295 U.S. at 628.

112. 457 U.S. 731, 754 (1982).

113. *See generally* Carter, *The Political Aspects of Judicial Power: Some Notes on the Presidential Immunity Decision*, 131 U. Pa. L. Rev. 1341 (1983). In this article, Professor Carter was more hospitable to the test of necessity for new checks on the President than he is here:

Suppose one branch of government, as a result of its own misconduct, the lassitude of the other branches, or simple cultural evolution, gradually increases its freedom of action, to the detriment of the other two. If the necessity for fresh remedies proves great enough, a good argument might be made in this narrow circumstance, the principle [that anything that upsets the balance is wrong] should be altered.

Id. at 1367 n. 106. He concludes that in these circumstances, new checks on the offending branch can be devised by Congress or even the courts if they are necessary to restore the balance between the branches.

114. Banks, *supra* Ch. 9, text accompanying notes 66–69.

115. Tiefer, *supra* Ch. 10, text preceding note 68.

116. Professor Ides would underscore the necessity by amending the FAS proposal to empower the committee to approve first use only if it finds that Congress as a whole is unavailable to convene for the purpose. Ides, *supra* Ch. 6, text following note 79.

117. Some would view *Bowsher v. Synar*, 106 S. Ct. 3181 (1986), as another such rejection, but that would make more of the concurring opinion of Justices Stevens and Marshall than of the majority opinion. *See supra* Summary, note 7. Balanced against their concurrence is Justice White's dissent, which asserts that, in light of the congressional judgment that the statute was necessary and proper to counteract a deficit crisis, the Court's role should be limited to determining whether the statute "so alters the balance of authority as to pose a genuine threat to the basic division between the lawmaking power and the power to execute the law." *Id.* at 3214.

118. Berney, *supra* Ch. 13, text accompanying notes 66–72.

119. *Id.* note 73 (quoting L. Tribe, *The American Constitution* iii (1978)).

120. Not the least of these is whether *either* the President or the Congress will have the opportunity to decide first use in light of the apparent subdelegation of first use authority from the President to his field commanders, *see, e.g.*, D. Ford, *The Button: The Pentagon's Command and Control System—Does It Work?* 121 (1985) ("half of the strategic [nuclear] forces can be fired without the President's direct order"), and the development of launch-on-warning technology.

121. Fisher, *supra* note 46, at 334.

Bibliography

Eleanor DeLashmitt

I. PERIODICALS

(Notes and Comments are listed alphabetically by title.)

Alford, Neill H. *The Legality of American Military Involvement in Viet Nam: A Broader Perspective*. 75 Yale Law Journal 1109–1121 (1966).

Allison, Graham T. *Making War: The President and Congress*. 40 Law and Contemporary Problems 86–105 (Summer 1976).

The Appropriations Power as a Tool of Congressional Foreign Policy Making. 50 Boston University Law Review 34–50 (1970).

Banks, William C. *First Use of Nuclear Weapons: The Constitutional Role of a Congressional Leadership Committee*. 13 Journal of Legislation 1–21 (1986).

Berdes, George R., and Robert T. Huber. *Making the War Powers Resolution Work: The View from the Trench (A Response to Professor Glennon)*. 17 Loyola of Los Angeles Law Review 671–81 (1984).

Berger, Raoul. *The Presidential Monopoly of Foreign Relations*. 71 Michigan Law Review 1–58 (1972).

———. *War-Making by the President*. 121 University of Pennsylvania Law Review 29–86 (1972).

———. *War, Foreign Affairs and Executive Secrecy*. 72 Northwestern University Law Review 309–45 (1977).

Bestor, Arthur. *Separation of Powers in the Domain of Foreign Affairs: The Intent of the Constitution Historically Examined*. 5 Seton Hall Law Review 527–665 (1974).

Bickel, Alexander M. *Congress, the President and the Power to Wage War*. 48 Chicago-Kent Law Review 131–47 (1971).

———. *The Constitution and War*. 54 Commentary 49–55 (July 1972).

Black, Charles L., Jr. *The Working Balance of the American Political Departments*. 1 Hastings Constitutional Law Quarterly 13–20 (1974).

Brawer, Charles N. *The Great War Powers Debate*. 7 International Lawyer 746–51 (1973).

Buchanan, G. S. *In Defense of the War Powers Resolution: Chadha Does Not Apply.* 22 Houston Law Review 1155–80 (1985).

Call, Joseph L. *Executive Power vs. Limited Government.* 9 Baylor Law Review 322–35 (1957).

Carter, Stephen L. *The Constitution and the Prevention of Nuclear Holocaust: A Reaction to Professor Banks.* 13 Journal of Legislation 206 (1986).

———. *The Constitutionality of the War Powers Resolution.* 70 Virginia Law Review 101–34 (February 1984).

Casper, Gerhard. *Response.* 61 Virginia Law Review 777–83 (1975). (A Response to Louis Henkin).

Congress, the President and the Power to Commit Forces to Combat. 81 Harvard Law Review 1771–1805 (1968).

Congressional Control of Presidential War-Making Under the War Powers Act: The Status of a Legislative Veto After Chadha. 132 University of Pennsylvania Law Review 1217–41 (1984).

The Constitution and the Use of Military Force Abroad. 10 Virginia Journal of International Law 32–117 (1969) (Symposium).

Craig, Barbara Hinkson. *The Power to Make War: Congress' Search for an Effective Role.* 1 Journal of Policy Analysis and Management 317–32 (Spring 1982).

Cruden, John C. *The War-Making Process.* 69 Military Law Review 35–143 (1975).

Darling, W. Stuart, and D. Craig Mense. *Rethinking the War Powers Act.* 7 Presidential Studies Quarterly 126–36 (Spring/Summer 1977).

Donahoe, Bernard, and Marshall Smelser. *The Congressional Power to Raise Armies: The Constitutional and Ratifying Conventions, 1787–1788.* 33 Review of Politics 202–11 (1971).

Eagleton, Clyde. *The Form and Function of the Declaration of War.* 32 American Journal of International Law 19–35 (1938).

Eagleton, Thomas F. *The August 15 Compromise and the War Powers of Congress.* 18 St. Louis University Law Journal 1–11 (Fall 1973).

———. *Congress and War Powers.* 37 Missouri Law Review 1–31 (Winter 1972).

———. *Whose Power Is War Power?* 8 Foreign Policy 1–32 (Fall 1972).

Ehrlich, Thomas. *The Legal Process in Foreign Affairs: Military Intervention—A Testing Case.* 27 Stanford Law Review 637–52 (1978).

———. *Response.* 61 Virginia Law Review 785–89 (1975). (A Response to Louis Henkin).

Emerson, J.T. *The War Powers Resolution Tested: The President's Independent Defense Power.* 51 Notre Dame Lawyer 187–216 (1975).

———. *War Powers, An Invasion of Presidential Prerogative.* 58 American Bar Association Journal 809–14 (1972).

———. *War Powers Legislation.* 74 West Virginia Law Review 53–119 (November-January, 1971–72).

Falk, Richard A. *International Law and the U.S. Role in the Viet Nam War.* 75 Yale Law Journal 1122–60 (1966).

———. *International Law and the United States Role in Viet Nam: A Response to Professor Moore.* 76 Yale Law Journal 1095–1158 (1967).

———. *Response.* 61 Virginia Law Review 791–96 (1975) (A Response to Louis Henkin).

Faulkner, S. *War in Vietnam: Is it Constitutional?* 56 Georgetown Law Journal 1132–43 (June 1968).

Firmage, Edwin Brown. *Law and the Indochina War: A Restrospective View.* 1974 Utah Law Review 1–24.

——. *The War Powers and the Political Question Doctrine.* 49 University of Colorado Law Review 65–101 (1977).

Fisher, Louis. *Delegating Power to the President.* 19 Journal of Public Law (now Emory L. J.) 251–82 (1970).

Franck, Thomas M. *After the Fall: The New Procedural Framework for Congressional Control Over the War Power.* 71 American Journal of International Law 605–41 (1977).

Friedman, David S. *Waging War Against Checks and Balances—The Claim of an Unlimited Presidential War Power.* 57 St. John's Law Review 213–73 (1983).

Fulbright, J. William. *American Foreign Policy in the Twentieth Century Under an 18th-Century Constitution.* 47 Cornell Law Quarterly 1–13 (1961).

——. *Congress, the President and the War Powers.* 25 Arkansas Law Review 71–84 (Spring 1971).

Ginnane, Robert W. *The Control of Federal Administration by Congressional Resolutions and Committees.* 66 Harvard Law Review 569–611 (1953).

Glennon, Michael J. *Strengthening the War Powers Resolution: The Case for Purse-Strings Restrictions.* 60 Minnesota Law Review 1–43 (1975).

——. *The War Powers Resolution: Sad Record, Dismal Promise.* 17 Loyola Los Angeles Law Review 657–70 (1984).

——. *The War Powers Resolution Ten Years Later: More Politics Than Law.* 78 American Journal of International Law 571–81 (July 1984).

Goldberg, Arthur J. *The Constitutional Limitations on the President's Powers.* 22 American University Law Review 667–716 (1973).

Goldman, Eric F. *The President, the People and the Power to Make War.* 21 American Heritage 4–35 (April 1970).

Goldwater, Barry M. *The President's Ability to Protect America's Freedoms—The War-making Power.* Law and Social Order 423–49 (1971).

——. *The President's Constitutional Primacy in Foreign Relations and National Defense.* 13 Virginia Journal of International Law 463–89 (1973).

Harris, Lester. *War Powers of the President.* 19 Florida Law Journal 221–27 (1945).

Harrison, Stanley L. *President and Congress: the War Powers Wrangle.* 54 Military Review 40–49 (July 1974).

Henkin, Louis. *"A More Effective System" for Foreign Relations: The Constitutional Framework.* 61 Virginia Law Review 751–76 (1975).

——. *Is There a "Political Question" Doctrine?* 85 Yale Law Journal 597–625 (1976).

——. *Viet-Nam in the Courts of the United States: "Political Questions."* 63 American Journal of International Law 284–89 (1969).

Henry, Donna Haynes. *The War Powers Resolution: A Tool for Balancing Power Through Negotiation.* 70 Virginia Law Review 1037–50 (June 1984).

Highsmith, Newell L. *Policing Executive Adventurism: Congressional Oversight of Military and Paramilitary Operations.* 19 Harvard Journal on Legislation 327–92 (1982).

Historical and Structural Limitations on Congressional Abilities to Make Foreign Policy. 50 Boston University Law Review 51–77 (1970) (Special Issue).

Hollander, Bennet N. *The President and Congress—Operational Control of the Armed Forces*. 27 Military Law Review 49–74 (1965).

Hoxie, R. Gordon. *The Office of the Commander in Chief: A Historical and Projective View*, 6 Presidential Studies Quarterly 10–36 (1976).

Hughes, Charles Evans, *War Powers Under the Constitution*. 85 Central Law Journal 206–14 (1917).

Hughes, Graham. *Civil Disobedience and the Political Question Doctrine*. 43 New York University Law Review 1–19 (1968).

Ides, Allan. *Congress, Constitutional Responsibility and the War Power*. 17 Loyola of Los Angeles Law Review 599–655 (1984).

———. *Congressional Authority to Regulate the Use of Nuclear Weapons*. 13 Hastings Constitutional Law Quarterly 233–69 (1986).

The Indochina War Cases in the United States Court of Appeals of the Second Circuit. 7 New York University Journal of International Law & Politics 137–61 (1974).

International Law and Military Operations Against Insurgents in Neutral Territory. 68 Columbia Law Review 1127–48 (1968).

Javits, Jacob K. *Congress and the President: a Modern Delineation of the War Powers*. 35 Albany Law Review 632–37 (1971).

———. *The War Powers Crisis*. 8 New England Law Review 157–80 (1973).

———. *War Powers Reconsidered*. 64 Foreign Affairs 130–40 (Fall 1985).

Jones, Harry Willmer. *The President, Congress, and Foreign Relations*. 29 California Law Review 565–85 (1941).

Jones, Thomas M. *After the Fall: the New Procedural Framework for Congressional Control Over the War Power*. 71 American Journal of International Law 605–41 (1977).

Kelley, Michael F. *The Constitutional Implications of the Mayaquez Incident*. 3 Hastings Constitutional Law Quarterly 301–38 (1976).

Keown, Stuart S. *The President, the Congress, and the Power to Declare War*. 16 University of Kansas Law Review 82–97 (November 1967).

King, Donald E., and Arthur B. Leavens. *Curbing the Dog of War: The War Powers Resolution*. 18 Harvard International Law Journal 55–96 (1977).

Kurland, Philip B. *The Impotence of Reticence*. Duke Law Journal 619–36 (1968).

Levitan, David M. *The Foreign Relations Power: An Analysis of Mr. Justice Sutherland's Theory*. 55 Yale Law Journal 467–97 (1946).

Lobel, Jules. *The Rise and Decline of the Neutrality Act: Sovereignty and Congressional War Powers in United States Foreign Policy*. 24 Harvard International Law Journal 1–71 (1983).

Lofgren, Charles A. *War-Making Under the Constitution: The Original Understanding*. 81 Yale Law Journal 672–702 (1972).

Lungren, Daniel E., and Mark L. Krotoski. *The War Powers Resolution After the Chadha Decision*. 17 Loyola of Los Angeles Law Review 767–802 (1984).

Malawer, Stuart S. *The Vietnam War Under the Constitution: Legal Issues Involved in the United States Military Involvement in Vietnam*. 31 University of Pittsburgh Law Review 205–41 (Winter 1969).

Mathews, Craig. *The Constitutional Power of the President to Conclude International Agreements*. 64 Yale Law Journal 345–89 (1955).

Meeker, Leonard C. *The Legality of United States Participation in the Defense of Viet*

Nam. 54 Department of State Bulletin 474–89 (1966), *reprinted in* 75 Yale Law Journal 1085–1108 (1966).

Mikva, Abner J. and Joseph R. Lundy, *The 91st Congress and the Constitution*. 38 University of Chicago Law Review 449–99 (Spring 1971).

Monaghan, Henry P. *Presidential War-Making*. 50 Boston University Law Review 19–33 (1970) (Special Issue).

Moore, John Norton. *Contemporary Issues in an Ongoing Debate: The Roles of Congress and the President in Foreign Affairs*. 7 International Lawyer 733–45 (1973).

———. *International Law and the United States Role in Viet Nam: A Reply*. 76 Yale Law Journal 1051–94 (1967).

———. *The Justiciability of Challenges to the Use of Military Forces Abroad*. 10 Virginia Journal of International Law 85–107 (1969).

———. *Legal Dimensions of the Decision to Intercede in Cambodia*. 65 American Journal of International Law 38–75 (January 1971).

———. *The National Executive and the Use of the Armed Forces Abroad*. 21 Naval War College Review 28–38 (1969).

1973 War Powers Legislation: Congress Re-Asserts Its Warmaking Powers. 5 Loyola University of Chicago Law Journal 83–106 (1974).

Patterson, James T. *The Rise of Presidential Power Before World War II*. 40 Law & Contemporary Problems 39–57 (Spring 1976).

Potter, Pitman B. *The Power of the President of the United States to Utilize Its Armed Forces Abroad*. 48 American Journal of International Law 458–59 (1954).

Presidential Power to Make War. 7 Indiana Law Review 900–24 (1974).

Putney, Albert H. *Executive Assumption of the War Making Power*. 7 National University Law Review 1–41 (1927).

Ratner, Leonard G. *The Coordinated Warmaking Power—Legislative, Executive and Judicial Roles*. 44 Southern California Law Review 461–89 (1971).

Ratner, Michael, and David Cole. *The Force of Law: Judicial Enforcement of the War Powers Resolution*. 17 Loyola of Los Angeles Law Review 715–66 (1984).

Rehnquist, William H. *The Constitutional Issues—Administration Position*. 45 New York University Law Review 628–39 (June 1970) (Special Issue).

Reveley, W. Taylor, III. *Constitutional Allocation of the War Powers Between the President and Congress: 1787–1788*. 15 Virginia Journal of International Law 73–147 (1974).

———. *Presidential War-Making: Constitutional Prerogative or Usurpation?* 55 Virginia Law Review 1243–1305 (1969).

Rogers, William D. *Congress, the President, and the War Powers*. 59 California Law Review 1194–1214 (September 1971).

Rogers, William D. *The Constitutionality of the Cambodian Incursion*. 65 American Journal of International Law 26–37 (January 1971).

Rostow, Eugene V. *Great Cases Make Bad Law: The War Powers Act*. 50 Texas Law Review 833–900 (1972).

———. *Response*. 61 Virginia Law Review 797–806 (1975). (A Response to Louis Henkin).

Rubner, Michael. *The Reagan Administration, the 1973 War Powers Resolution, and the Invasion of Grenada*. 100 Political Science Quarterly 627–47 (Winter 1985–86).

Rushkoff, Bennett C. *A Defense of the War Powers Resolution*. 93 Yale Law Journal 1330–54 (1984).

Schlesinger, Arthur, Jr. *Congress and the Making of American Foreign Policy.* 51 Foreign Affairs 78–113 (October 1972).

Schwartz, Warren F., and Wayne McCormack. *The Justiciability of Legal Objections to the American Military Effort in Vietnam.* 46 Texas Law Review 1033–53 (1968).

Scriber, Jeffrey L. *The President Versus Congress on War Making Authority.* 52 Military Review 87–96 (April 1972).

Sofaer, Abraham D. *The Presidency, War, and Foreign Affairs: Practice Under the Framers.* 40 Law and Contemporary Problems 12–30 (Spring 1976).

Spong, William B., Jr. *Can Balance Be Restored in the Constitutional War Powers of the President and Congress?* 6 University of Richmond Law Review 1–47 (1971).

——. *Organizing the Government to Conduct Foreign Policy: The Constitutional Questions.* 61 Virginia Law Review 747–50 (1975) (Introduction).

——. *The War Powers Resolution Revisited: Historic Accomplishment or Surrender?* 16 William & Mary Law Review 823–82 (1975).

Stone, Jeremy J. *Presidential First Use Is Unlawful.* 56 Foreign Policy 94–112 (1984).

The Supreme Court as Arbitrator in the Conflict Between Presidential and Congressional War-Making Powers. 50 Boston University Law Review 78–116 (1970) (Special Issue).

Thomson, Harry C. *The War Powers Resolution of 1973: Can Congress Make It Stick?* 139 World Affairs 3–9 (Summer 1976).

Thurow, Glen E. *Presidential Discretion in Foreign Affairs.* 7 Vanderbilt Journal of Transnational Law 71–91 (1973).

Tigar, Michael E. *Judicial Power, the "Political Question Doctrine," and Foreign Relations.* 17 UCLA Law Review 1135–79 (June 1970).

Tower, John G. *Congress Versus the President: The Formulation and Implementation of American Foreign Policy.* 60 Foreign Affairs 229–46 (1981).

Tuley, Deanna M. *The War Powers Resolution: The Questionable Solution.* 25 Air Force Law Review 244–74 (1985).

Turner, Robert F. *The War Powers Resolution: Unconstitutional, Unnecessary, and Unhelpful.* 17 Loyola of Los Angeles Law Review 683–713 (1984).

U.S. Department of State. *Authority of the President to Repel the Attack in Korea.* 23 Department of State Bulletin 173–80 (1950).

Van Alstyne, William. *Congress, the President and the Power to Declare War: A Requiem for Vietnam.* 121 University of Pennsylvania Law Review 1–28 (1972).

Vance, Cyrus R. *Striking the Balance: Congress and the President Under the War Powers Resolution.* 133 University of Pennsylvania Law Review 79–95 (1984).

Velvel, Lawrence R. *The War in Viet Nam: Unconstitutional, Justiciable, and Jurisdictionally Attackable.* 16 University of Kansas Law Review 449–503(e) (1968).

Waikart, Robert A. *Applying Chadha: The Fate of the War Powers Resolution.* 24 Santa Clara Law Review 697–741 (Summer 1984).

Wald, Martin. *The Future of the War Powers Resolution.* 36 Stanford Law Review 1407–45 (July 1984).

Wallace, Don, Jr. *The War-Making Powers: A Constitutional Flaw?* 57 Cornell Law Review 719–76 (1972).

The War-Making Powers: The Intentions of the Framers in the Light of Parliamentary History. 50 Boston University Law Review 5–18 (1970) (Special Issue).

The War Powers Resolution. 17 Loyola Los Angeles Law Review 579–802 (1984) (Symposium).

The War Powers Resolution: An Act Facing "Imminent Hostilities" a Decade Later. 16 Vanderbilt Journal of Transnational Law 915–1051 (Fall 1983).

Wormuth, Francis D. *The Nixon Theory of the War Power: A Critique*. 60 California Law Review 623–703 (1972).

Wright, Quincy. *The Power of the Executive to Use Military Forces Abroad*. 10 Virginia Journal of International Law 43–52 (1969).

Zablocki, Clement J. *War Powers Resolution: Its Past Record and Future Promise*. 17 Loyola of Los Angeles Law Review 579–89 (1984).

Zuta, Robert. *The Recapture of the S.S. Mayaguez: Failure of the Consultation Clause of the War Powers Resolution*. 8 New York University Journal International Law and Politics 457–78 (Winter 1976).

II. BOOKS

Austin, Anthony. *The President's War*. Philadelphia: J.B. Lippincott, 1971.

Barnet, Richard J. *Roots of War*. New York: Atheneum Publishers, 1971.

Berdahl, C. A. *War Powers of the Executive in the United States*. Urbana: University of Illinois Press, 1922.

Bessette, Joseph M., and Jeffrey Tulis, eds. *The Presidency in the Constitutional Order*. Baton Rouge: LSU Press, 1981.

Bickel, Alexander M. *The Least Dangerous Branch: The Supreme Court at the Bar of Politics*. Indianapolis: Bobbs-Merrill, 1962.

Burns, James MacGreger. *Presidential Government: The Crucible of Leadership*. Boston: Houghton Mifflin, 1966.

———. *The Deadlock of Democracy*. Englewood Cliffs, N.J.: Prentice-Hall, 1963.

Caraley, Demetios, ed. *The President's War Powers: From the Federalists to Reagan*. New York: Academy of Political Science, 1984.

Collier, Ellen C. *Nuclear Weapons Use: International Law and the United States Position*. Washington, D.C.: Congressional Research Service, 1984.

———. *War Powers Resolutions*. Washington, D.C.: Congressional Research Service, 1984.

Congress, the President, and Foreign Policy. Washington, D.C.: American Bar Association, Standing Committee on Law and National Security, 1984.

Corwin, Edward S. *The President: Office and Power, 1787–1984: History and Analysis of Practice and Opinion*. New York: New York University Press, 1984.

———. *Total War and the Constitution*. New York: Alfred A. Knopf, 1947.

Cox, Henry Bartholomew. *War, Foreign Affairs and Constitutional Power: The Origins*. (Vol. 2). Cambridge, Mass.: Ballinger, 1976.

Dahl, Robert. *Congress and Foreign Policy*. New York: Harcourt, Brace and Company, 1950.

Daly, John Charles, Moderator. *War Powers and the Constitution*. Washington, D.C.: American Enterprise Institute, 1984.

Dverin, Eugene, ed. *The Senate's War Powers; Debate on Cambodia from the Congressional Record*. Chicago: Markham Publishing, 1971.

Eagleton, Thomas F. *War and Presidential Power: A Chronicle of Congressional Surrender*. New York: Liveright, 1974.

Falk, Richard A. *The Six Legal Dimensions of the Viet Nam War*. Princeton: Center for International Studies, 1968.

————. *The Vietnam War and International Law*. New York: Oxford University Press, 1979.

Friedman, Leon, and Burt Neuborne. *Unquestioning Obedience to the President*. New York: Norton, 1972.

Fulbright, J. William. *The Arrogance of Power*. New York: Random House, 1967.

Glennon, Michael J., and Thomas M. Frank. *United States Foreign Relations Law*. New York: Oceana, 1980.

Guggenheimer, Jay Caesar. "The Development of the Executive Departments, 1775–1789" in *Essays in the Constitutional History of the United States in the Formative Period 1775–1789* (Jameson J. Franklin, ed.). Boston: Houghton Mifflin, 1889.

Henkin, Louis, *Foreign Affairs and the Constitution*. Mineola, N.Y.: Foundation Press, 1972.

Holt, Pat M. *The War Powers Resolution: The Role of Congress in U.S. Armed Intervention*. Washington, D.C.: American Enterprise Institute, 1978.

Hull, Roger, and John C. Novogrod. *Law and Vietnam*. Dobbs Ferry, N.Y.: Oceana, 1968.

Javits, Jacob K. *Who Makes War: the President Versus Congress*. New York: Morrow, 1973.

Kotzsch, Lothar. *The Concept of War in Contemporary History and International Law*. Geneva: E. Droz, 1956.

Macridis, Roy C., ed. *Foreign Policy in World Politics*. 6th ed. Englewood Cliffs, N.J.: Prentice-Hall, 1985.

Maurice, John Frederick. *Hostilities Without Declaration of War: An Historical Abstract of the Cases in Which Hostilities Have Occurred Between Civilized Powers Prior to Declaration of War From 1700 to 1870*, London: HMSO, 1883.

May, Ernest. *The Ultimate Decision: The President as Commander in Chief*. New York: George Braziller, 1960.

Miller, A., and H. Bart Cox. *Congress, the Constitution, and First Use of Nuclear Weapons*. Lawyers' Committee on Nuclear Policy, Inc., 1986 (to appear in 48 Review of Politics 211–45 (Spring 1986)).

Moore, John Norton. *Law and the Indochina War*, New Jersey: Princeton University Press, 1972.

Neustadt, Richard E. *Presidential Power, the Politics of Leadership*. New York: Wiley & Sons, 1960.

Odell, Talbot. *War Powers of the President*. Washington, D.C.: Washington Service Bureau, 1942.

Pelsby, Nelson W. *Congress and the Presidency*. Englewood Cliffs, N.J.: Prentice-Hall, 1964.

"President's War Powers—I & II," in *C.Q. Guide to Current American Government*. Washington, D.C.: Congressional Quarterly, 1968.

Reveley, W. Taylor, III. *War Powers of the President and Congress: Who Holds the Arrows and Olive Branch?* Charlottesville: University of Virginia Press, 1981.

Rossiter, Clinton L. *The American Presidency*. New York: Harcourt Brace Jovanovich, 1963.

————. *The Supreme Court and the Commander-in-Chief*. (expanded ed.). New York: Cornell University, 1976.

Russell, Robert W. *The United States Congress and the Power to Use Military Force*

Abroad. (thesis: Fletcher School, 1967) available on microfilm. Cambridge, Mass.: MIT Libraries, 1972.

Schasre, James. A. *One Lawyer's Reflections on the War Power*. Spokane: James Schasre, 1970.

Schlesinger, Arthur, Jr. *The Imperial Presidency*. Boston: Houghton Mifflin, 1973.

Schlesinger, Arthur, Jr. and Alfred De Grazia. *Congress and the Presidency: Their Role in Modern Times*. Washington, D.C.: American Enterprise Institute, 1967.

Sofaer, Abraham D. *War, Foreign Affairs and Constitutional Power: The Origins*. (vol. 1). Cambridge, Mass.: Ballinger, 1976.

Sullivan, John H. *The War Powers Resolution: A Special Study of the Committee on Foreign Affairs*. Washington, D.C.: U.S. G.P.O., 1982.

Taft, Robert A. *A Foreign Policy for Americans*. Garden City, N.Y.: Doubleday, 1951.

Thomas, Ann Van Wynen, and A.J. Thomas, Jr. *The War-Making Powers of the President*. Dallas: Southern Methodist University Press, 1982.

Tugwell, Rexford G. *The Enlargement of the Presidency*. New York: Doubleday, 1960.

Tugwell, Rexford G., and Thomas E. Cronin, eds. *The Presidency Re-Appraised*. (2d. ed.). New York: Praeger, 1977.

Turner, Robert F. *The War Powers Resolution: Its Implementation in Theory and Practice*. Philadelphia: Foreign Policy Research Institute, 1983.

Velvel, Lawrence. *Undeclared War and Civil Disobedience: the American System in Crisis*. New York: Dunellen, 1970.

Wechsler, Herbert. *Principles, Politics and Fundamental Law*. Cambridge, Mass.: Harvard University Press, 1961.

Whiting, William. *The War Powers Under the Constitution of the United States*. New York: DaCapo Press, 1972 (reprint of 1871 rev. ed.).

Wilcox, Francis O. *Congress, the Executive, and Foreign Policy*. New York: Harper & Row for the Council on Foreign Relations, 1971.

Wilcox, Francis O., and Richard A. Frank, eds. *The Constitution and the Conduct of Foreign Policy: an Inquiry by a Panel of the American Society of International Law*. New York: Praeger, 1976.

Wormuth, Francis D. *The Vietnam War: The President Versus the Constitution* (occasional paper). Santa Barbara: Center for the Study of Democratic Institutions, April 1968.

——— and Edwin B. Firmage. *To Chain the Dog of War*. Dallas: Southern Methodist University Press, 1986.

III. SELECTED GOVERNMENT PUBLICATIONS

House Committee on Foreign Affairs. *Grenada War Powers: Full Compliance Reporting and Implementation*. 98th Cong., 1st. Sess., 1983.

House Subcommittee on International Security and Scientific Affairs of the Committee on International Relations. *Hearing on War Powers: A Test of Compliance Before the Subcommittee on International Security and Scientific Affairs of the House Committee on International Relations*. 94th Cong., 1st Sess., 1975.

House Subcommittee on International Security and Scientific Affairs of the Committee on International Relations. *Hearings on Congressional Oversight of War Powers Compliance: Zaire Airlift Before the Subcommittee on International Security and Scientific Affairs*. 95th Cong., 2d Sess., 1978.

House Subcommittee on International Security and Scientific Affairs of the Committee on International Relations. *The War Powers Resolution: Relevant Documents, Correspondence, Reports*. 94th Cong., 2d Sess., 1976.

House Subcommittee on International Security and Scientific Affairs of the Committee on International Relations. *War Powers: A Test of Compliance Relative to the Donang Sealift, the Evacuation of Phnom Penh, the Evacuation of Saigon, and the Mayaquez Incident*. 94th Cong., 1st. Sess., 1975.

House Subcommittee on National Security Policy and Scientific Developments of the Committee on Foreign Affairs. *Hearings before the Subcommittee on National Security Policy and Scientific Developments*. 91st Cong., 2d. Sess., 1970.

Multinational Force in Lebanon: Report to Accompany S.J. Res. 159. S. Rept. 98–242. Washington, D.C.: GPO, 1983.

Senate Committee on Foreign Relations. *Hearing before the Committee on Foreign Relations: Markup to Consider Three Joint Resolutions Relating to Lebanon and the War Powers Resolution*. 98th Cong., 1st Sess., 1983.

Senate Committee on Foreign Relations. *Hearings on a Review of the Operation and Effectiveness of the War Powers Resolution Before the Senate Committee on Foreign Relations*. 95th Cong., 1st Sess., 1977.

Senate Committee on Foreign Relations. *Hearings on War Powers Legislation Before the Senate Committee on Foreign Relations*. 92nd Cong., 1st Sess., 1971.

Senate Committee on Foreign Relations. *War Powers Resolution Hearing*. 98th Congress, 1st Sess., Washington, D.C.: GPO, 1975.

Staff of House Committee on Foreign Affairs. *Report on the War Powers Resolution: A Special Study of the Committee on Foreign Affairs*. 97th Cong., 2d Sess., Washington, D.C.: GPO Committee Print, 1982 (Sullivan Study).

Staff of House Subcommittee on International Security and Scientific Affairs of the House Committee on Foreign Affairs. *The War Powers Resolution: Relevant Documents, Correspondence, Reports*. 98th Cong., 1st Sess., Washington, D.C.: GPO Committee Print, 1983.

Veto Message From the President of the United States. H.R. Doc. No. 171, 119 Cong. Rec. 34,990 (1973).

Index

Reid v. Covert, 99
Repel sudden attacks, power to, 4, 9, 10,
  27, 39, 77–78, 88 n.46, 95–96, 100–
  101, 125 n.20, 127 n.58
Reports, from President to congressional
  nuclear planning committee, 12
Revolutionary War, 5, 28
Rio Treaty and automatic commitment,
  64 n.4
Roosevelt, Franklin D., 19, 56, 181
Rostow, Eugene, 27
Rules for government of armed forces,
  29, 40, 217
Rush, Kenneth, 3

Schechter Poultry Corp. v. United States,
  55
Schlesinger, Arthur, 42
Schlesinger, James, 10
SEATO Treaty, 54
Second strike, 16, 18
Secretary of State, 14, 30, 35 n.19, 38,
  58, 174
Secretary of Defense, 7, 14, 30, 35 n.19
Select Committee on Intelligence, 90–91
  n.79, 189
Senate Foreign Relations Committee, 38,
  ix
Separation of powers: balancing test,
  224–26; purposes of, 134–36
Seward, William, 55
Shortcuts, constitutional, 12
Soviet Union, 18, 23
Standing armies, 75–76, 88 n.37, 219
Steel Seizure Case, 57–58, 59, 71, 87
  n.16, 136, 152
Stewart, Potter, 56, 200
Story, Joseph, 55, 133
Strategic equivalence, 23
Subdelegation of first use authority, 232
  n.120
Sudden attack. *See* Repel sudden attacks,
  power to
Surprise attack. *See* Repel sudden at-
  tacks, power to
Sutherland, George, 56
Swaim v. United States, 29, 40, 217

Tactical nuclear weapons or uses, 18
Tactical command decisions, 5, 29
Taft, Robert, 42
Taft, William Howard, 41
Talbot v. Seeman, 44
*Thomas v. Union Carbide Agricultural
  Products Co.*, 132
Tonkin Gulf Resolution, 44, 45, 79–80,
  157, 199
Treaty power, 52
Treaty ratification, 19, 52
Troop movements, 41–42
Truman, Harry S., 5, 6, 58, 60
"Tuesday lunch group," 181
Twilight Zone of Shared Powers, 73,
  132, 136, 139 n.33, 219

Undeclared wars, 5, 10
United Nations Charter, 24, 25, 26, 43,
  114
United States v. Nixon (Tapes Case), 225
*United States v. Curtiss–Wright Export
  Corp.*, 39, 56, 59, 148–49
United States v. Lovett, 105
United States v. Klein, 105

Vandenberg, Robert, 61, 62
Veto. *See* Legislative veto
Vietnam War, ix, 6, 9, 42, 44, 54, 152,
  196; decisions by the courts, 198–201;
  fund cut-off, 6

Wald v. Regan, 58
War, power to make, 78, 112. *See also*
  Congress; Constitution; President
War powers. *See* Congress; Constitution;
  President
War Powers Act, ix; no first use amendment to, ix. *See also* War Powers Resolution
War Powers Resolution, 5, 9, 31, 47,
  103, 116–18, 120, 134, 152, 157, 189,
  192, 223, 229 n.42; and *Chadha*, 117;
  constitutionality of, 27; impossibility of
  specifying standards, 157–58; judicial
  review of presidential compliance with
  reporting provisions of, 202; reporting
  requirement, 27

About the Editor and Contributors

WILLIAM C. BANKS is Professor of Law and Director of Center for Interdisciplinary Legal Studies, Syracuse University College of Law. He is the author of a forthcoming constitutional law casebook for Matthew Bender (1986), and articles on the legislative veto, federal system and public law topics.

ARTHUR L. BERNEY is Professor of Law, Boston College Law School, and a member of the Board of Directors of Lawyers Alliance for Nuclear Arms Control. He is the author of articles on constitutional law and forthcoming materials on arms control law.

STEPHEN L. CARTER is Associate Professor of Law, Yale University, and author of articles on presidential immunity, the War Powers Resolution, and constitutional interpretation.

ELEANOR DeLASHMITT is Associate Librarian for Research, National Law Center, George Washington University, and former Acting Head of Reference, University of Texas School of Law.

MICHAEL J. GLENNON is Professor of Law, University of Cincinnati College of Law; formerly Legal Counsel, Senate Foreign Relations Committee and Assistant Counsel, Office of the Legislative Counsel for the U.S. Senate. He is author of *United States Foreign Relations Law* and articles on War Powers Resolution and U.S. foreign relations.

ALLAN IDES is Associate Dean and Professor of Law, Loyola Law School, and author of articles on War Powers Resolution and nuclear war powers.

WILLIAM G. MILLER is President of the American Committee on US-Soviet Relations, and formerly senior aide in the Senate on national security matters and staff director of three senate committees, including the Senate Select Committee on Intelligence. He was Associate Dean and Professor of International Relations at The Fletcher School of Law and Diplomacy and a fellow of The John F. Kennedy School of Government.

JOHN NORTON MOORE is Walter L. Brown Professor of Law, University of Virginia Law School; Director, Centers for Oceans Law and Policy and National Security; Chairman, American Bar Association Standing Committee on Law and National Security; Chairman, NSC Interagency Task Force on the Law of the Sea; and Counselor on International Law to the Department of State.

PETER RAVEN-HANSEN is Professor of Law and Faculty Associate in Public Policy, National Law Center, George Washington University and formerly a National Council Member of the Federation of American Scientists. He is the author of articles on presidential power and administrative law.

EDWIN M. SMITH is Professor of Law, University of Southern California Law Center, and the author of articles on international law and superpower crises.

JEREMY J. STONE is Director, Federation of American Scientists, and the author of *Containing the Arms Race* and *Strategic Persuasion*.

CHARLES TIEFER is Deputy General Counsel to Clerk of the U.S. House of Representatives, and formerly Assistant Senate Legal Counsel. He is the author of articles on the constitutionality of independent officers as checks on executive abuse.

ROBERT F. TURNER is President, U.S. Institute for Peace; formerly Senior Fellow, Center for Law and National Security, University of Virginia School of Law; three-term Chairman of the Committee on Executive-Congressional Relations of the American Bar Association's Section of International Law and Practice; Principal Deputy Assistant Secretary of State for Legislative and Intergovernmental Affairs; and author of *The War Powers Resolution: Its Implementation in Theory and Practice* (1983); *Congress, the Constitution, and Foreign Affairs* (forthcoming, 1986).